IMAGES
of America

THE CONWAYS

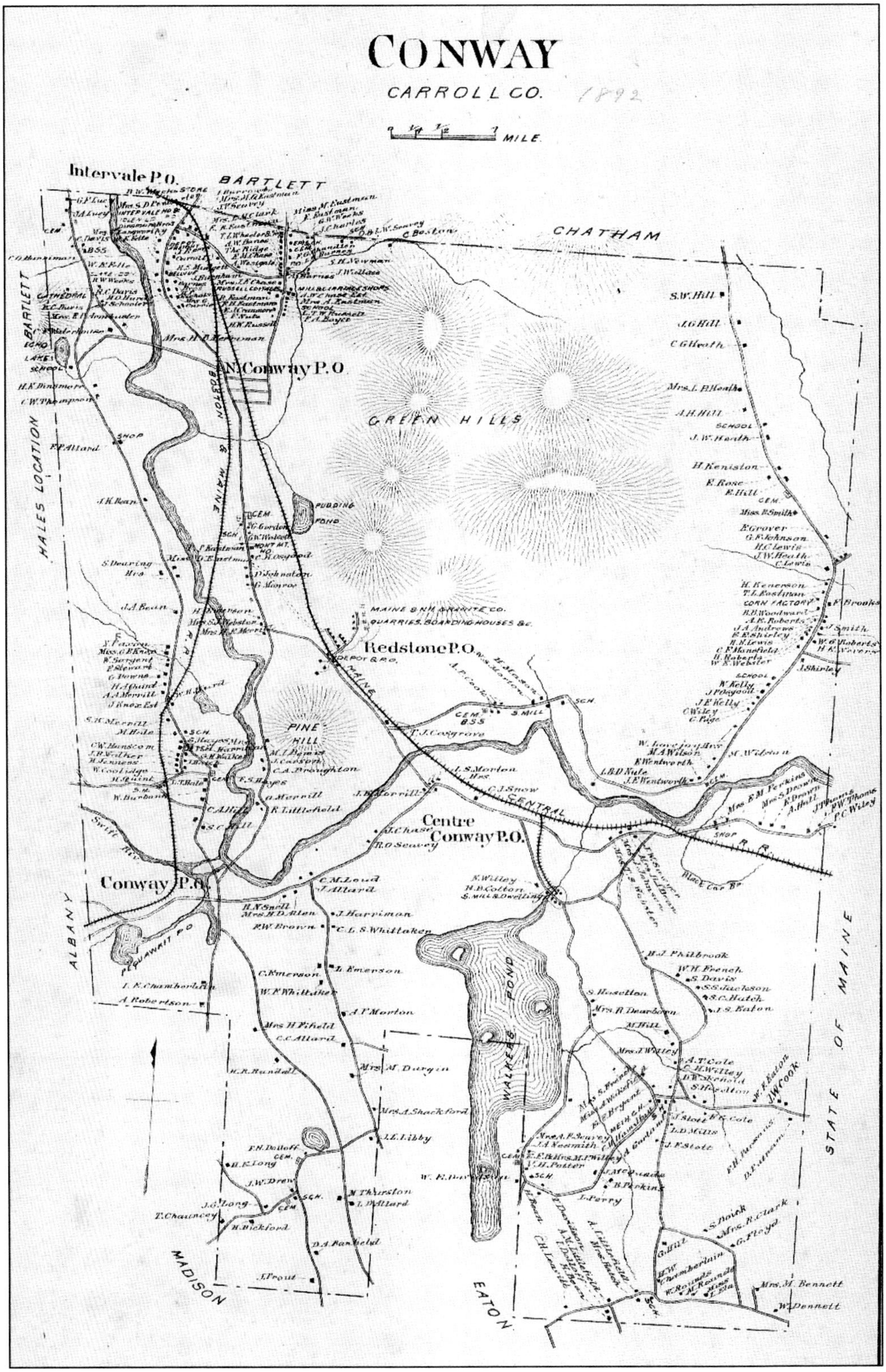
CONWAY
CARROLL CO.
1892
MILE
Intervale P.O.
BARTLETT
CHATHAM
N. Conway P.O.
GREEN HILLS
PUDDING POND
Redstone P.O.
MAINE & N.H. GRANITE CO.
QUARRIES, BOARDING HOUSES &c.
PINE HILL
Centre Conway P.O.
Conway P.O.
WALKERS POND
HALES LOCATION
ALBANY
MADISON
EATON
STATE OF MAINE
MAINE CENTRAL R.R.
BOSTON & MAINE R.R.

IMAGES
of America

THE CONWAYS

David Emerson

ARCADIA
PUBLISHING

ISBN 978-0-7385-6256-8

Published by Arcadia Publishing
Charleston, South Carolina

Printed in the United States of America

Library of Congress Catalog Card Number: 2008932681

For all general information contact Arcadia Publishing at:
Telephone 843-853-2070
Fax 843-853-0044
E-mail sales@arcadiapublishing.com
For customer service and orders:
Toll-Free 1-888-313-2665

Visit us on the Internet at www.arcadiapublishing.com

Developed and presented
by the
Nella Braddy Henney History Room
of the
Conway Public Library

Contents

ACKNOWLEDGMENTS

The photographs in this volume are from the collections of the Conway Public Library, the Conway Historical Society, and the private collection of Thom Steele. Much appreciation is extended to Thom and to the Historical Society for loaning these rare and wonderful images to the Library for inclusion in this book. Thank you, also, to the ever patient staff of the Conway Public Library for their support and encouragement, to Adrian E. Hurd for sharing his staggering knowledge of Conway Village history, and to Suzanne C. Levesque for her proofreading.

INTRODUCTION

The quiet valley, nestled among the twists and turns of the Saco River, has attracted hunters and gatherers for thousands of years. The first Europeans to visit were attracted for many of the same reasons as the first Native Americans. After Benning Wentworth, by the grace of George III, granted 6 square miles of land to be divided into 69 equal shares, the proprietors met in a tavern in Chester to hear the surveyor's report. On December 2, 1765, Conway, New Hampshire, was named in honor of Henry Seymour Conway, British statesman and colonial sympathizer.

Many of the original proprietors never visited their lands in Conway, but those who did found rich and fertile soil along the banks of the Saco River. The first farms were plagued by spring freshets and in 1787, Squire Eastman and his neighbors moved to higher ground. Landscape had much to do with the layout of the town. Water was the only source of power for mills. Villages sprang up around the mills. Rivers were very real geographical barriers and roads were dependent on river fords.

As the winding paths became roads and the rivers were bridged, travel became more practical. The trickle of adventurers and naturalists became a steady flow of hardy souls seeking fresh air and mountain views. When Benjamin Champney began to invite artists to join him in North Conway, the entire Northeast became aware of the rugged beauty of the eastern slope of Mt. Washington. With the coming of the railroad, the flow of visitors became a torrent. The valley was experiencing a new form of freshet.

Grand hotels sprang up from the rocky soil and a tourism industry was born. Others were quick to succumb to the lure of the virgin forests and fine granite deposits. The influx of European immigrants made possible the growth of world-class industries. The golden age of the Conways was born.

All was not idyllic in the valley. The weather could be brutal, floods were regular visitors, and fires were a constant threat. Mills were often closed for extended periods due to the vagaries of weather, supply, and demand. The tourist economy demanded a constant supply of visitors and snow.

Divisions between the seven sections that make up the Conways were more than geographical. Petty jealousies as well as cultural and class differences were always near the surface. The political make-up of the town was and is complicated by the precinct system, separating fire departments, water services, and lighting districts into semi-autonomous mini governments—one town, divided by common interests.

Despite their differences, for the past two centuries the Conways have managed to work through a multitude of challenges to create a much sought after quality of life. The community has grown and prospered. This volume is a sampler of a rich and varied past presented through the lenses of local photographers.

One

Sticks and Stones: Agriculture and Lumbering

It was the fertile soil and abundant forests that lured the first settlers to the Conway valley. Farms had to be self sufficient, making good use of the natural bounty of the area. Not all land was equally productive. The village of Kearsarge earned the designation "Hard Scrabble" because of the difficulty of farming the rocky soil. Floods and marauding wild life were of constant concern. The weak and unwilling were soon weeded out, leaving a thriving agricultural community.

Trees, at first, were both a curse and a blessing. Necessary for building and warmth, the old growth timber had to be cleared from the fields before tilling could begin. Later, the seemingly endless supply of timber was harvested on a grand scale. Logging railroads were built. Throughout the White Mountains, logging towns sprang up, prospered, and disappeared when the timber was gone. Lumbering and agriculture were driving forces, shaping life in the valley.

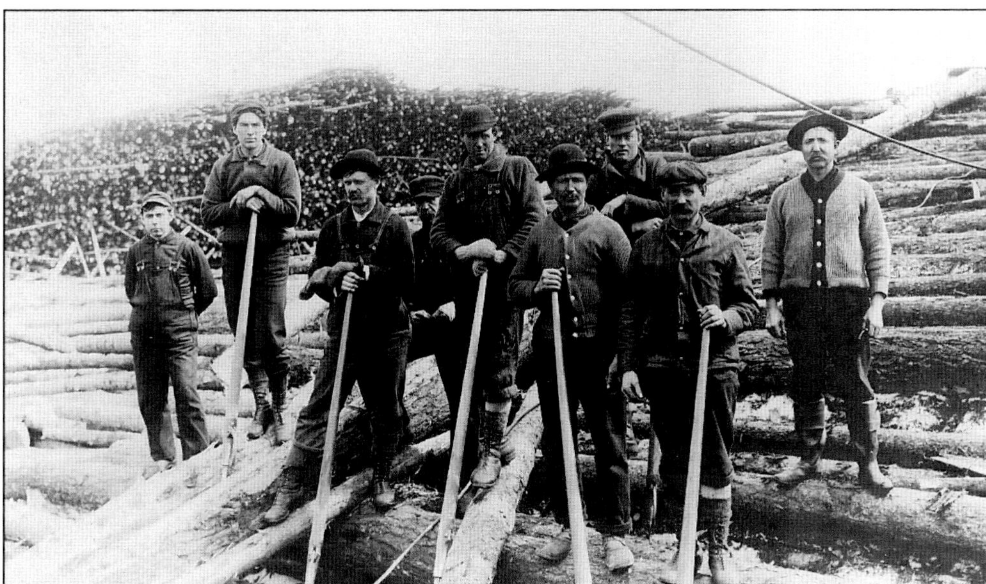

THE CONWAY LUMBER COMPANY, *c.* 1910. The vast acreage of old growth timber surrounding Conway fueled several wood-related businesses including a box factory, spool factory, and peg mill.

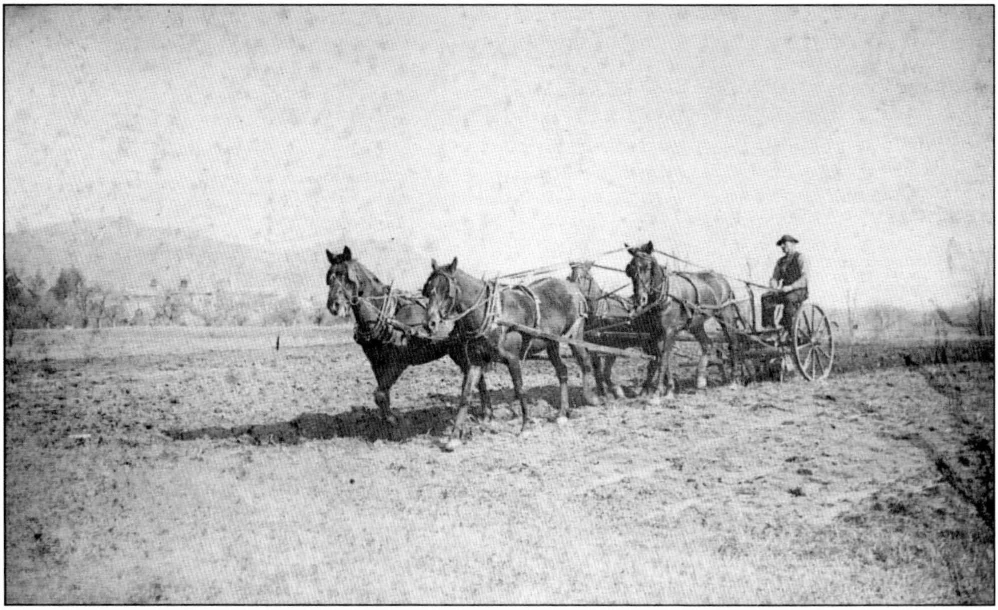

FOUR-HORSE HITCH. Horsepower was an important part of farm life well into the nineteenth century. The configuration shown in this T.E.M. White photograph, with one team ahead of the other, is called "four up."

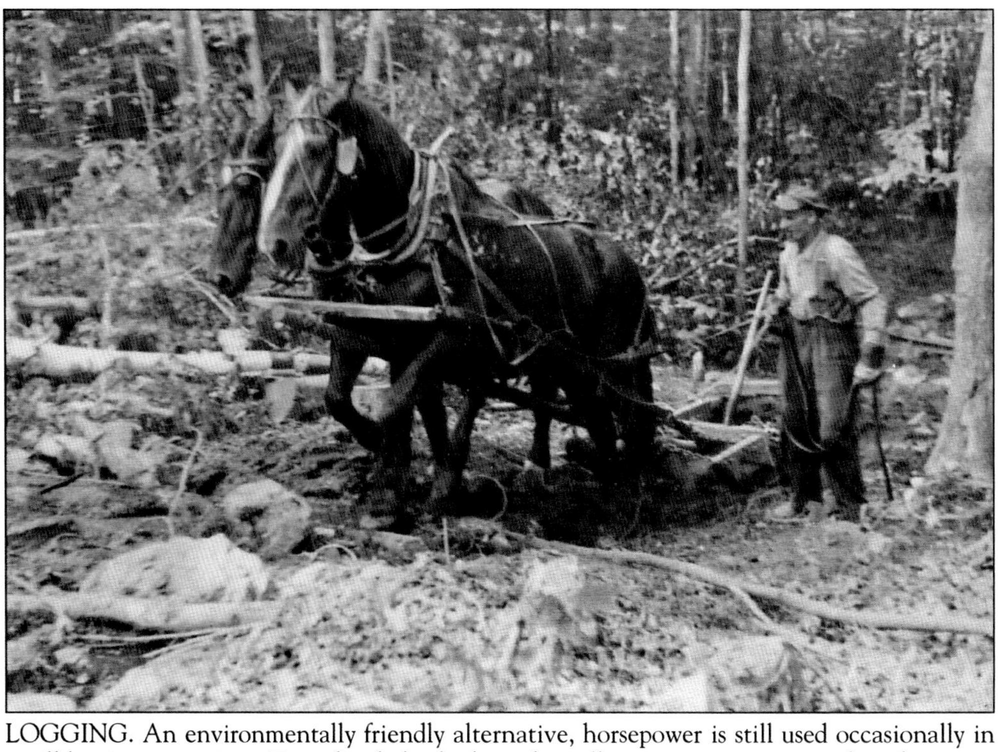

LOGGING. An environmentally friendly alternative, horsepower is still used occasionally in small logging operations. Note the sled, which works well on snow, wet grass, and mud.

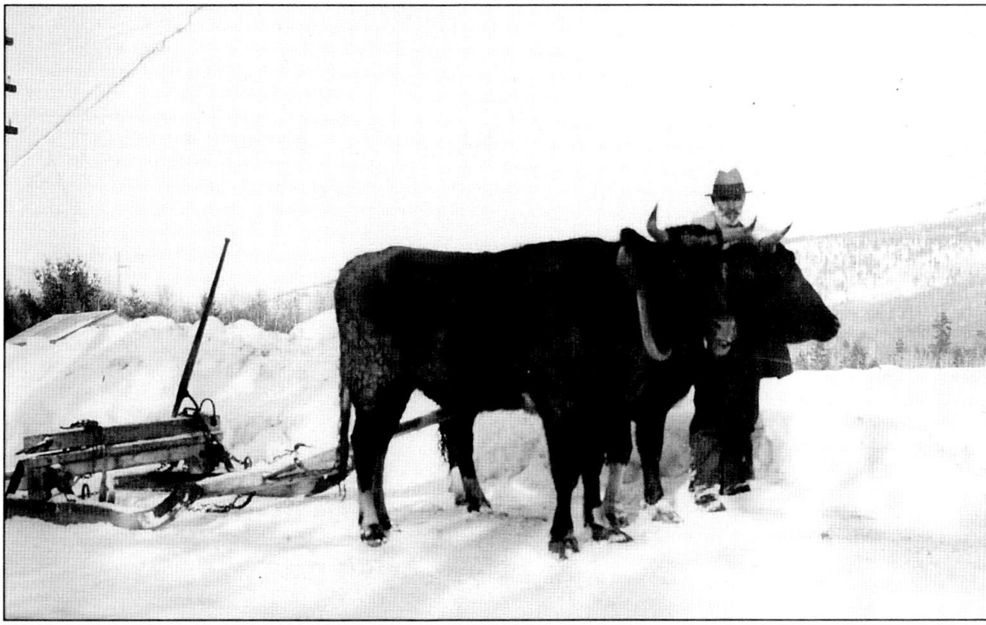

OX TEAM, NORTH CONWAY. A cheaper and steadier alternative to horses, oxen were a vital segment of the work force. The team above was driven by Irving Eastman.

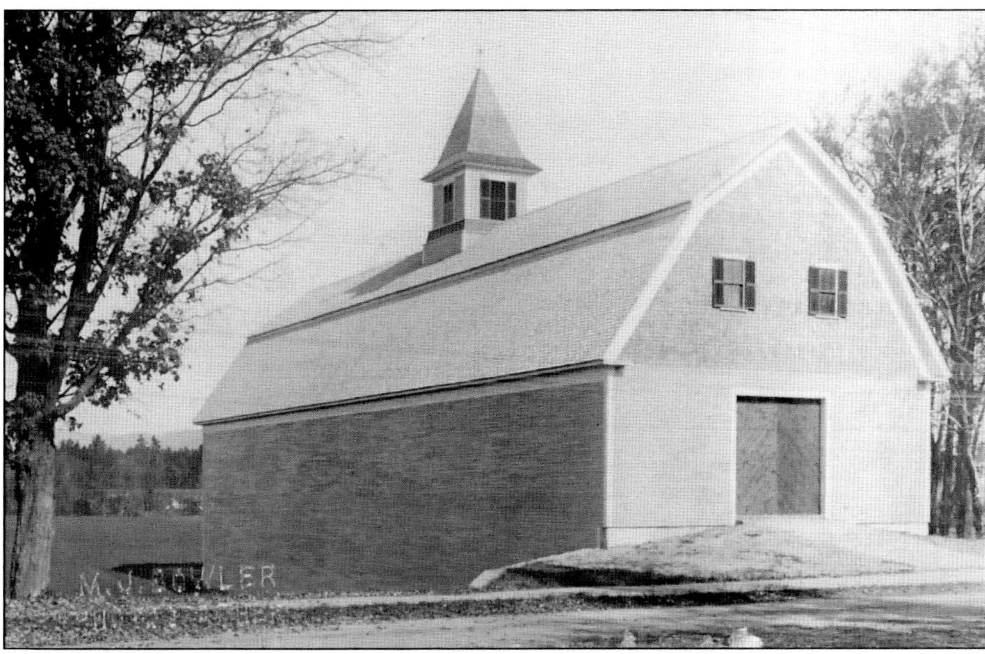

THE KENNETT BARN, MAIN STREET, CONWAY VILLAGE. This barn, used by the Kennett family for hay storage, stood on the lot now occupied by St. Charles Church. The cupola was salvaged for use on the Redmen's Hall on VFW Street in Conway.

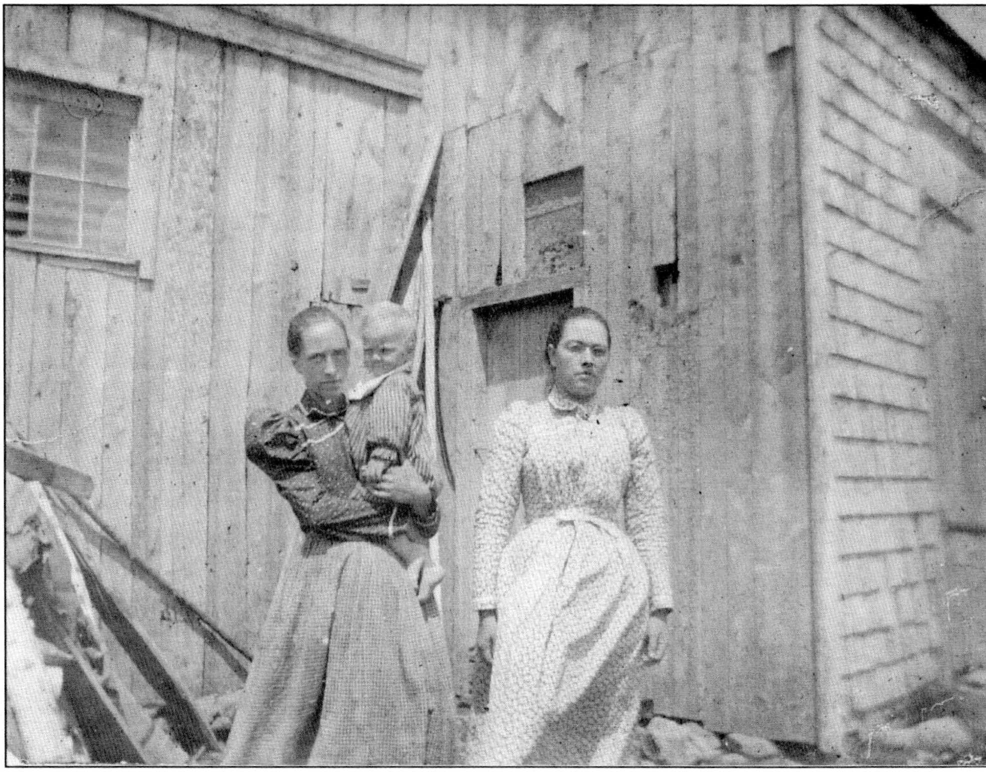

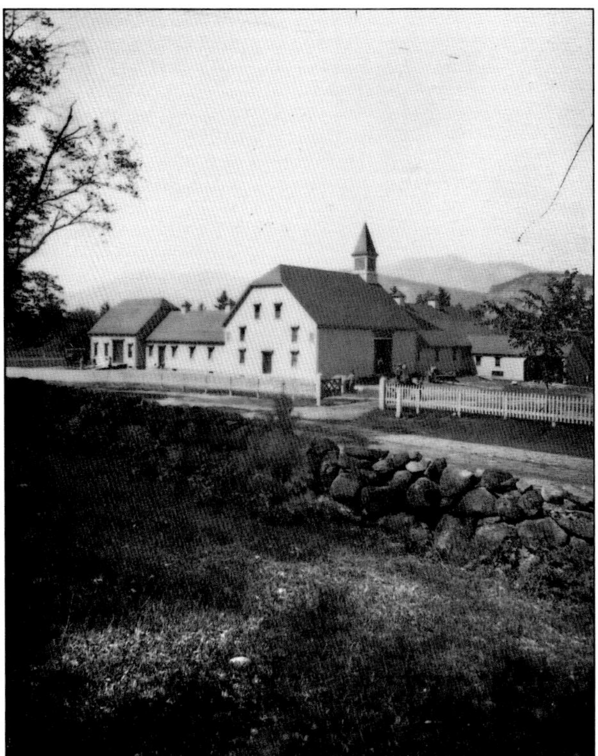

FARM WOMEN. Women fought the loneliness, monotony, and hard labor of rural life by sharing jobs whenever possible. The year was filled with quilting bees, corn husking, apple drying, and any other activity that could be shared with willing neighbors.

THE BIGELOW MERRIMAN BARN, *c.* 1875. While the Bigelow Merriman summer cottage (now Stonehurst) was the center of social activity in North Conway, the accompanying farm was a model of up-to-date agriculture. The barn later became the Carriage Inn.

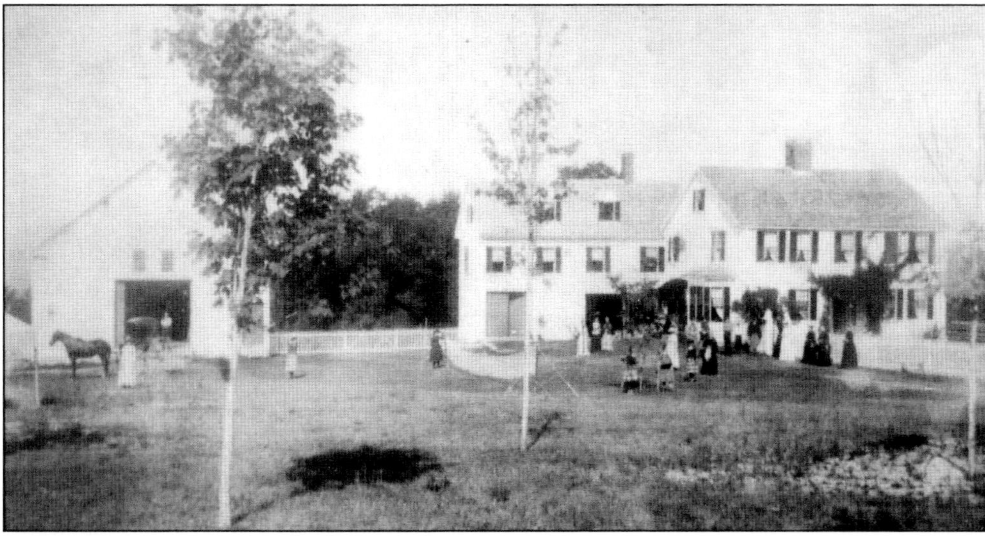

THE ATHERTON FARM, SOUTH CONWAY. Danforth and Lucy Atherton were pioneers in housing South Conway summer boarders. The house boasted two flush toilets before they were common in the Conways. Among their early guests were Louisa May Alcott and her family. Miss Alcott wrote much of *Eight Cousins* while staying at the farm. The pine tree under which she sat to write was a local landmark for many years.

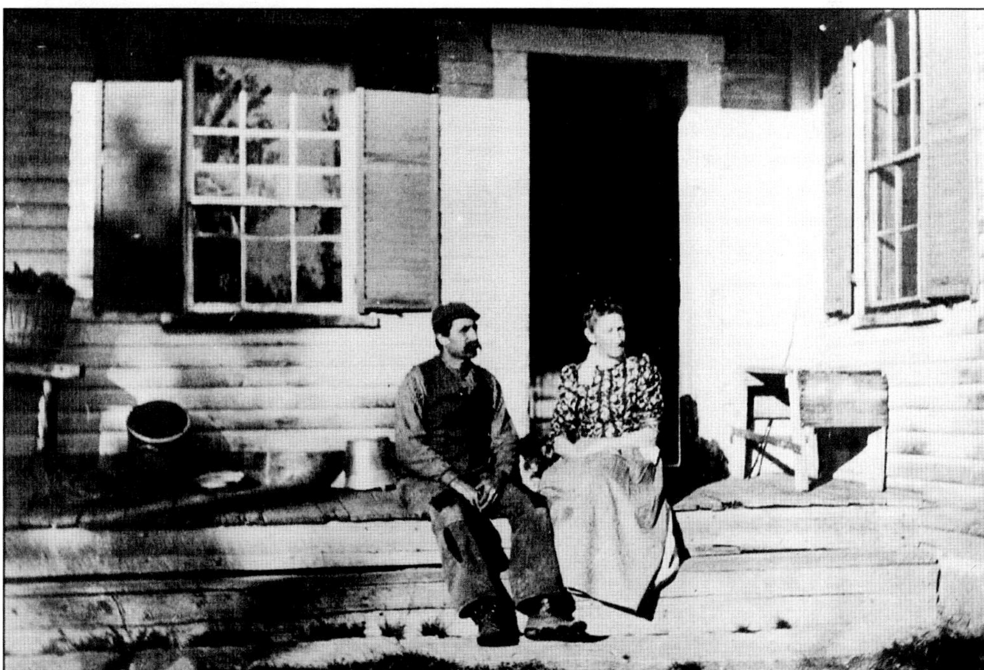

AUNT GUSTIE AND UNCLE JOHN LEGARE OF GOSHEN. Hannah Wakefield Legare, lifelong resident of the South Conway neighborhood called Goshen, was a sickly child. After her father's illness necessitated her taking over the farm work, she developed a robust constitution that lasted for the rest of her life. At age sixty-three, she married John Legare, a forty-seven-year-old French-Canadian. Aunt Gustie, as she was known to her friends and neighbors, wandered the lanes of Goshen until her death at the age of ninety-two.

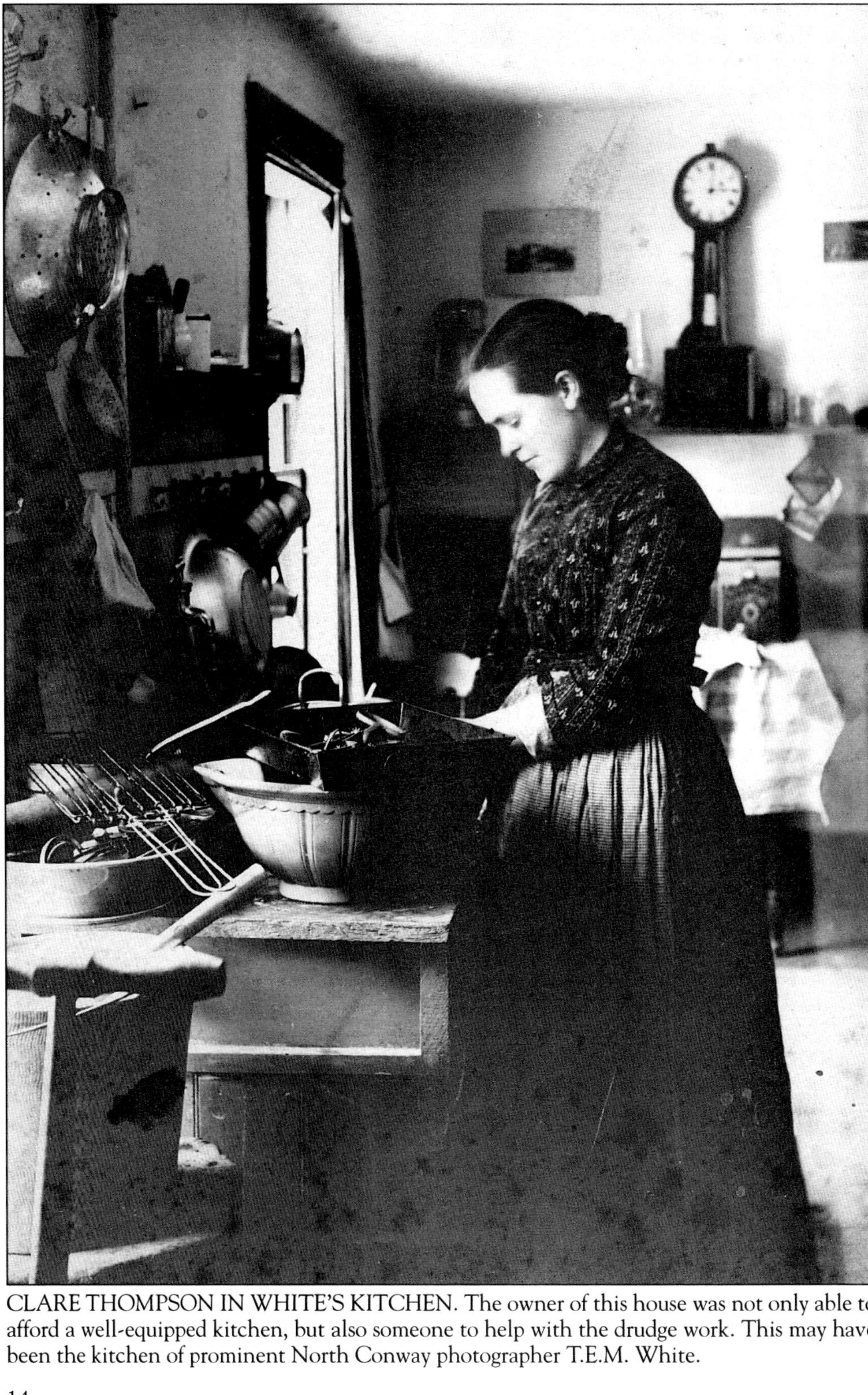

CLARE THOMPSON IN WHITE'S KITCHEN. The owner of this house was not only able to afford a well-equipped kitchen, but also someone to help with the drudge work. This may have been the kitchen of prominent North Conway photographer T.E.M. White.

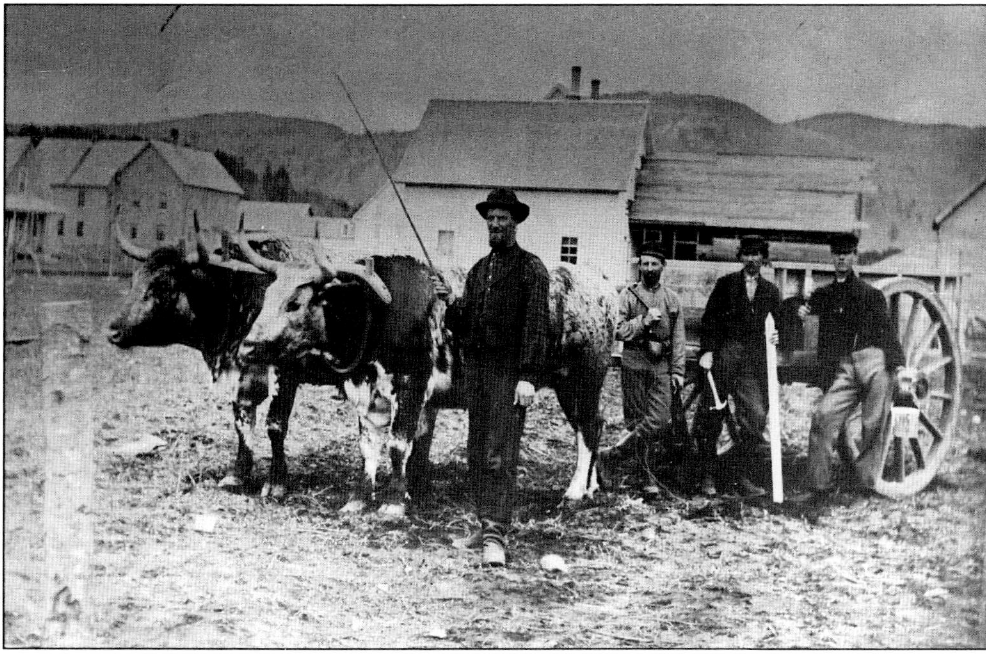

HERBERT (GUS) WHITAKER, *c.* 1880. Herbert Whitaker, the son of William Franklin and Mary (Thomas) Whitaker, is shown driving an ox team and cart. The Whitakers lived in Stark Neighborhood.

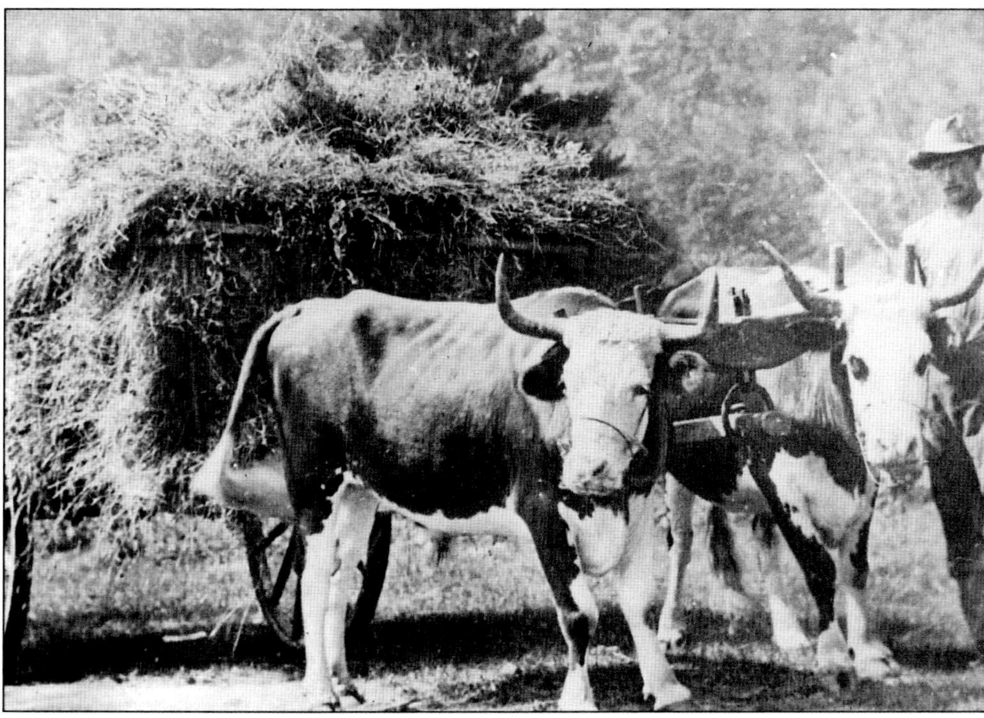

HAYING. Herbert Thompson is shown with a team of oxen hauling a load of loose hay. The two-wheeled ox cart was a common farm vehicle. When farmers traded labor, a day with a team of oxen counted as two days of labor.

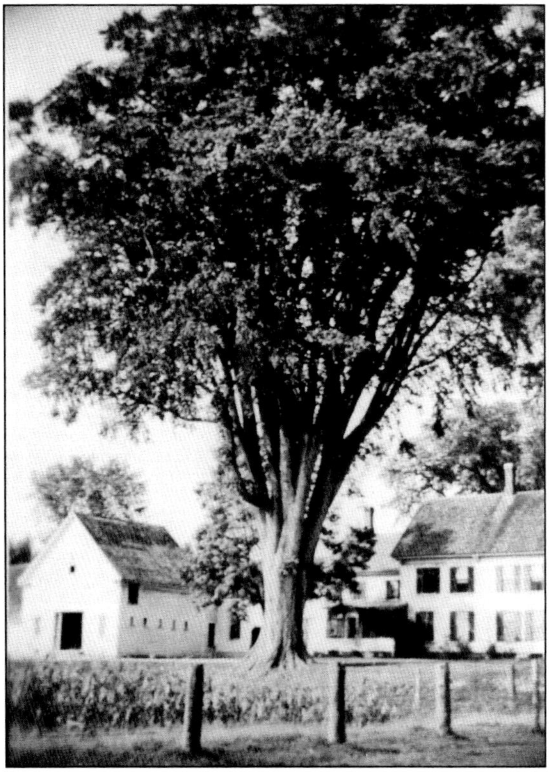

THE ALLARD FARM, WEST SIDE ROAD. Tradition says that Leavitt Hill planted this elm as a sapling in 1780. When it was removed in August 1966, it was the largest elm in the state, with a stump measuring 6-by-8-feet in diameter.

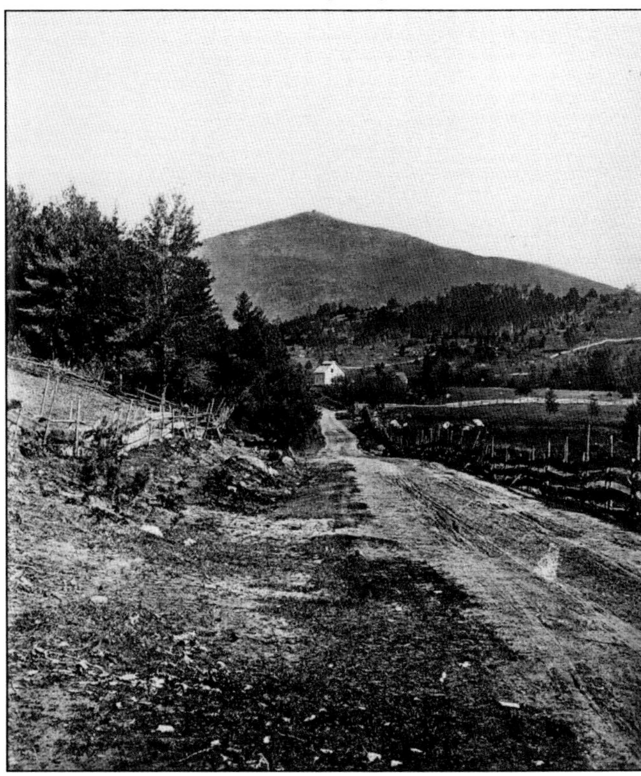

"HARD SCRABBLE." This Kearsarge scene is in stark contrast to the flat, fertile bottom land along the banks of the Saco.

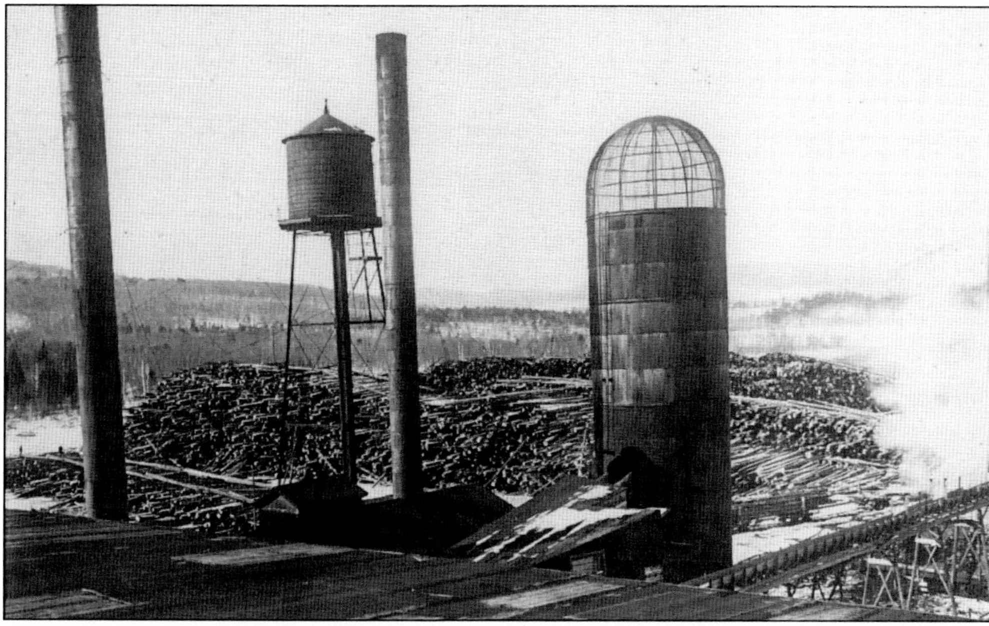

THE CONWAY LUMBER COMPANY, *c.* 1910. The "Big Mill," as the Conway Lumber Company was commonly known, was served by three railways bringing old growth lumber from the area that would later become the White Mountain National Forest. In February 1916, eighty car loads were brought to the mill in just two days.

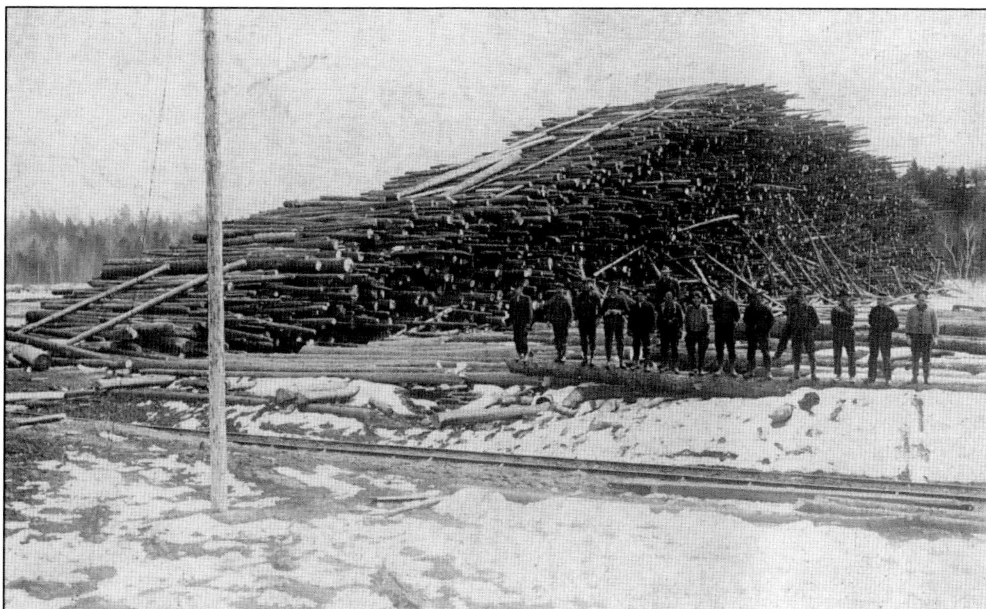

THE CONWAY LUMBER COMPANY, *c.* 1910. On March 16, 1916, *The White Mountain Reporter* related the following: "Patrick Murphy fell over the guard fence on the saw mill slip and landed in a pile of snow about thirty feet below. A steam pipe broke his fall . . . Ike Tewksbury met with a peculiar loss last Sunday morning, while tending to his work as fireman at the big mill, he sneezed and a set of teeth were ejected from their usual resting place and found everlasting rest in the fire box."

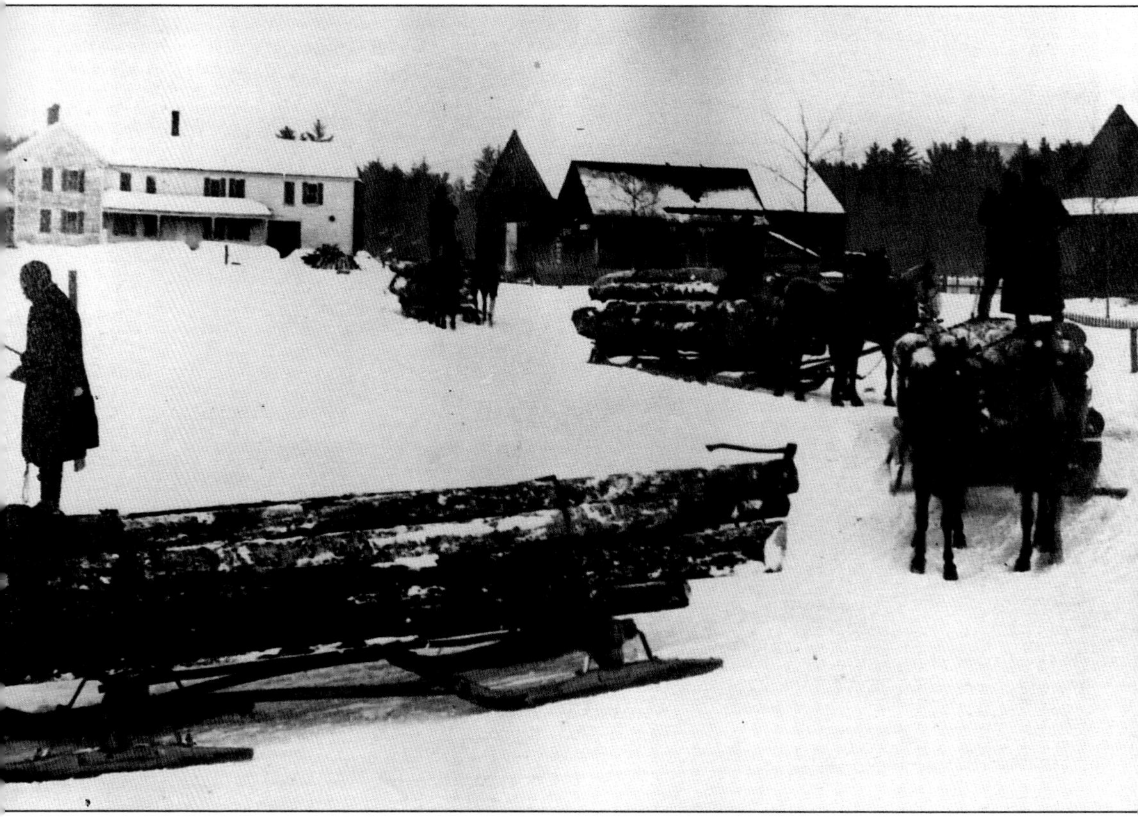

LOGGING TEAMS, WHITAKER HOMESTEAD. Logging was easier in winter when sleds could be used. Mills were sometimes closed because lack of snow affected the timber supply.

Two

Troubled Waters: Bridges, Rivers, and Floods

Travel was difficult in early Conway. Rivers and brooks sliced the landscape into isolated wedges. During periods of high water, crossings were dangerous or impossible. In nearby Passaconaway, those wishing to cross the Swift River without a long detour used a basket suspended from cables to traverse the flooded stream. After floods drove the settlers to build on higher ground, they continued to plague farmers by ruining crops and drowning livestock. Periodically, sections of Conway are still cut off by rising flood waters.

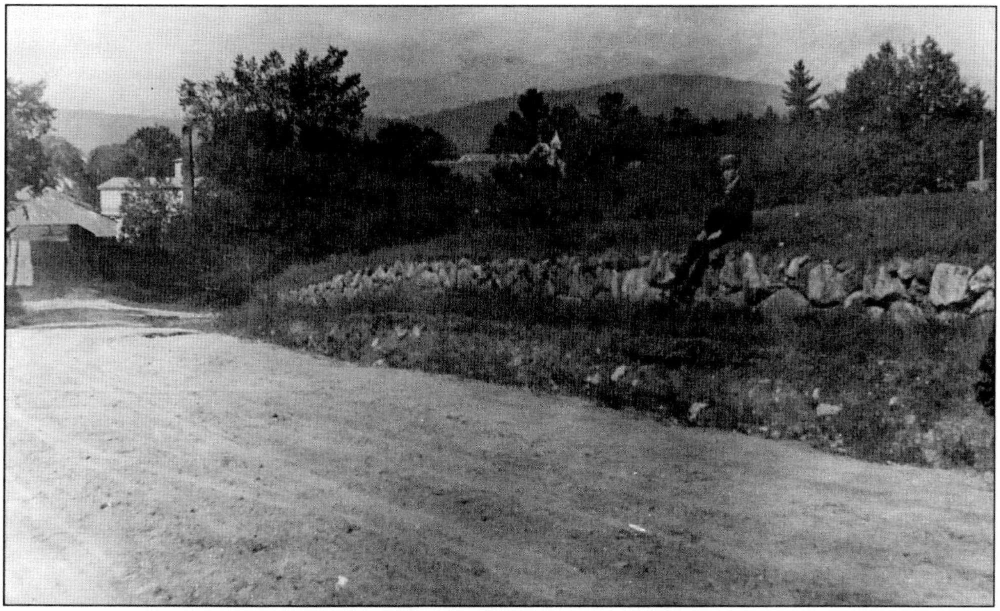

THE SACO RIVER BRIDGE. In 1869, the Swift River Bridge washed away for the second time, taking with it the Saco River Bridge. When the Chair and Ladder Factory, shown beside the bridge, burned in 1890, the fire spread to the Toll House and Saco River Bridge. All three structures were destroyed. When the Chair Factory again burned in December 1903, the new bridge was spared. The Saco River Bridge was renovated in 1988.

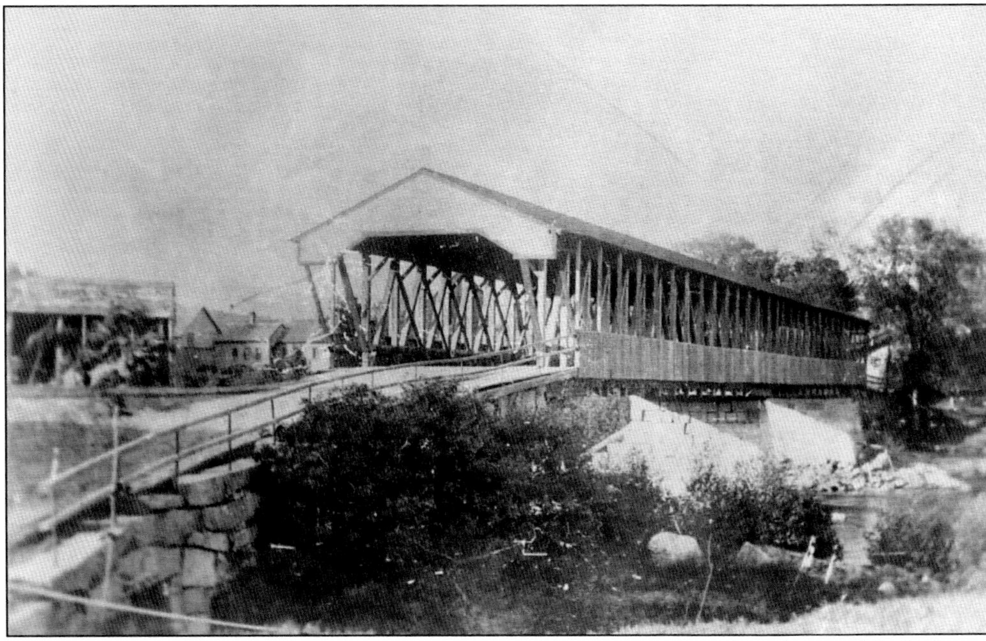

THE SACO RIVER COVERED BRIDGE, CONWAY VILLAGE. This Paddleford-truss bridge was built by Charles and Frank Broughton in 1890 to replace one destroyed by fire. The structure boasts two sidewalks.

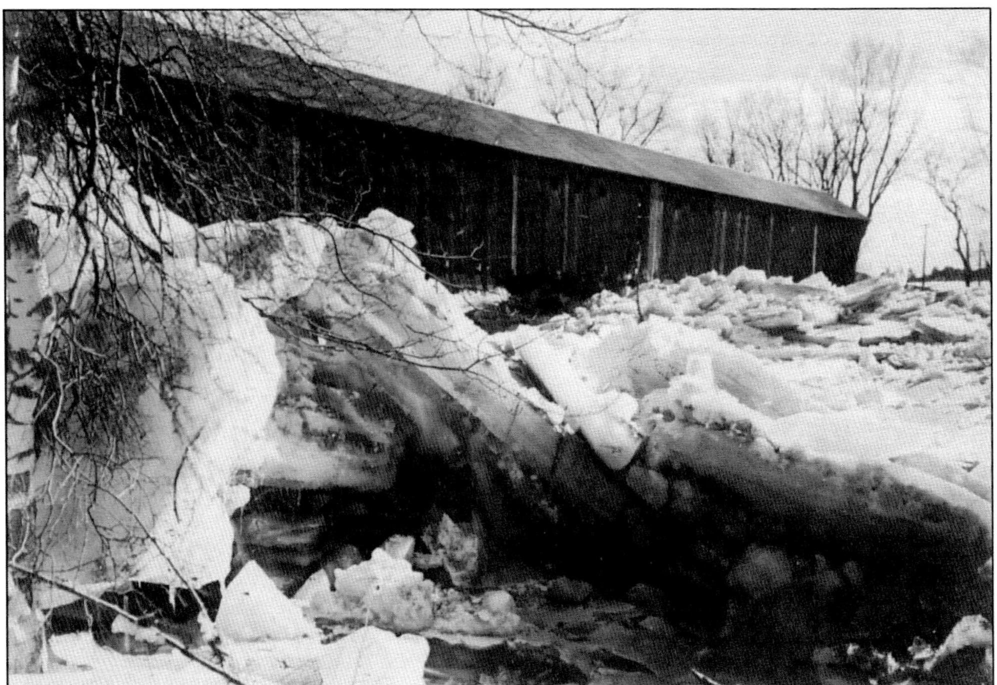

THE JOEL EASTMAN BRIDGE. Early bridges were destroyed with great regularity. The first bridge at this site in Center Conway was built in the winter of 1797 and washed away the next fall. The next one, built at Odell's Falls, lasted only four days. The Smith-Eastman Bridge was destroyed by arsonists in 1976.

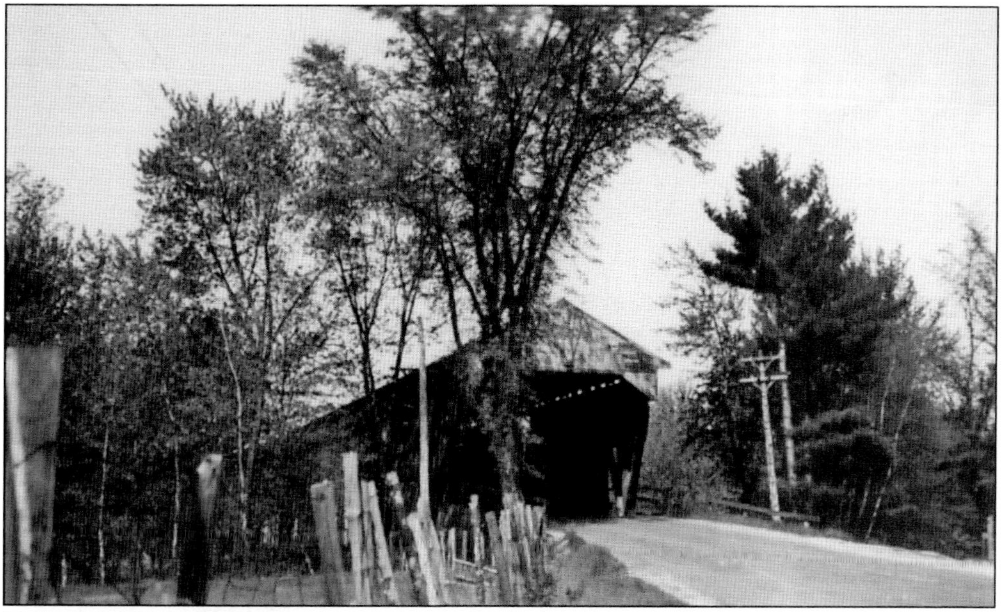

THE NORTH CONWAY COVERED BRIDGE. During the 1940s, the upstream arch had begun to sag and in 1950, the town voted to replace this bridge with a modern one. During the previous year, the covered railroad bridge on the West Side was replaced. Timber from the railroad bridge was used in the construction of the nearby Dennison home (later destroyed by flood).

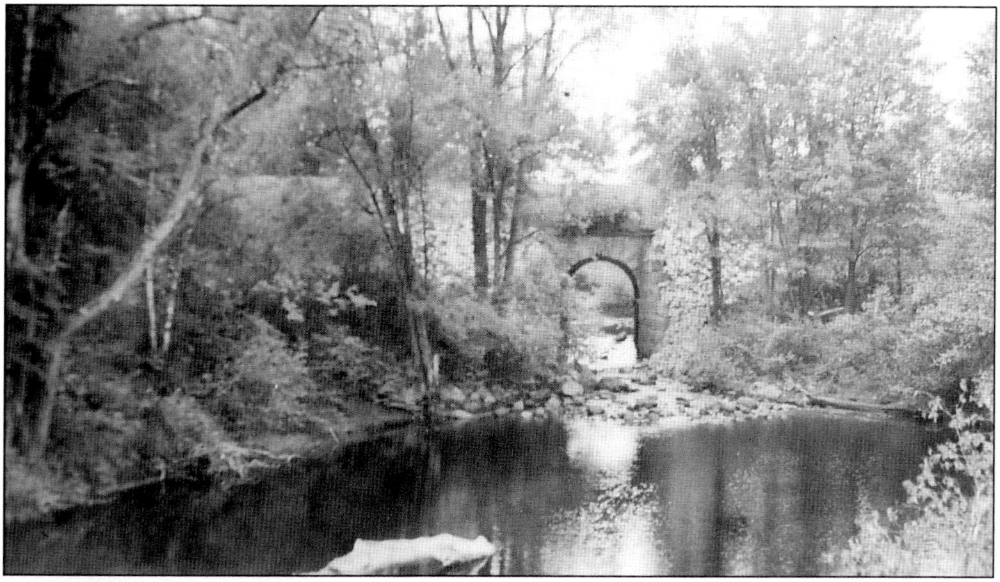

AN OLD STONE BRIDGE, CONWAY CENTER. The Conways were rich in stonecutters, quarry men, and the raw materials essential to their crafts. There are many fine examples of their skills scattered throughout the valley. In 1854, Edmund Wentworth was paid $105 for building a stone bridge in District #1 and Andrew Dinsmore was paid $25 for furnishing and laying stone at the ends of the Swift River Bridge.

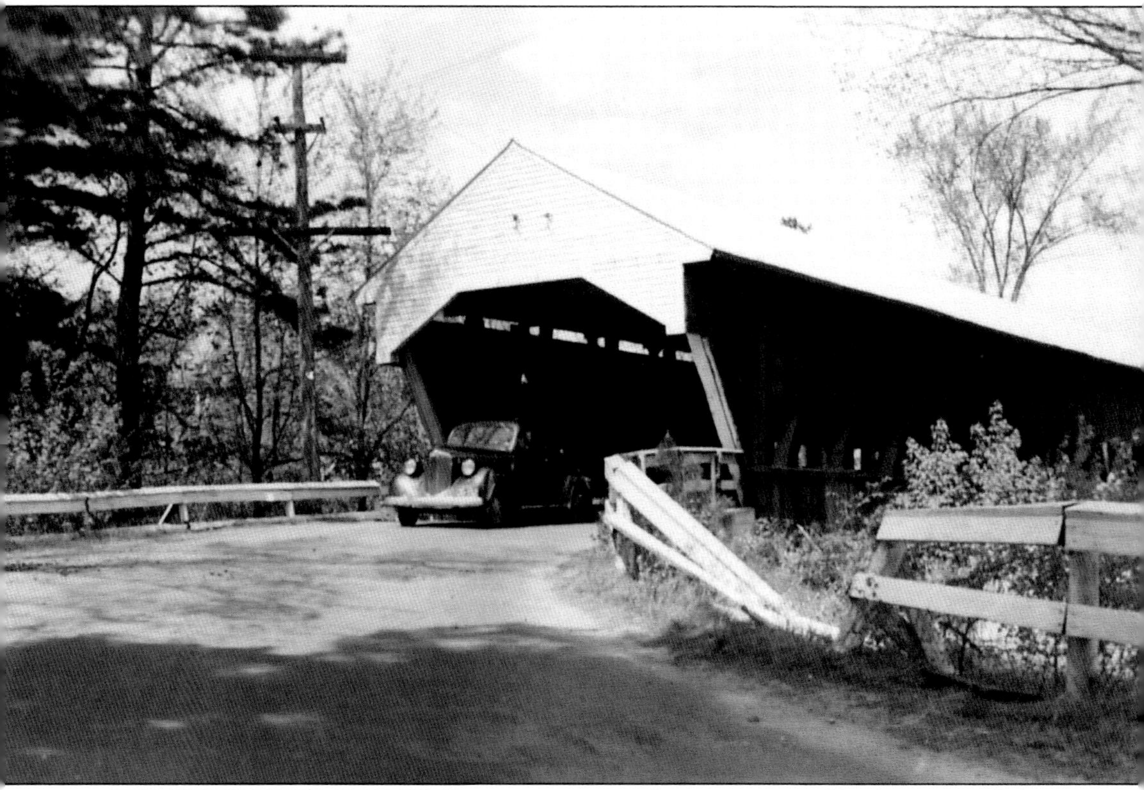

THE SWIFT RIVER BRIDGE. Horses were required to cross covered bridges at a walk because the vibrations caused by a trotting team could damage the structure. Men were hired to "snow" covered bridges to allow sleigh travel. Built in 1869 to replace the 1850 bridge carried away by floods, the Swift River Bridge was saved from imminent destruction by a fund raising campaign in 1990.

Three

A Room with a View: Arts, Artists, and Scenic Views

It is not surprising that the White Mountains have attracted artists. One has only to view the earliest representations of the "Crystal Hills" to realize the impressions that they made. Many early maps and sketches portray them as taller and steeper than the Alps, covering the entire center of the state. Later depictions were more true to fact, but seldom free from artistic license.

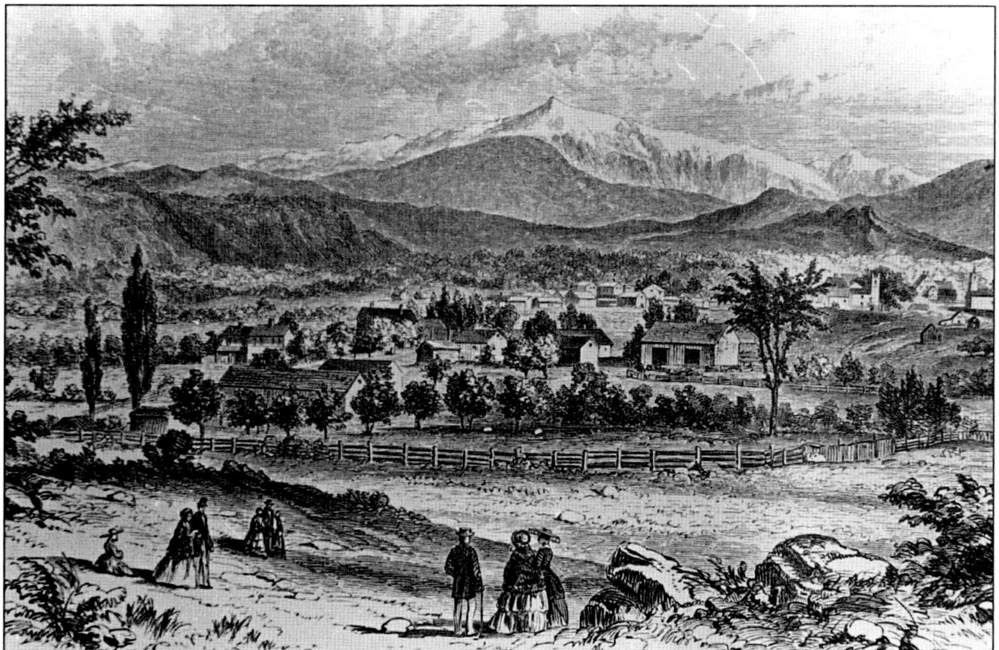

CONWAY AND THE WHITE MOUNTAINS. Early publicity for the Conways stressed the rugged pastoral beauty of the White Mountains. This Currier and Ives print took some liberties with the landscape.

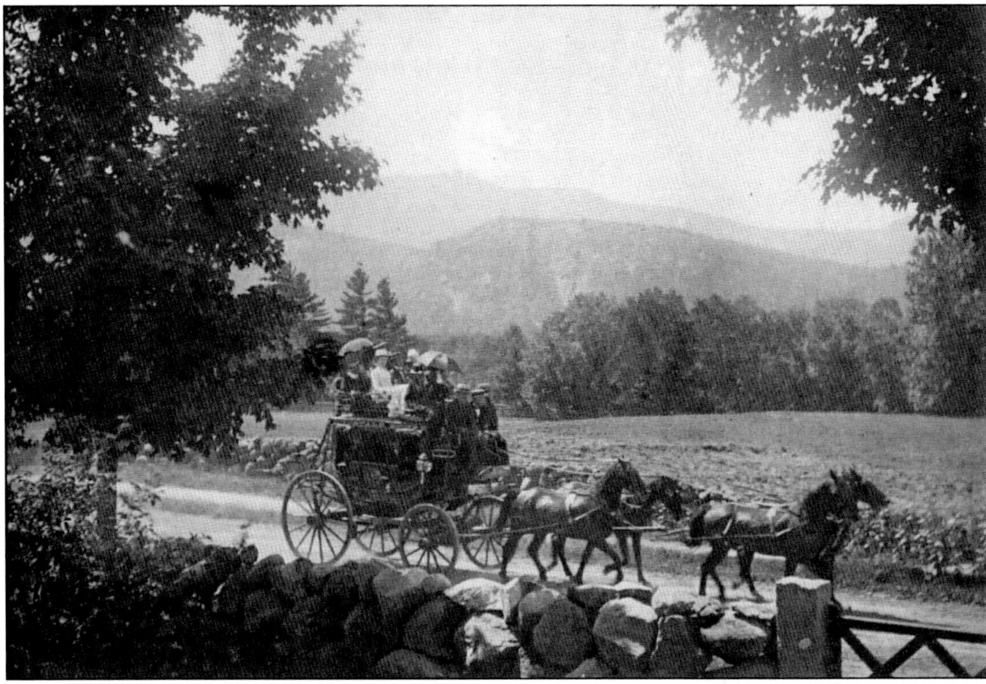

AN INTERVALE HOUSE COACH. The Intervale House advertised "pure spring water and perfect drainage" with telephone and telegraph offices as well. They were famed for the handsome turnouts provided by their livery.

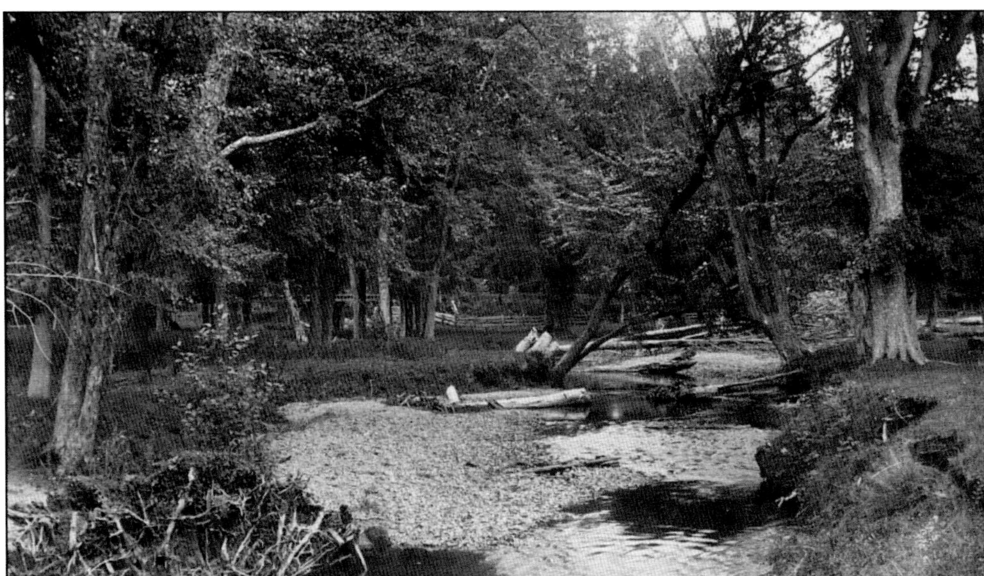

THE RAMBLE'S, ARTIST'S BROOK. The valley became a mecca for artists and photographers seeking bucolic vistas. Several spots were named in honor of their popularity with the artistic community.

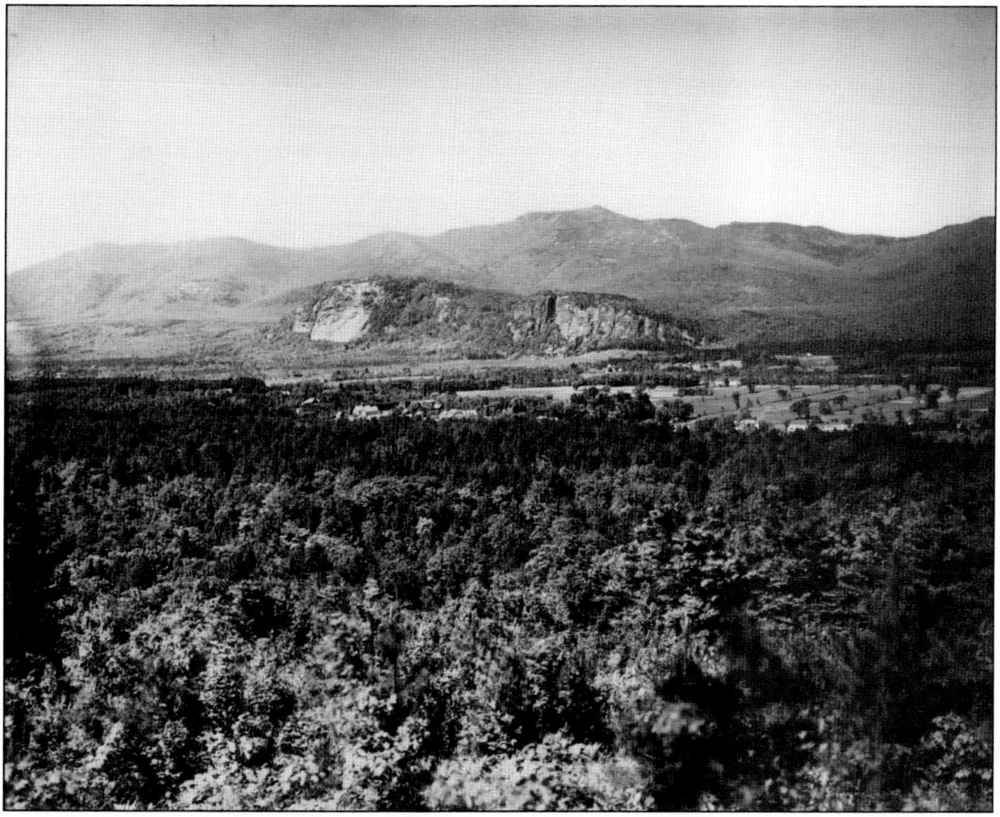

A VIEW FROM MT. KEARSARGE. The Cathedral and White Horse Ledges, backed by the Moats, form one of the most photographed scenes in the Conways.

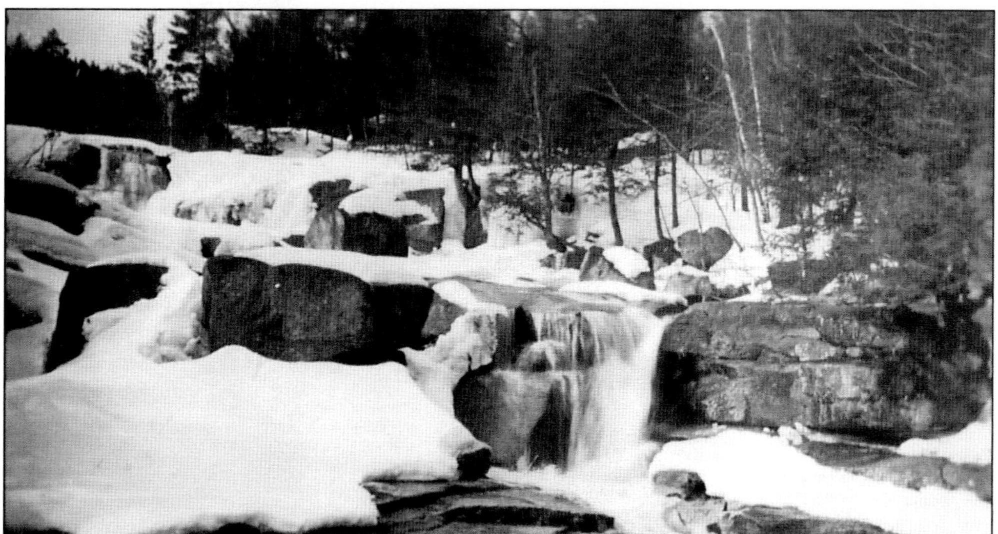

DIANA'S BATHS. Once a source of power for a sawmill, Diana's Baths developed a reputation as a prime tourist attraction. Although several theories have been advanced, no one seems sure of the origin of the name.

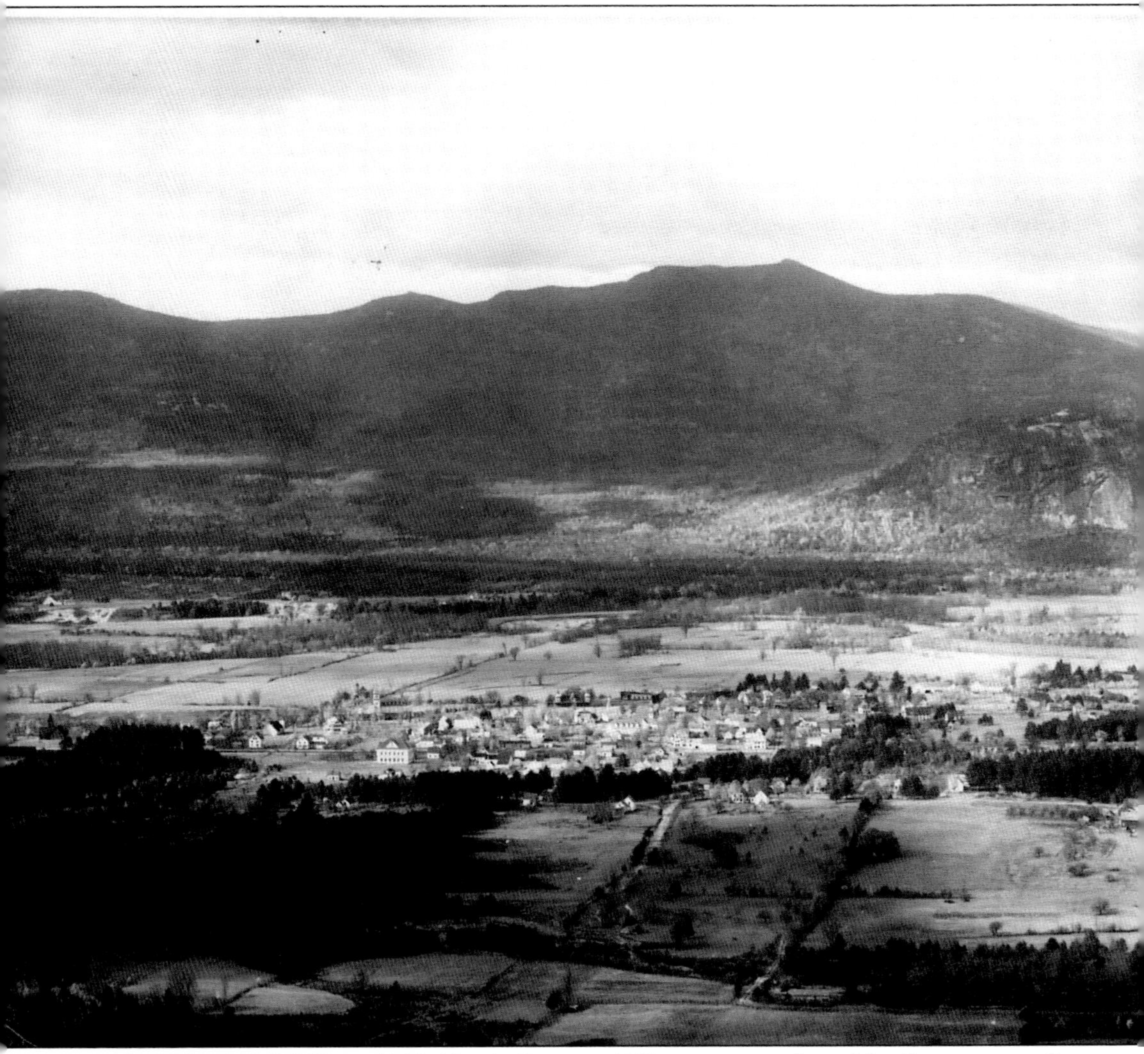

NORTH CONWAY, *c.* 1910. North Conway Village, as seen from Mt. Cranmore, radiates the aura of a turn-of-the-century resort. The railroad station can be seen in the center with the Kearsarge House to the left and the Randall House to the right.

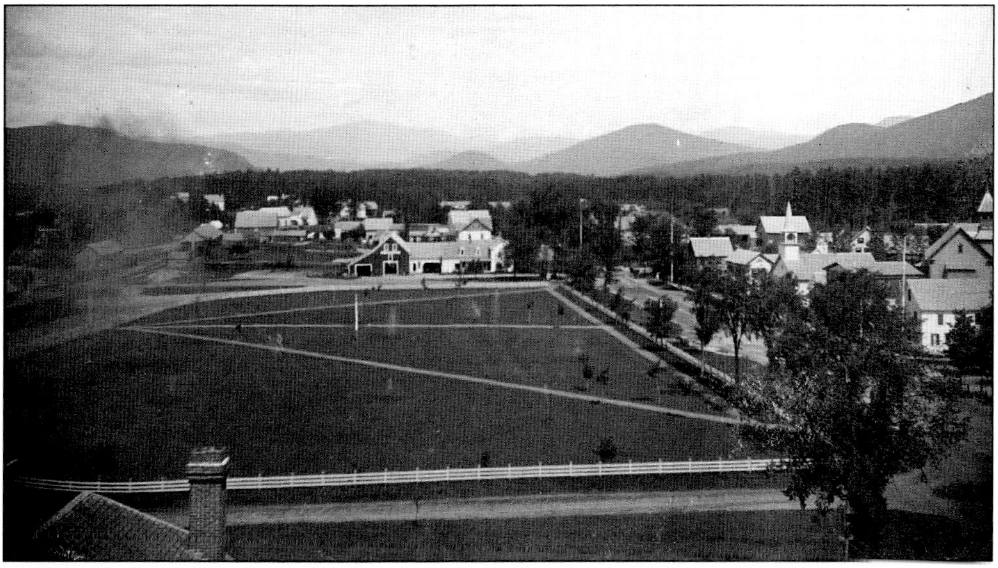

NORTH CONWAY FROM THE KEARSARGE HOUSE. Guests at the Kearsarge, once located near the site now occupied by the North Conway Community Center, were treated to spectacular mountain views without leaving their rooms. This is probably the view from the tower.

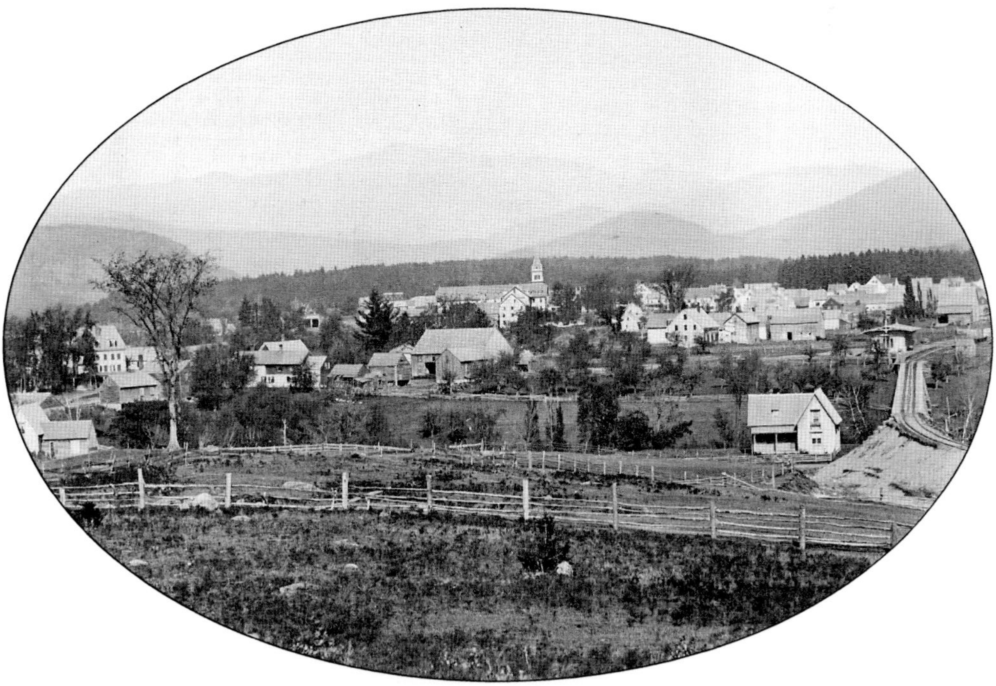

NORTH CONWAY VILLAGE FROM SUNSET HILL, *c.* 1870. This rare photograph of North Conway was taken before the familiar profile of the North Conway station appeared. The Kearsarge House, seen in the center, offered special rates to artists with up to fifteen staying at the hotel at one time. The artists, in turn, lured more tourists to North Conway. Conway Village, in order to compromise North Conway's success, sent coaches up the west side of the river, avoiding North Conway.

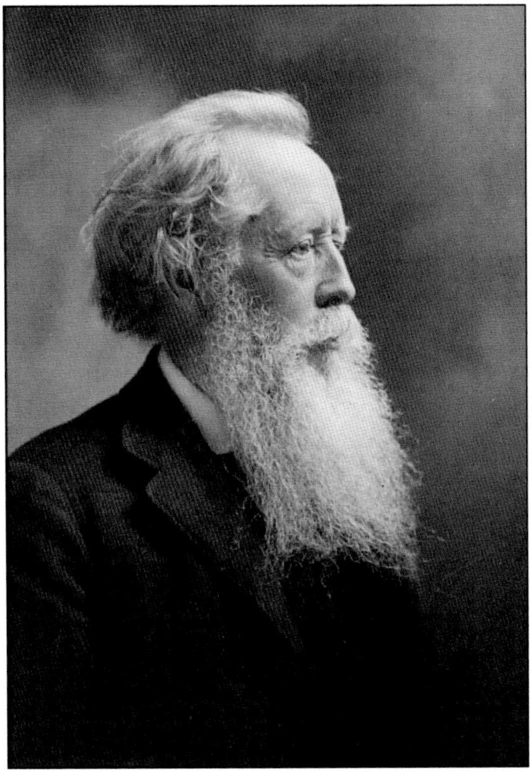

T.E.M. WHITE. Photographer Thomas Edward Mulliken White, along with his painter wife, Gabriella Eddy White, was a leading artistic force in North Conway. An avid swimmer, White was described, rising from the water and shaking his silver mane and beard, as looking like Neptune rising from the sea.

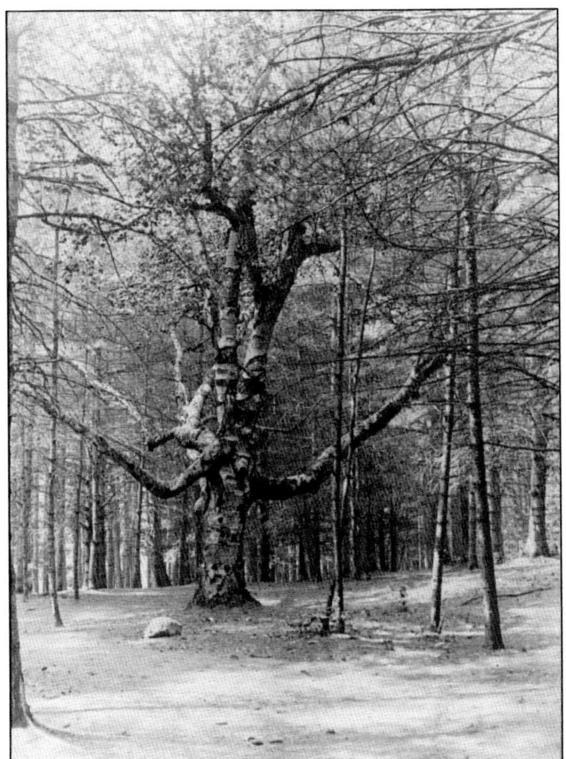

THE WIZARD BIRCH. The massive gnarled birch known as the "Wizard" grew in the section of Intervale called Cathedral Woods. Several groves became popular attractions, including Cathedral Woods and Enchanted Woods. One wooded section was maintained in North Conway Village for the pleasure of hotel guests.

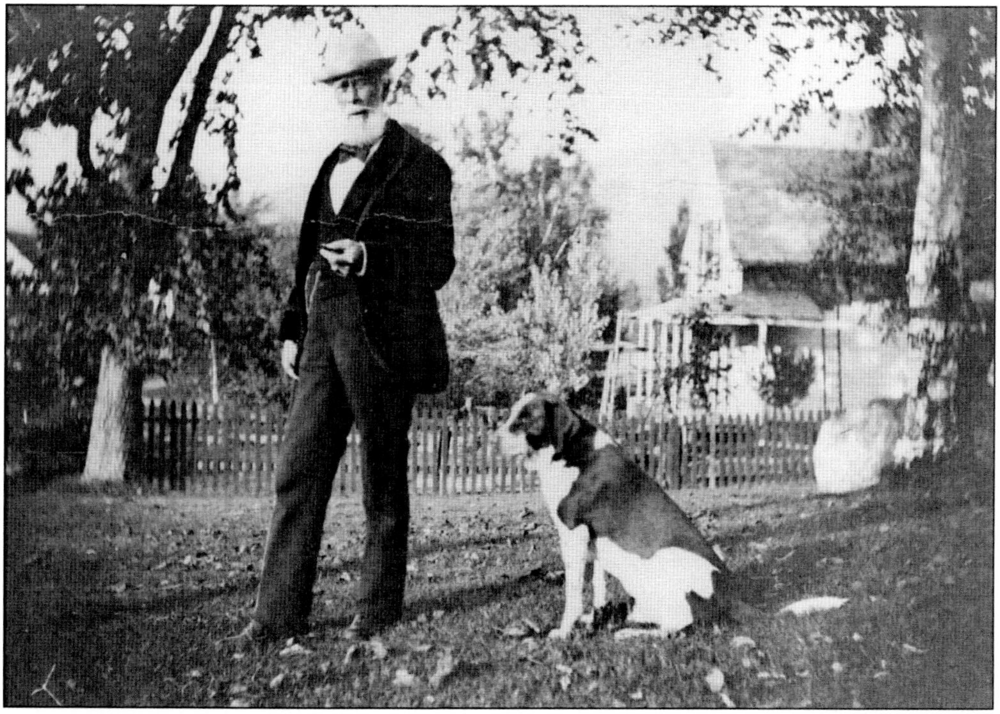

BENJAMIN CHAMPNEY. Champney was instrumental in bringing other artists to North Conway. He also gave art lessons to many locals. After touring Europe, he painted a massive diorama of the French Revolution which would be unrolled across a stage while Champney narrated. When it was destroyed by fire, he expressed a certain degree of relief.

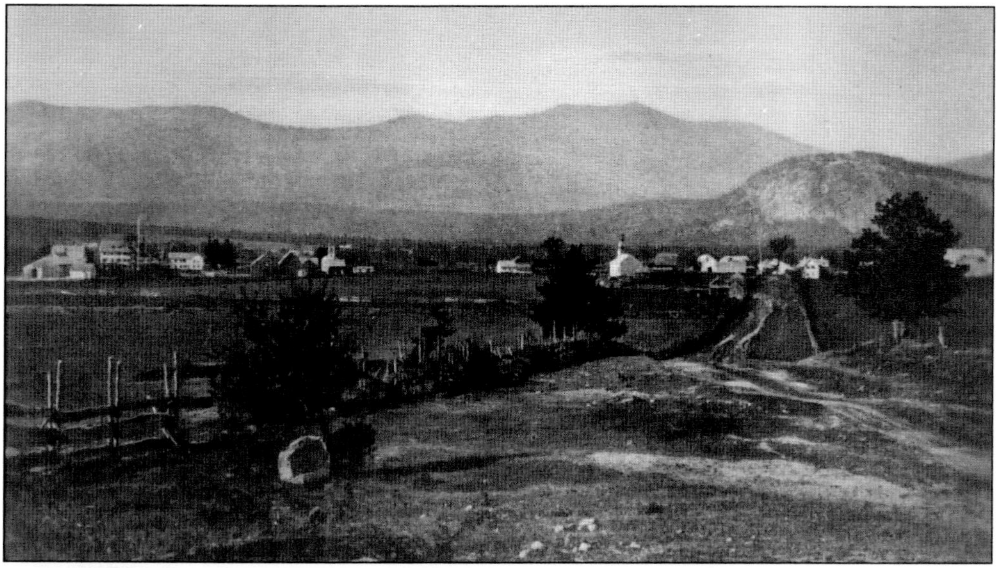

A COUNTRY ROAD, 1861. It was the popularity of the automobile that forced the improvement of roads. Well into the twentieth century, many roads became impassable quagmires in the spring. Horse or ox-drawn rollers were used to break roads for winter travel. Autos were put away for the winter and horses were used until the roads dried out. As automobiles became more important, roads were paved and plowed.

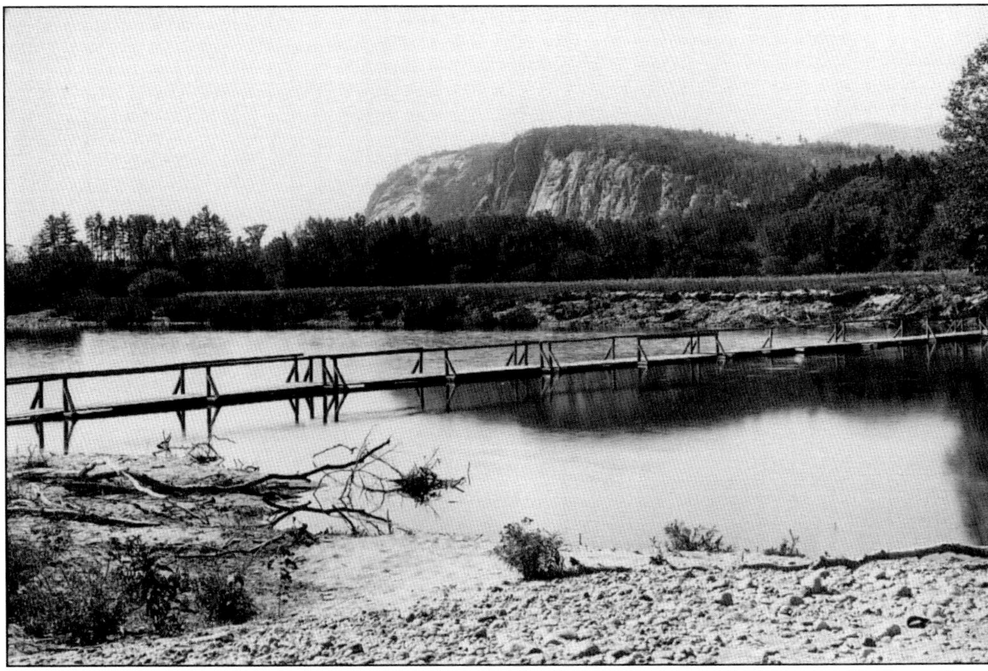

THE FOOTBRIDGE, INTERVALE. A floating footbridge was installed across the Saco River intervale for the convenience of tourists wishing to walk to the ledges.

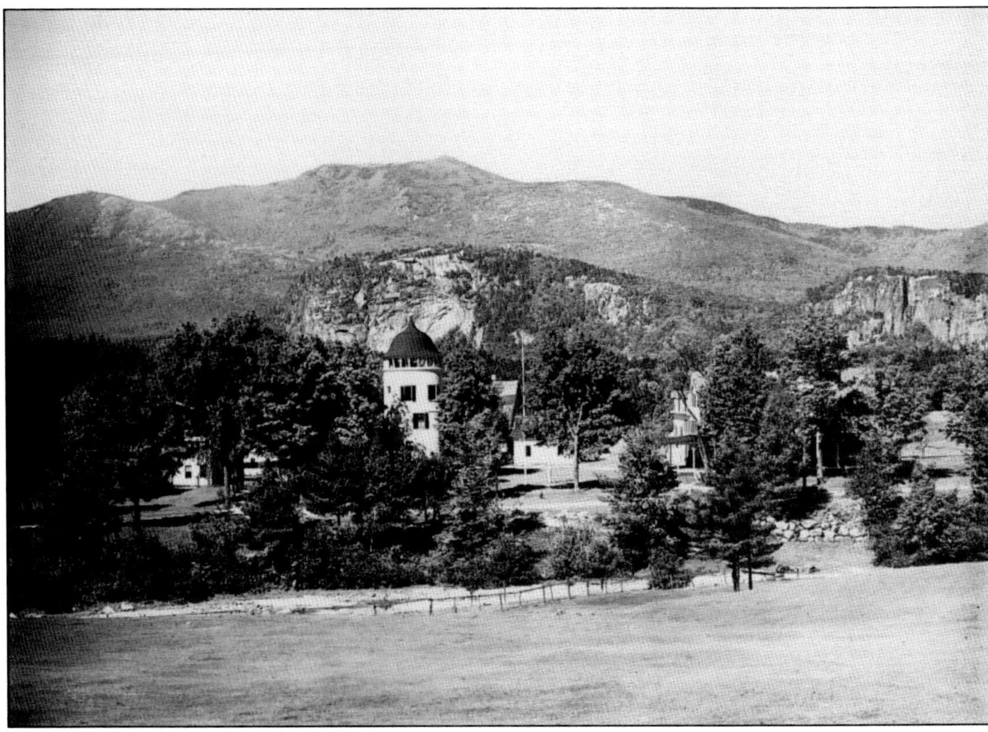

RUSSELL COTTAGES, KEARSARGE. With accommodations for up to 140 guests, Russell Cottages was, for many years, a popular boarding place. Their motto read "The proof of the pudding is in the eating thereof."

Four

A Plan for eAll Seasons: Tourism and Recreation

The first European visitors to the Conways were hardy explorers and hunters. The first tourists must have been hardy souls, as well. Roads were abominable or non existent; accommodations were often worse. Beds were rented to full capacity. A weary traveler might find himself sharing a bed with a drunken teamster, roving salesman, or possibly both. As the number of tourists grew, larger and more commodious inns were built, peaking in the era of the "Grand Hotels." With guests staying on for weeks or months, ways had to be found to entertain them. A new industry was born.

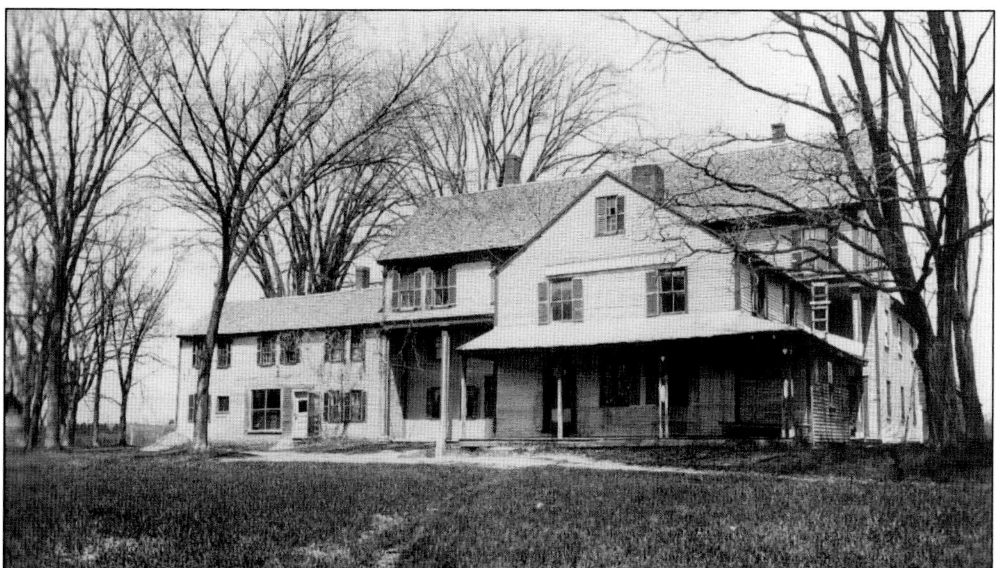

THE PEQUAWKET HOUSE, 1909. The Pequawket House, originally a one-story tavern built by Thomas Abbott around 1800, was enlarged by Asa Adams (Adams Hotel) and then sold to Colonel John Hill. The daughter of Daniel Pendexter, one of the last owners, maintained that Abraham Lincoln stayed at the hotel. She used as proof one of the hotel registers. John Shorey, the final owner, ran it as a boarding house for Polish mill workers. It was razed in 1923 to make room for Kennett High School.

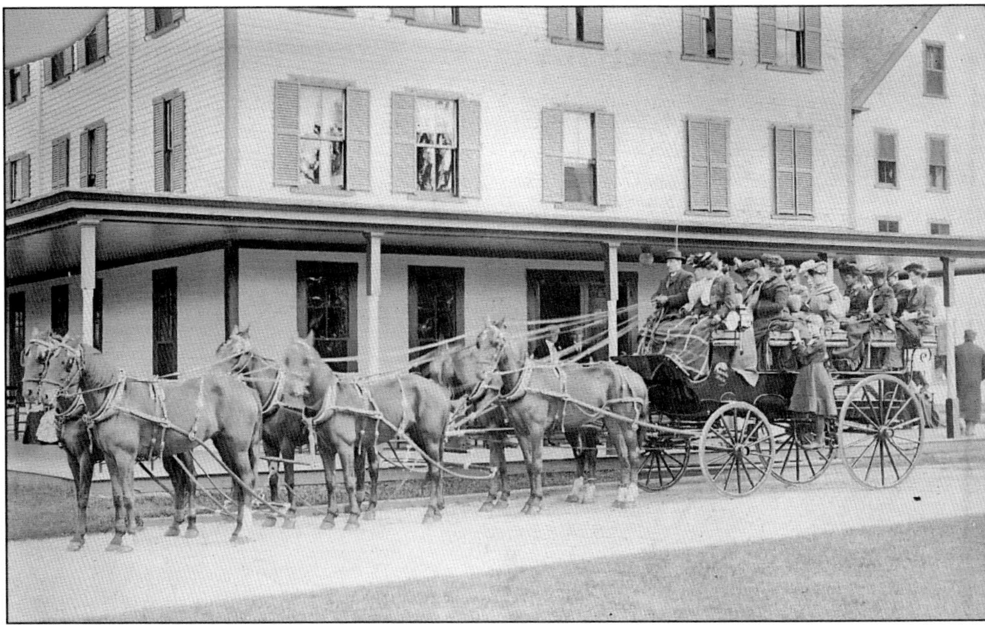

A COACH AND SIX. The Intervale House coach is top heavy with guests waiting for an afternoon excursion. Because guests stayed for long periods, hotels were obligated to offer diversions.

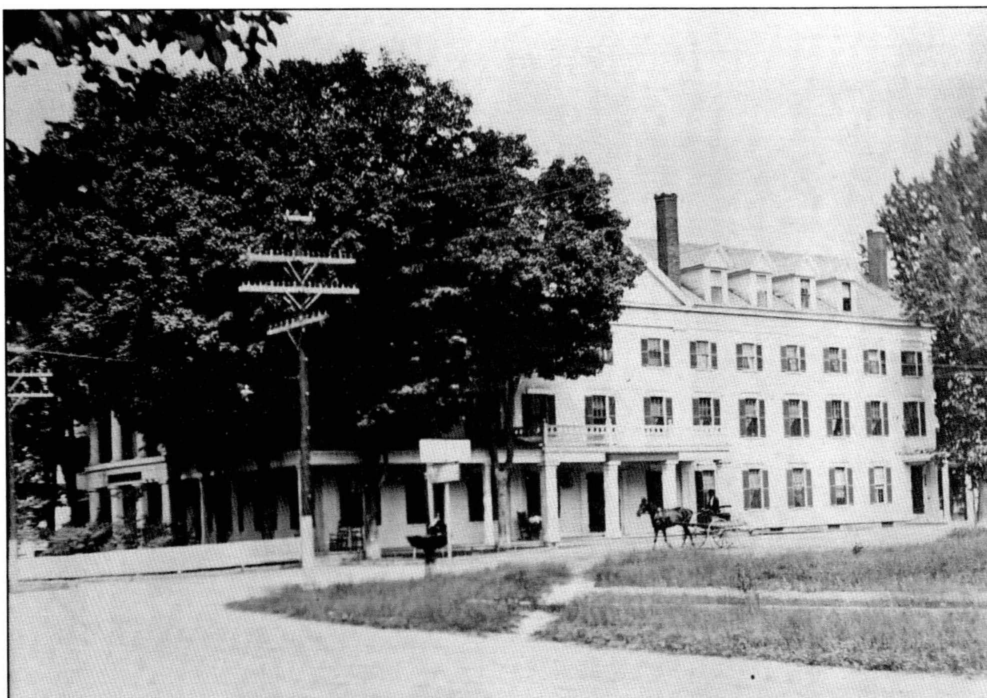

THE CONWAY HOUSE. Built in 1850 by the owners of the stage coach route, the Conway House burned in 1912. It stood on the corner of Main and Washington Streets in Conway Village. When renowned hotel manager Horace Fabyan was brought in as manager, a North Conway innkeeper sniped that he had come to "clean out the bedbugs."

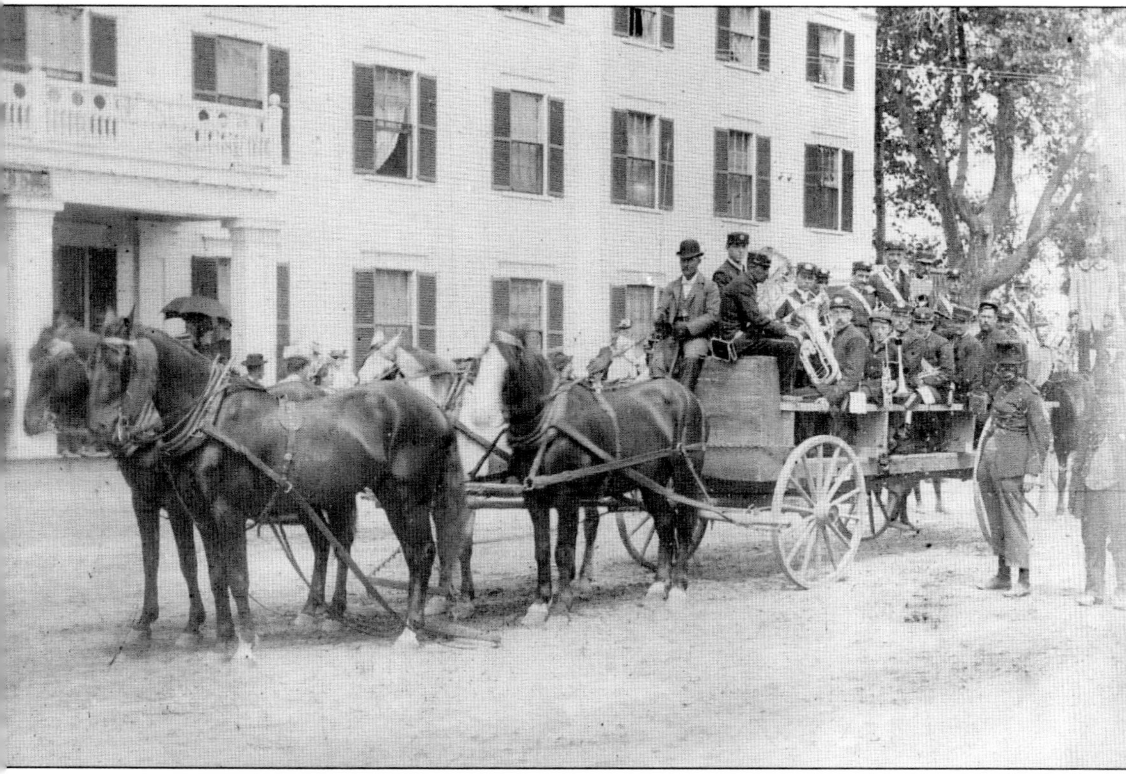

THE CONWAY HOUSE BAND. Included in this happy group were Mark Snow, Helen Snow, and Willis Bean.

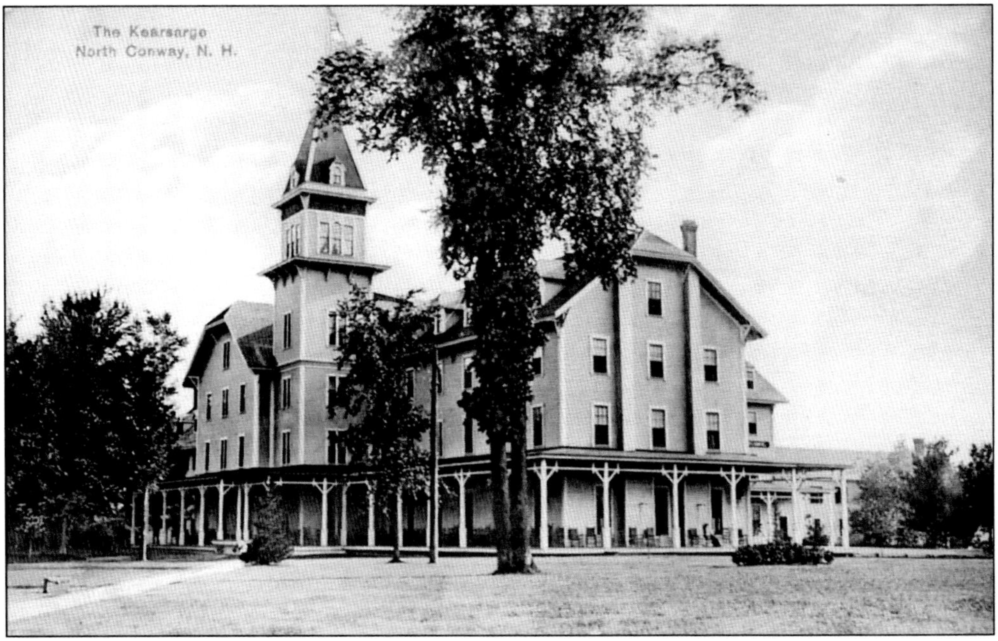

THE KEARSARGE HOUSE, NORTH CONWAY. In 1853, a large delegation of ladies, complete with chaperons, arrived from Boston to spend the summer at the Kearsarge House. Weekly board, including washing, came to $2.50 per person.

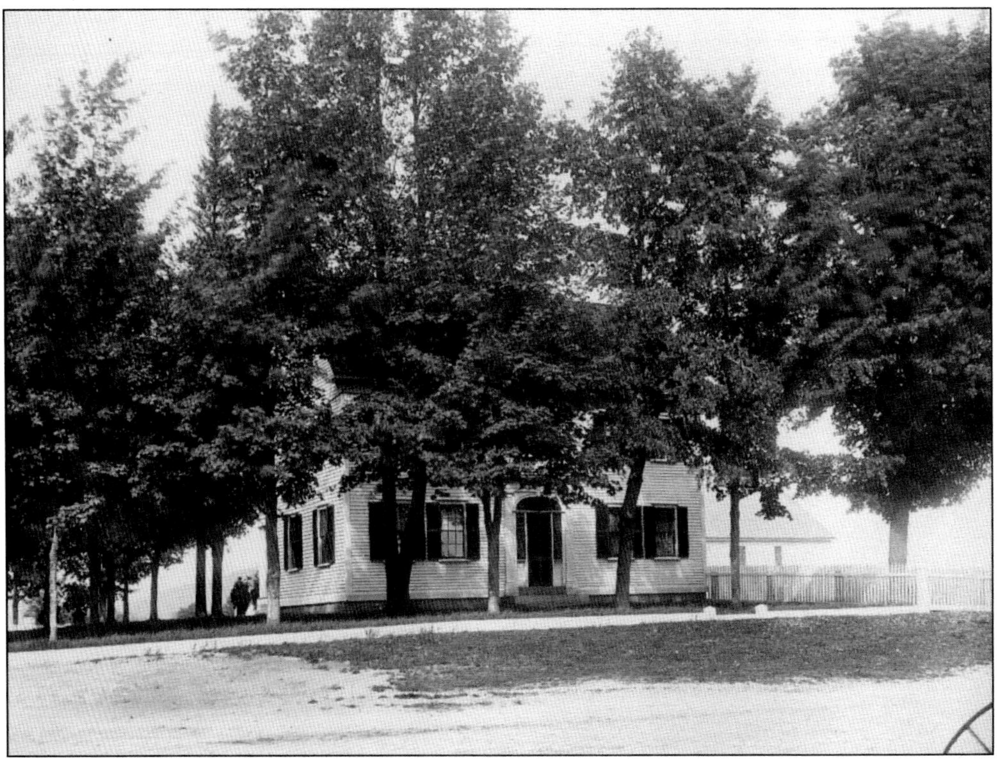

THE RICHARD THOM HOUSE, FOUR CORNERS, CONWAY VILLAGE. This portion of the rambling Thom house was retained to become part of the Presidential Inn.

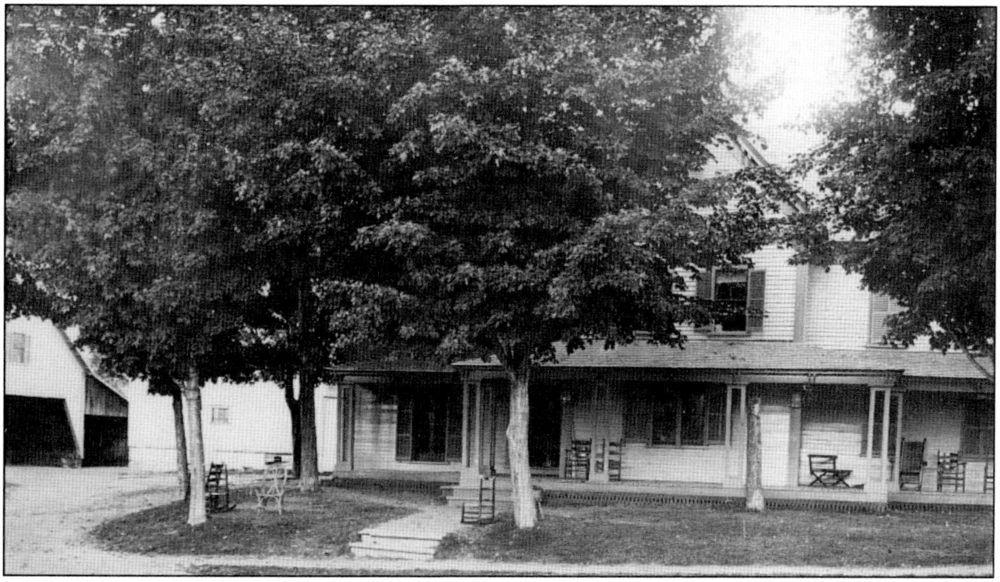

THE SUMMER HOUSE, KEARSARGE. Originally built across from the post office by Albert Barnes, the Summer House was moved, in 1885, back onto the ridge and aptly renamed "The Ridge." It offered electric bells, telephone service, and "water constantly running through the closets and drains."

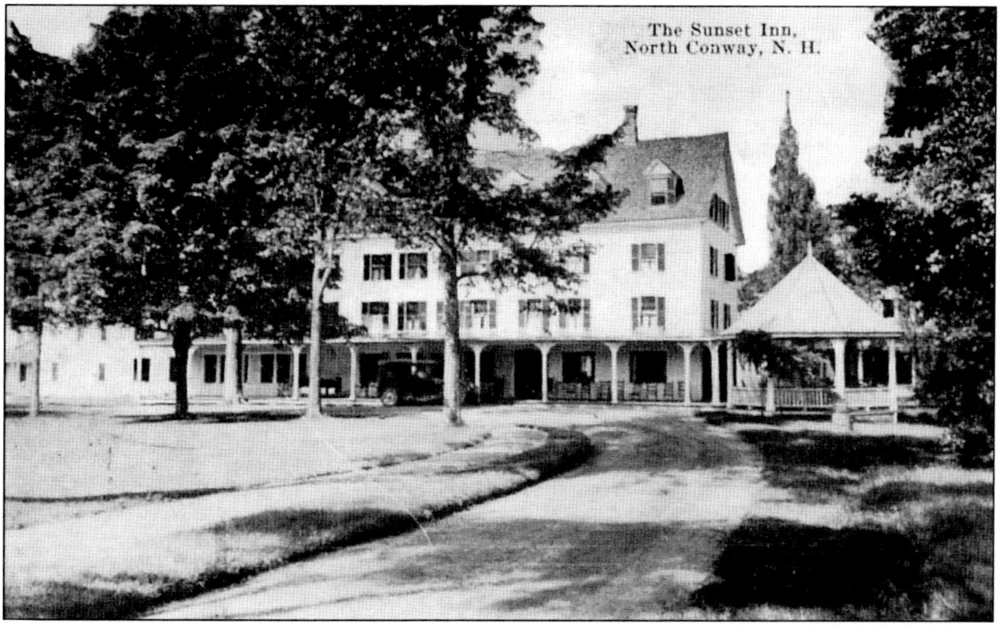

THE SUNSET INN, NORTH CONWAY. The Sunset Pavilion, built in 1869 by Frank and Mahlon Mason, stood just north of the Randall House (Eastern Slope Inn). After the hotel burned in 1940, the accompanying music hall became The Eastern Slope Playhouse.

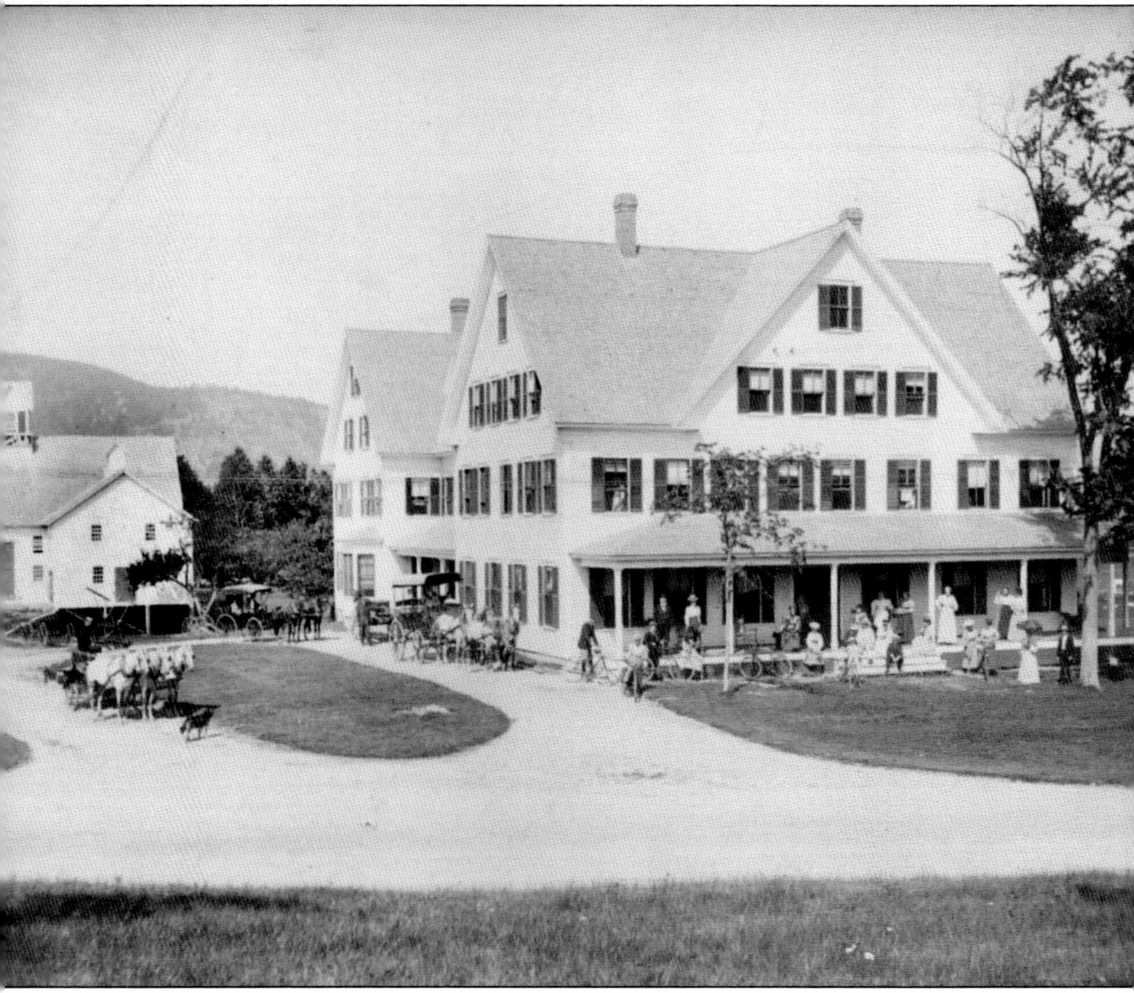

THE FAIRVIEW, INTERVALE, AUGUST 26, 1897. Opened in 1854 and rebuilt in 1894, the Fairview Hotel burned in 1919. Regular guests included the Parkers of Parker Bros. Games, the Harpers of Harpers Magazine, and Roger Babson of Babson College. Other guests were Mary Todd Lincoln and President Franklin Pierce.

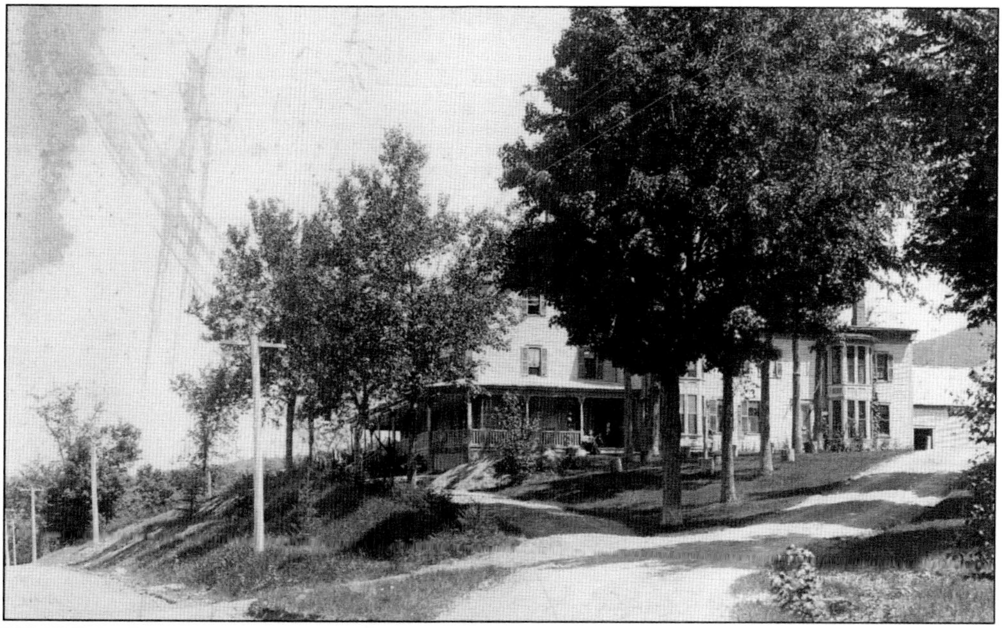

PENDEXTER MANSION, INTERVALE. In 1874, Samuel Pendexter opened his farmhouse to summer boarders. Over time, the house became the Pendexter Mansion. The oldest part of the house was advertised as "coeval with the settlement of the town of Bartlett." The 100-acre farm, wide piazzas, croquet ground, and lawn tennis court were attractive incentives to summer boarders.

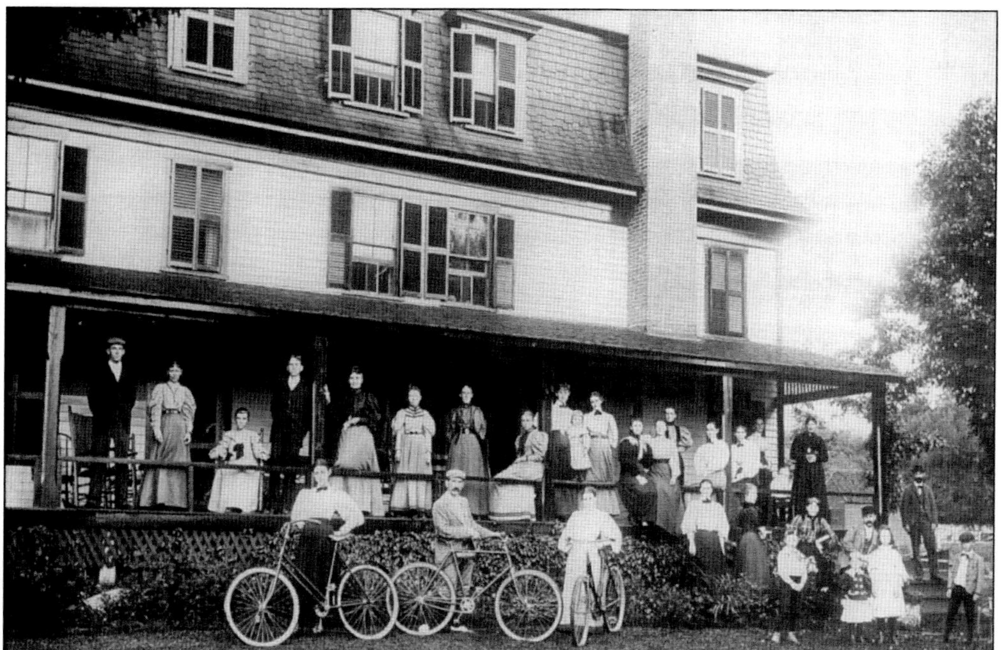

ARCADIAN COTTAGE, AUGUST 1896. Kearsarge Village's Arcadian Cottage, situated on high ground at the base of Mt. Kearsarge, offered commanding views of the countryside. A farm was connected with the facility, providing fresh produce for the guests.

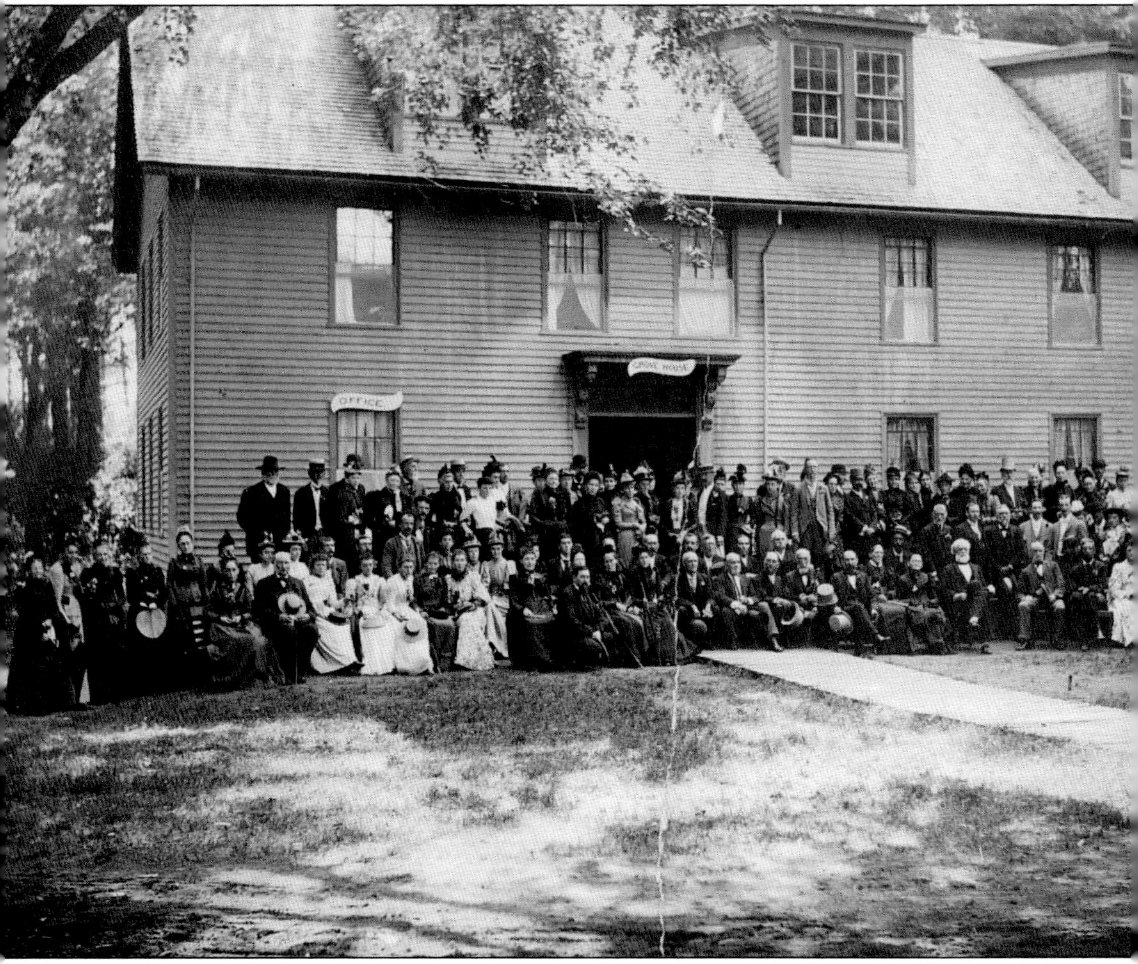

THE GROVE HOUSE. The Grove House, located on Washington Street in Conway Village, burned during the 1880s. There is no record of why this dour group of people was assembled.

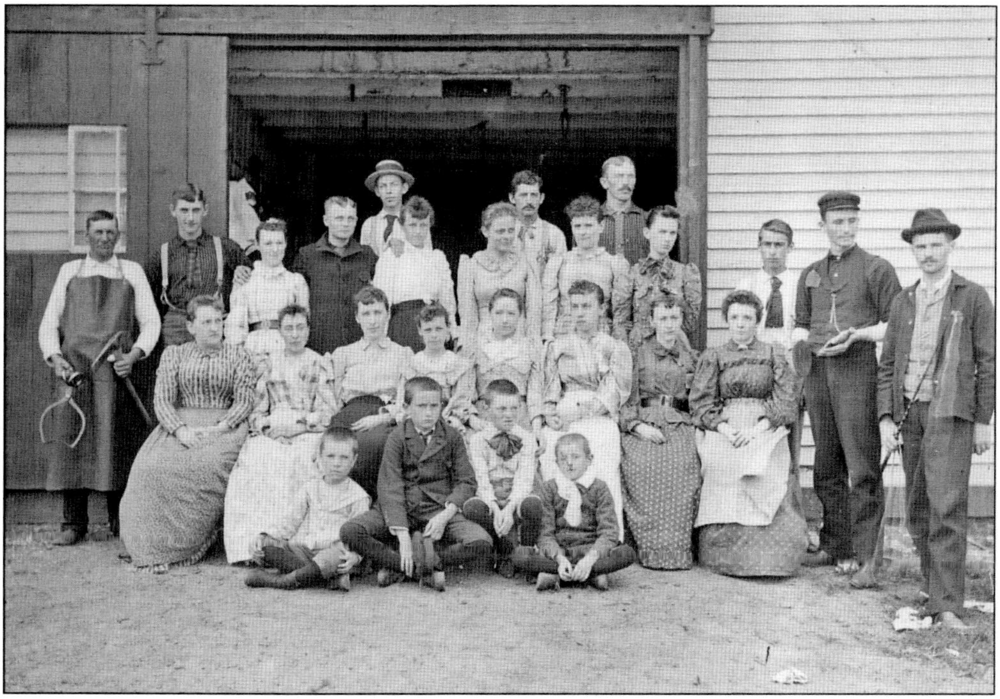

THE HIRED HELP AT RUSSELL'S COTTAGES. Arthur Randall is shown in the straw hat, Fred Eastman is in right rear, and Edward Lowd is at left with ice tongs.

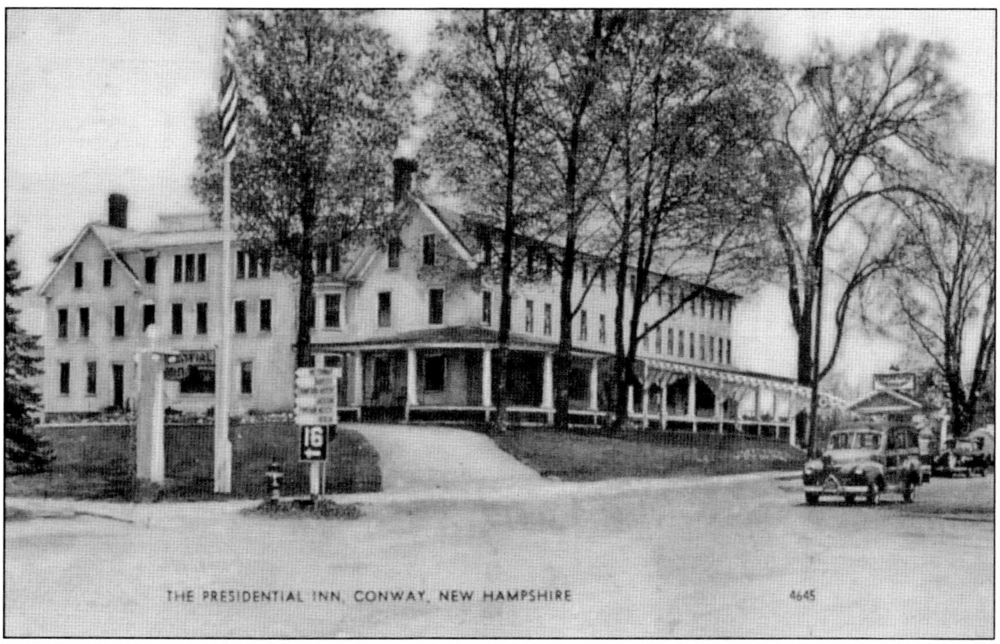

THE PRESIDENTIAL INN, FOUR CORNERS, CONWAY VILLAGE. Originally the Thoms house (1826), the Presidential Inn opened in 1917. It was razed in 1971.

Kiarsarge House.

ARRIVAL AND DEPARTURE OF TRAINS AND STAGES.

DEPARTURES.

BOSTON, via Eastern R. R.		7.20 A. M.	2.45 P. M.
PORTLAND and BOSTON, via P. & O. R. R.	6 45 A. M.,	12.35 P. M.,	5.30 P. M.
GLEN HOUSE, Stage,		8 A. M.	2.30 P. M.
CRAWFORD HOUSE,		9.40 A. M.	3.25 P. M.

ARRIVALS.

BOSTON, via Eastern R. R.		1.33 P. M.	8.08 P. M.
PORTLAND, via P. & O. R. R.	9.40 A. M.	3.25 P. M.	8.00 P. M.
GLEN HOUSE, Stage,		12.30 P. M.	7.00 P. M.
CRAWFORD HOUSE,		12.30 P. M.	5.30 P. M.

HOURS FOR MEALS.

BREAKFAST,	7 to 10 o'clock.
DINNER,	1 to 3 "
SUPPER,	7 "

EARLY BREAKFAST, 5.30 and 6.30.

SUNDAYS.

BREAKFAST,	8 o'clock.
DINNER,	2 "

No notice given of meals except early Breakfast.

☞ Guests leaving on Morning Trains or Stages, are requested to give notice at the office, the evening previous. ☜

Guests requiring extra seats at the Table, will give early notice at the office, and seats will be reserved.

Meals, Lunches or Fruit sent to rooms, will be charged extra.

Children occupying seats at regular table, or servants occupying first class rooms, full price. A private Dining Room is provided for children and nurses.

BREAKFAST,	7 o'clock.
DINNER,	1 "
SUPPER,	6.30.

A menu from the Kearsarge House, September 1873. The Kearsarge, still spelled with an "i" in

Dinner Bill of Fare.

SUNDAY, SEPT. 7, 1873.

Soups.

Tomato. English Split Pea.

Fish.

Boiled Cod, Egg Sauce. Baked Halibut, Port Wine Sauce.

Boiled.

Fowls, with Pork. Turkey, Egg Sauce. Leg of Mutton, Caper Sauce.
Phipp's Ham. Neat's Tongue. Corned Beef.

Roast.

Ham, Wine Sauce. Lamb, Mint Sauce. Spring Chicken, Giblet Sauce.
Ribs of Beef, Brown Sauce. Young Goose, Apple Sauce.
Leg of South-down Mutton, Jelly Sauce.

Cold Dishes.

Ham. Beef. Spring Lamb. Neat's Tongue. Boiled Mutton.
Chicken. Corned Beef.

Entrees.

Macaroni au Gratin. Rice Croquets, Vanilla Flavor. Stewed Lambs Kidneys
Currie of Chicken's Wings, with Rice. Potted Pigeon. Macaroni, with Cream.
Macaroni Fritters, Sweet Sauce. Stewed Giblets, with fine herbs.
Baked Pork and Beans. Rice in Form with Tomatoes.
Poulette of Tripe. Stewed Lambs Tongues. Harricott of Mutton.

Vegetables.

Onions. Egg Plant. Squash. New Beets. String Beans.
Mashed Potatoes. Shelled Beans. Boiled Potatoes. Boiled Rice.
Turnips. Stewed Tomatoes, Green Corn. Plain Macaroni.

Relishes.

Sliced Tomatoes. Cucumbers. Pickles. Olives. Chow-Chow.
Pickled Onions. Gherkins. Worcestershire Sauce.
Pine Apple Cheese, Roquefort Cheese. English Dairy Cheese.

Pastry.

Baked Indian Pudding. Cold Custard Pudding.
Blackberry Pie. Lemon Pie. Pumpkin Pie. Blueberry Pie.
Pound Cake. Jelly Cake. Kiarsarge Cake, White Mt. Cake. Green Apple Pie.

Dessert.

Lemon and Vanilla Ice Cream. Layer Raisins. Figs. English Walnuts.
Pecan Nuts. Soft Custard. Apple Meringues. Almonds.
Wine Jelly. Cocoanut Cake. Kisses. Floating Islands. Filberts.
Apples. Grapes. Musk Mellons. Charlotte Rnsse.
Coffee. Tea. Chocolate.

1873, listed train schedules as well as food choices on its menu.

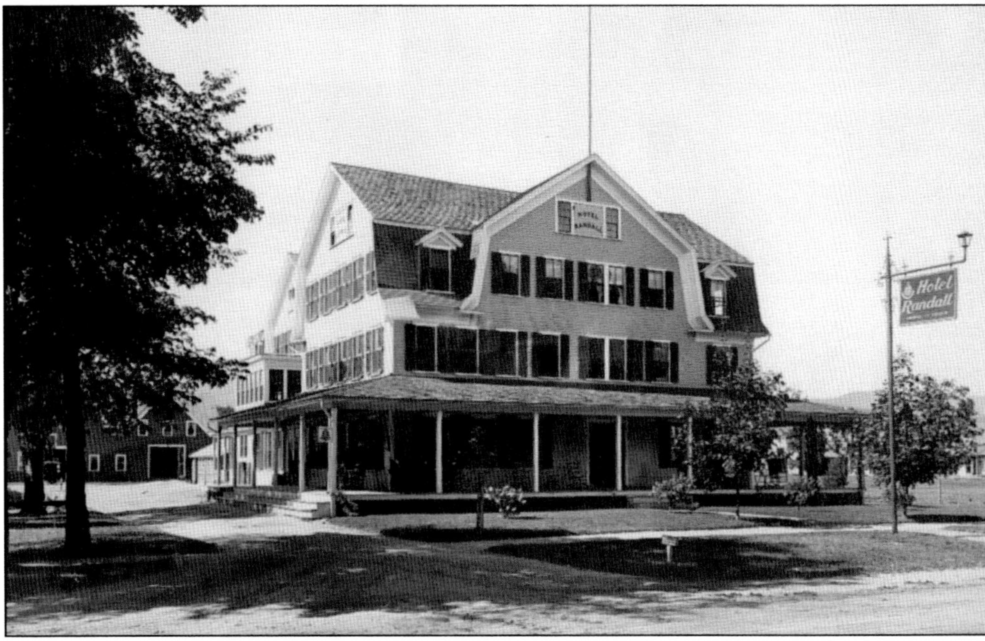

THE RANDALL HOUSE, NORTH CONWAY. The second Randall House, built in 1903 to replace one burned in 1902, was itself destroyed by fire in 1925. The new Hotel Randall was purchased in 1926 by Harvey Dow Gibson and renamed The Eastern Slope Inn.

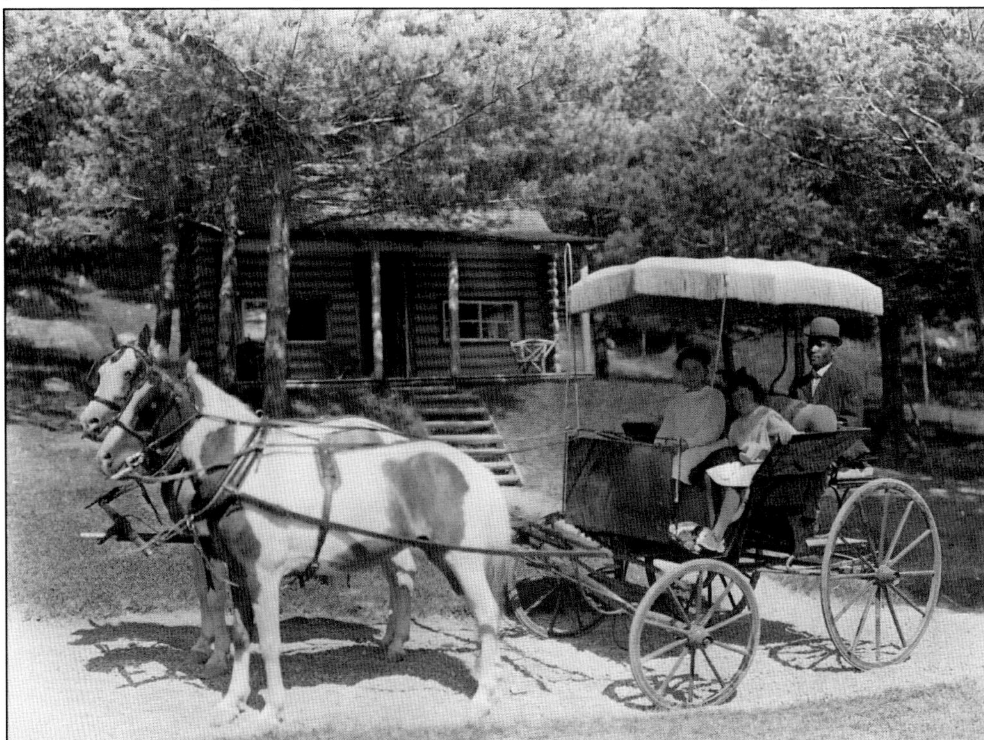

SUMMER PEOPLE. Many people of means summered in the Conways bringing their families and servants.

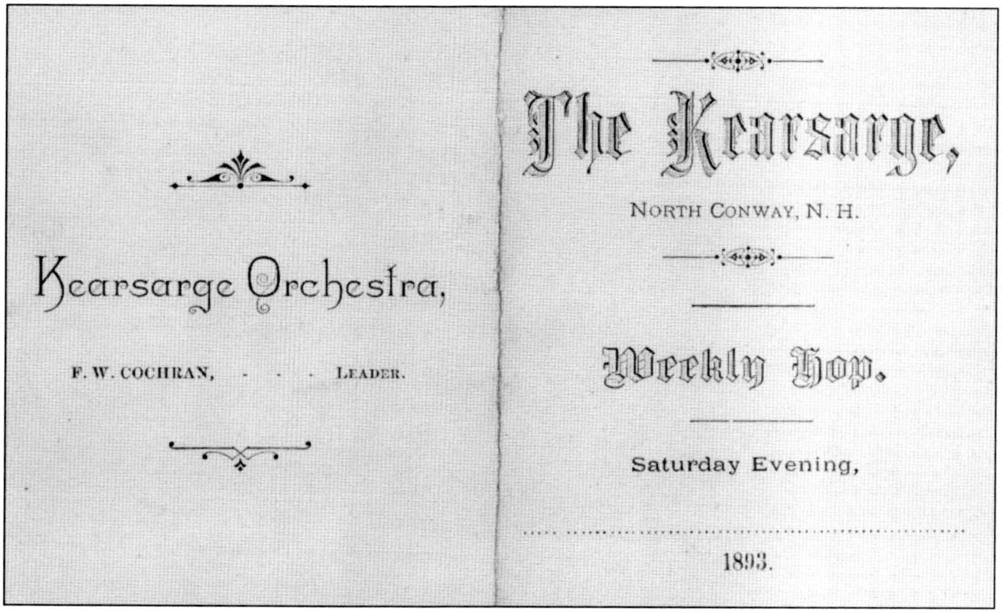

A DANCE CARD FROM THE KEARSARGE HOTEL. Once located on a site near the North Conway Community Center, the predecessor of the Kearsarge House was one of the earliest North Conway inns. Samuel W. Thompson built a small inn on the site to take advantage of the teamsters traveling from New Hampshire and Vermont to Portland, Maine. The inn was enlarged four times and by 1871 had accommodations for three hundred guests. In 1893, the Kearsarge Orchestra performed at the hotel's weekly "hop."

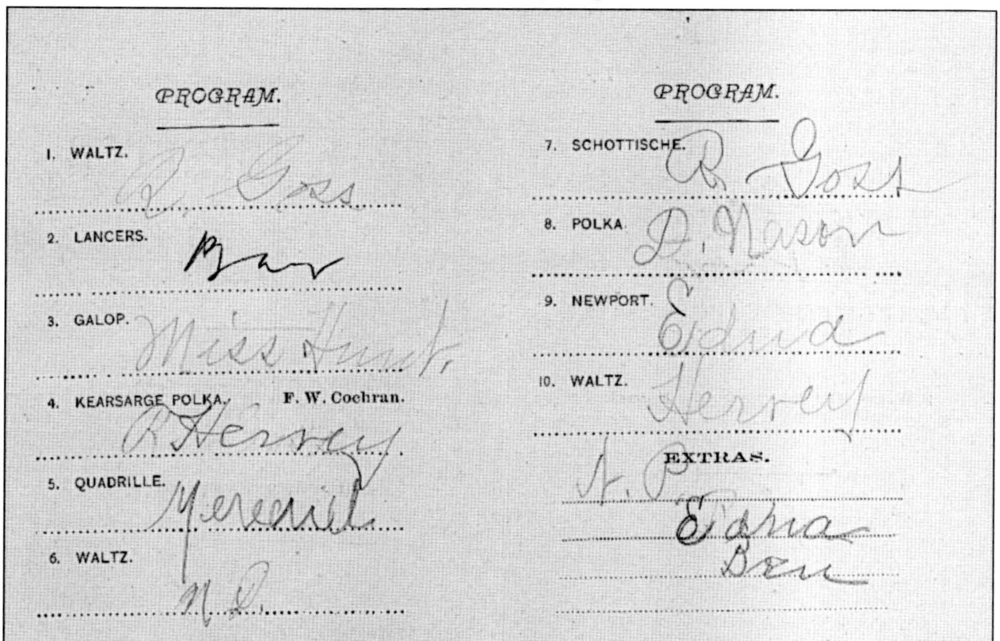

THE REVERSE SIDE OF THE ABOVE DANCE CARD. This dancer at the Kearsarge House "hop" must have been a popular partner. Her program was completely filled, including "extras." The house specialty was the Kearsarge Polka, sandwiched between the galop and the quadrille.

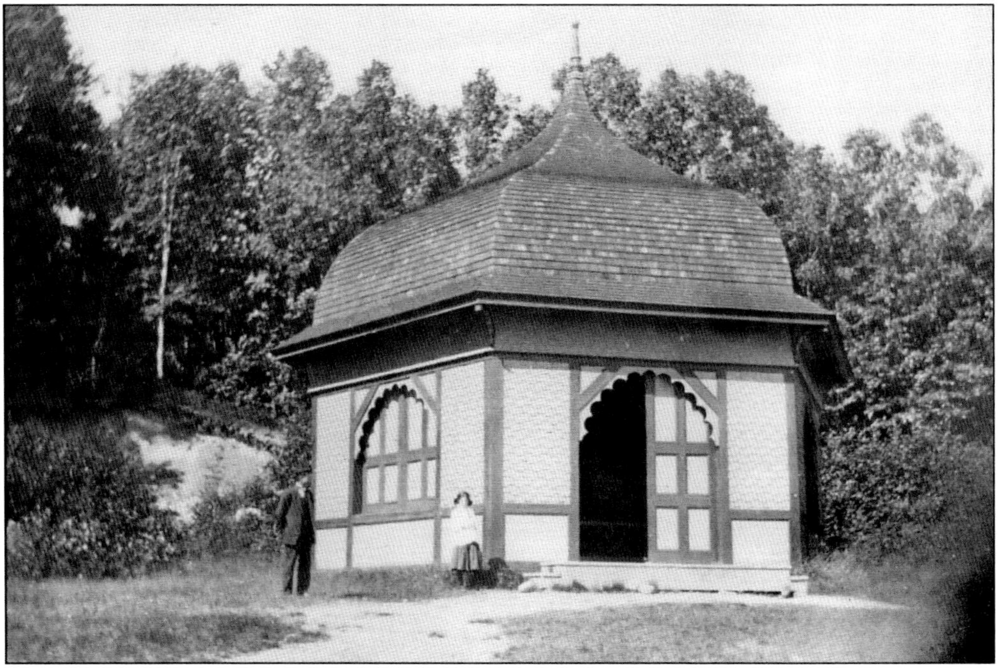

WHITE MT. MINERAL SPRING, PINE HILL. The spring sheltered by this hexagonal building was touted as having curative properties by merit of its magnesia, lithium carbonate, and sulphate of potassium. The water was bottled and sold at the turn of the century.

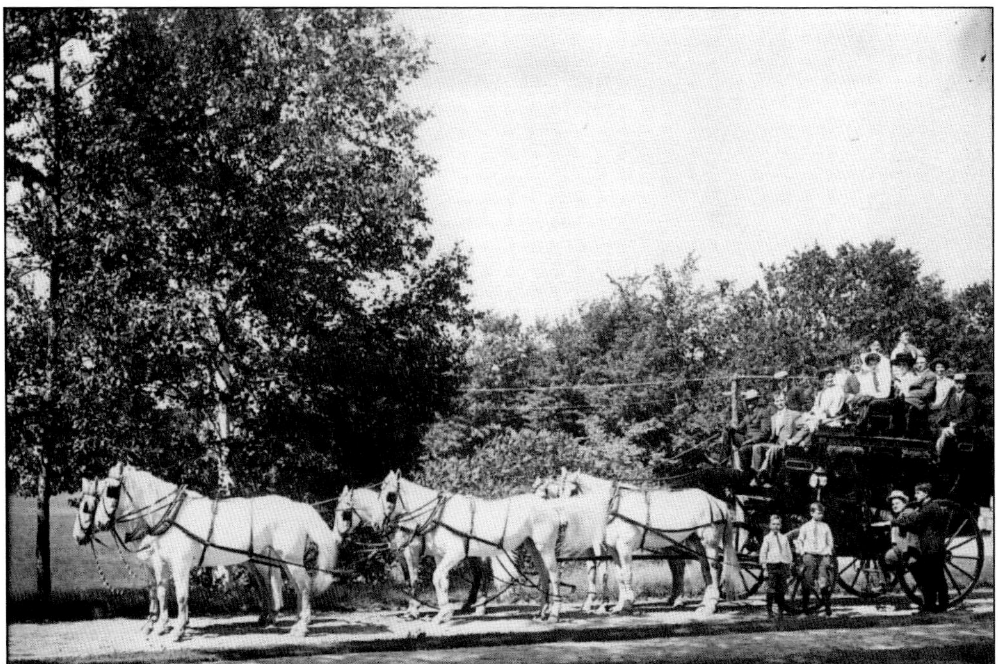

BELLEVUE HOUSE COACH. The Bellevue accommodated 100 guests and boasted running water on 2 floors, bathrooms, and 300 hundred feet of broad piazzas. Beds were furnished with woven wire springs and hair mattresses.

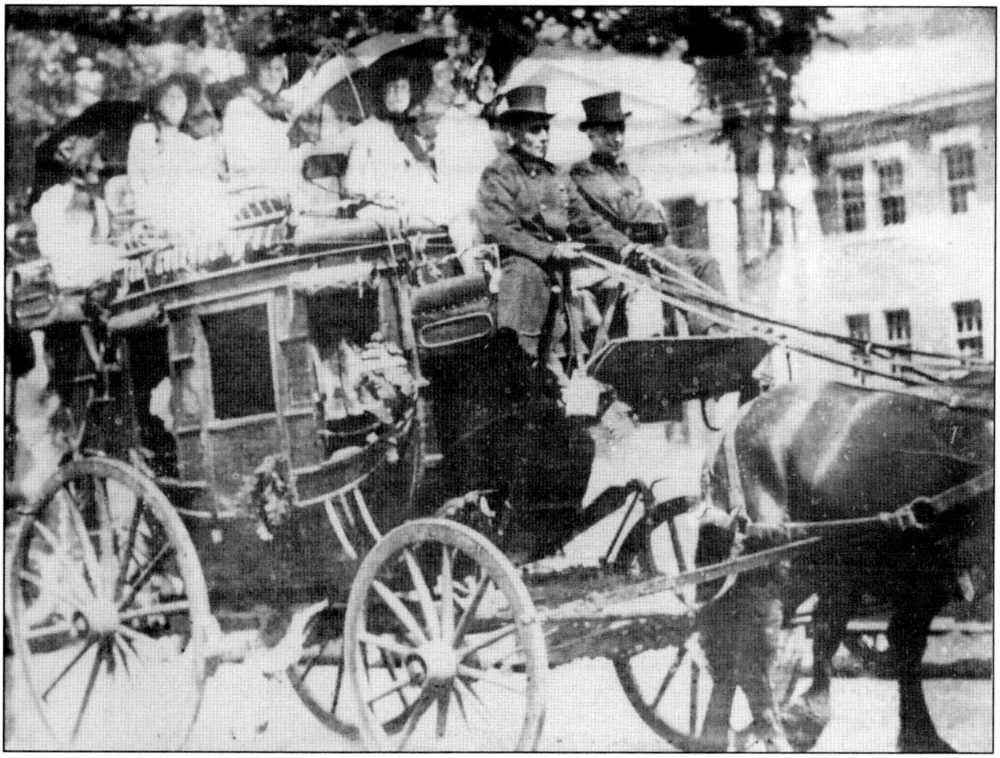

COACHING PARADES. Throughout the 1890s, hotels sponsored coaching parades. Along with the gaily-decorated coaches and passengers, there were festooned hayracks and wagons drawn by horses and oxen. The East Side parades ended at the Kearsarge House where prizes and speeches would be presented, highlighted by an address from the governor. Note the decorated inn in the background of the bottom photograph.

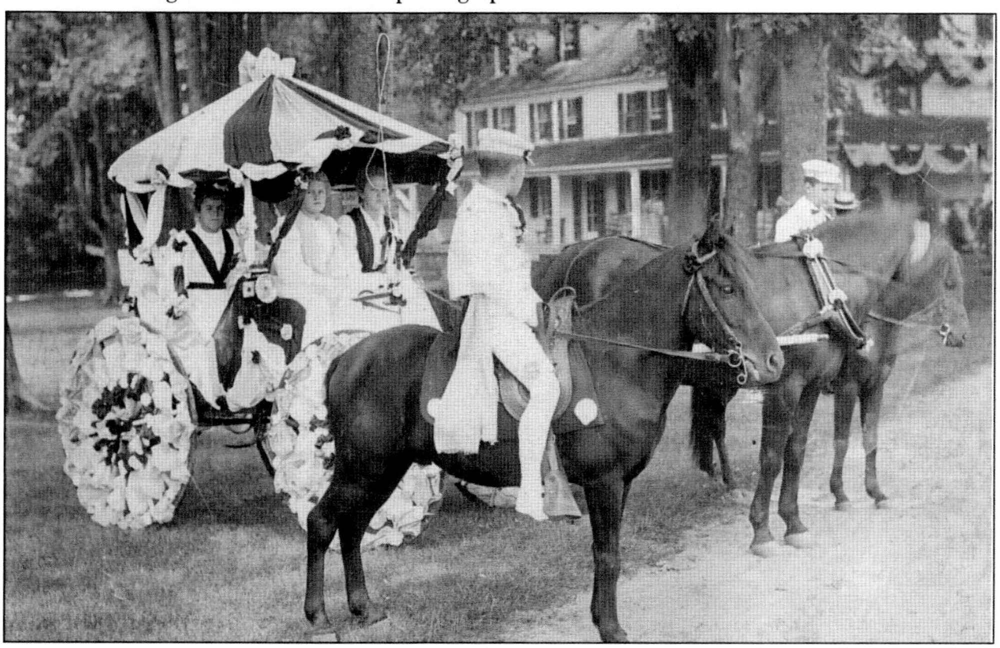

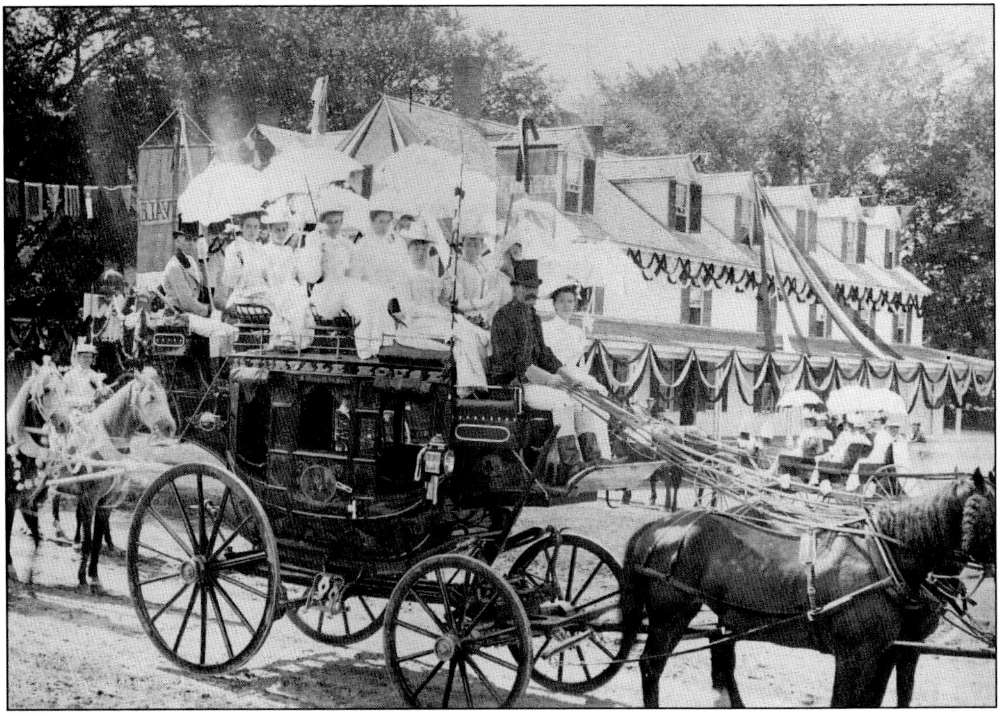

A COACHING PARADE. The Intervale House coach stands in front of the McMillan House with Tim Eastman driving. The McMillan House stood across from the present Red Jacket, offering "The grandest views of the White Mountains and the broad meadows of the Saco."

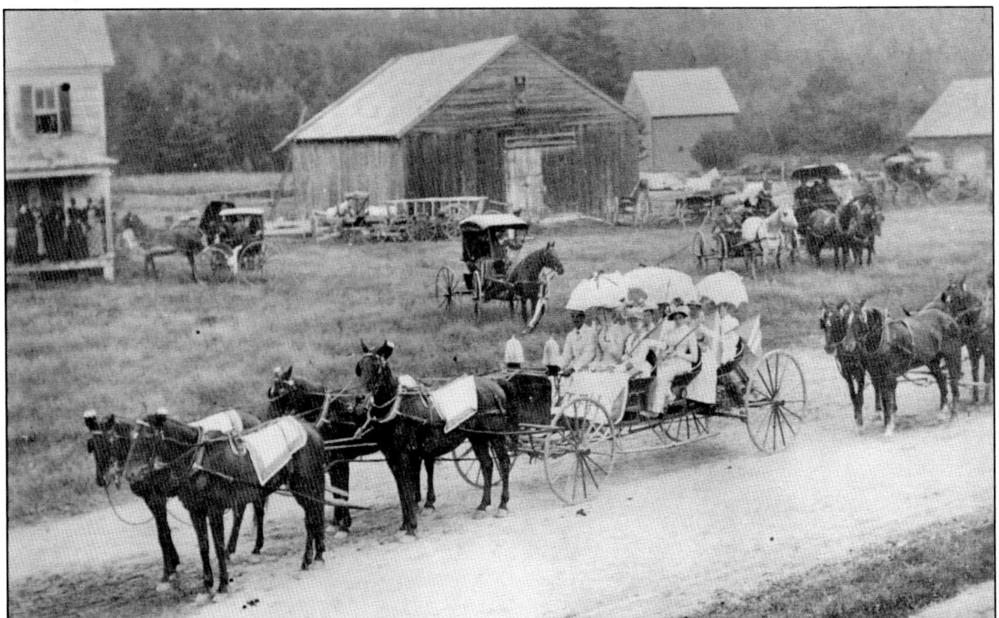

A COACHING PARADE, NORTH CONWAY. A coaching parade entry pauses before the Whitaker homestead. The parades were popular diversions for hotel guests and a favorite spectacle for locals.

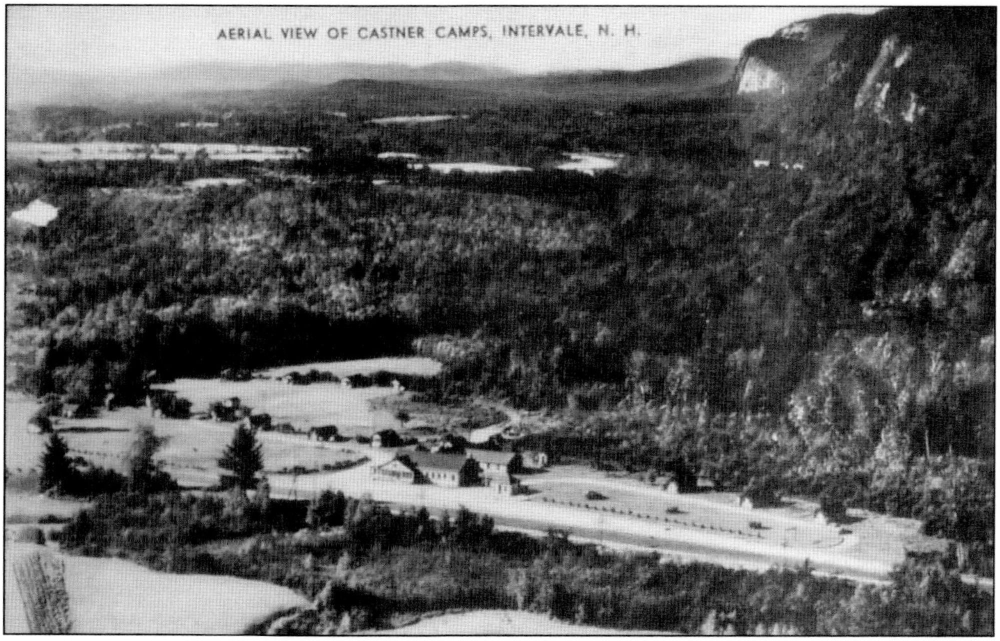

CASTNER CAMPS, INTERVALE. This aerial view depicts Castner's restaurant and overnight cabins located on the west side of Route 16 in Intervale.

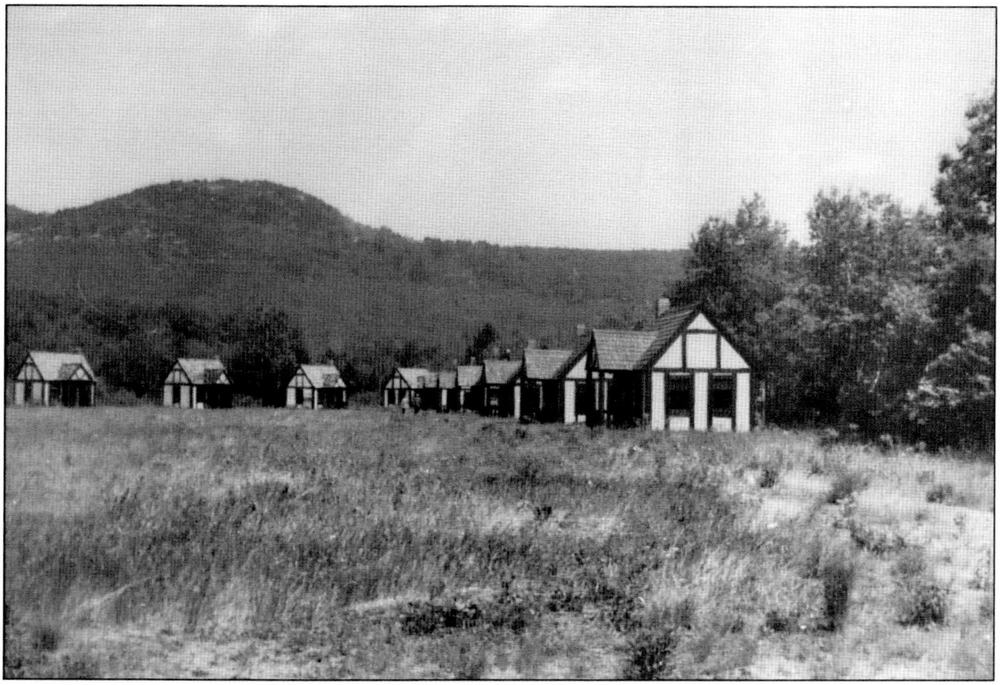

BONNET TOP, NORTH CONWAY. Timbers from the barn at the "old Baily place" in South Conway were used during the construction of these overnight cabins, once located along North Conway's "Strip."

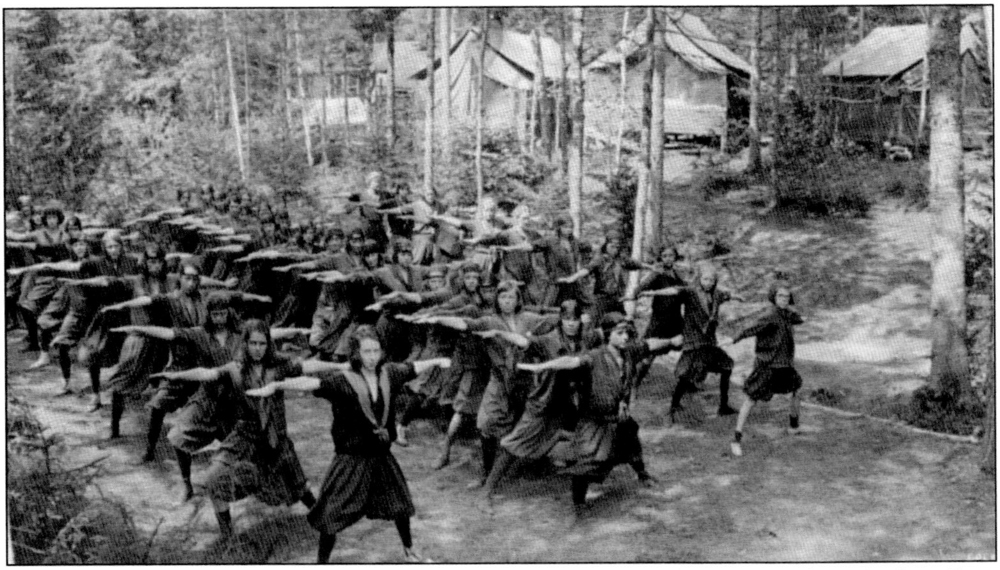

PINE KNOLL CAMP, ALBANY. Once the summer home of Frances White Bucher, Pine Knoll Camp for girls in nearby Albany was sold around 1940 and converted to a boys camp. Here, campers exercise in their brown serge middy blouses and bloomers. Boys' and girls' camps offered a bucolic retreat, replete with arts, crafts, and nature study. Similar camps still dot the countryside.

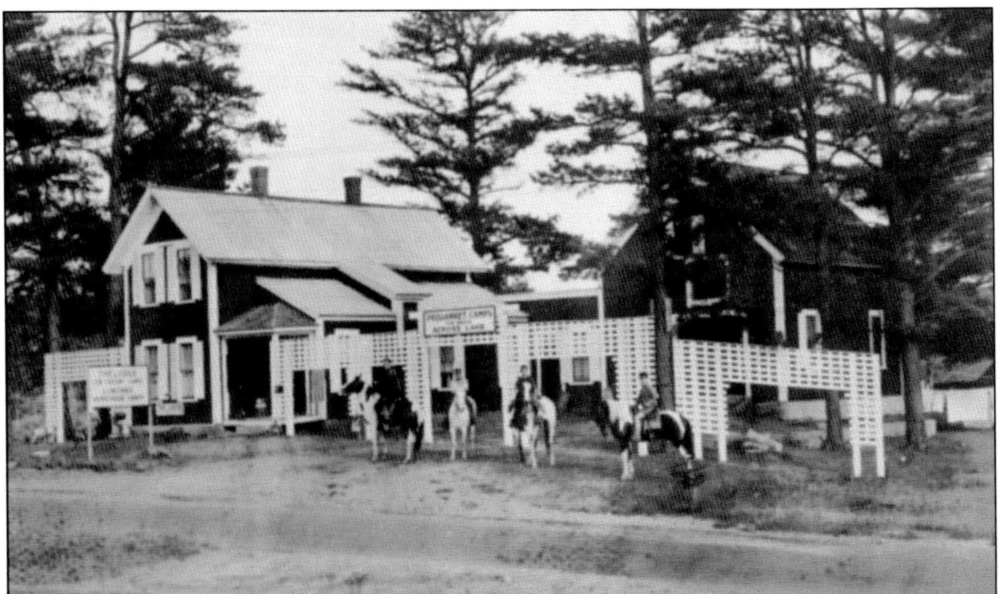

SWANWIER, *c.* 1930. On the shores of Pequawket Pond, Swanwier was once known as the Lodge. Campers from Pequawket Camp are shown in the foreground.

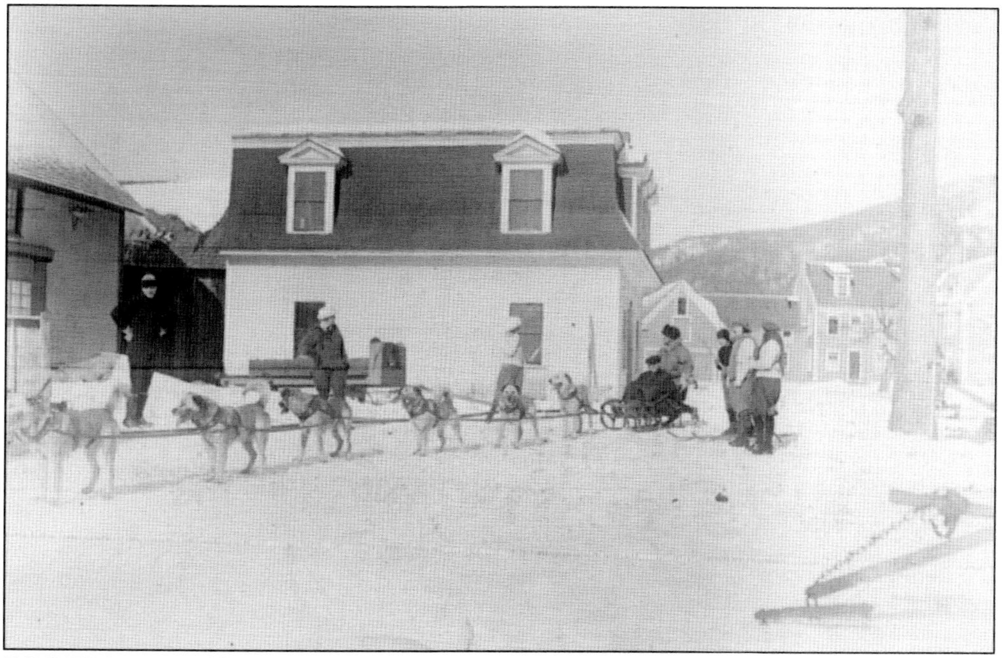

DOG TEAM. Harold Pendergast, at left, watches a dog-team driver from Manitoba put Chinook sled dogs through their paces.

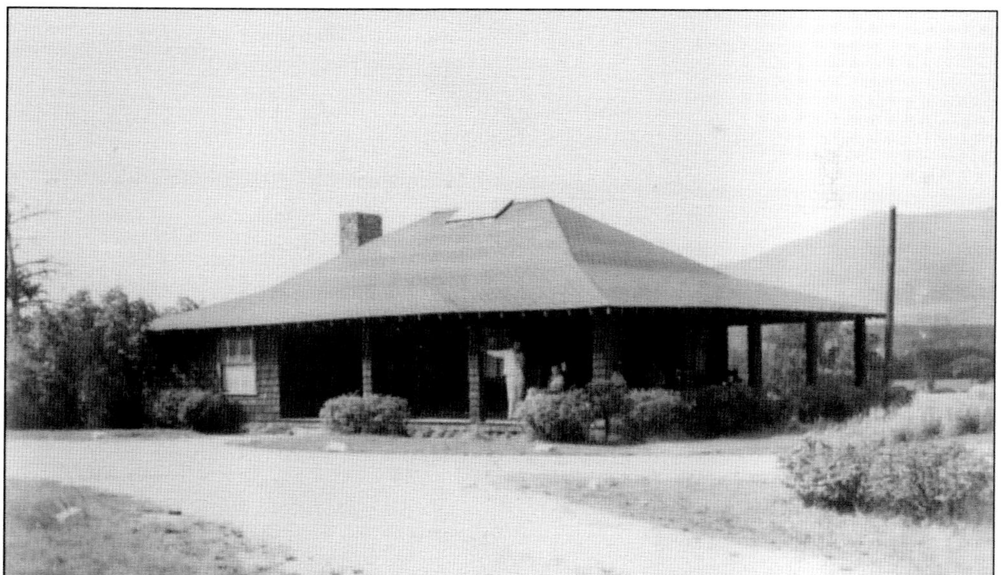

THE NORTH CONWAY COUNTRY CLUB GOLF COURSE, NORTH CONWAY. Originally the Kearsarge House Links, installed about 1895, this golf course became the North Conway Country Club after the hotel burned in 1917.

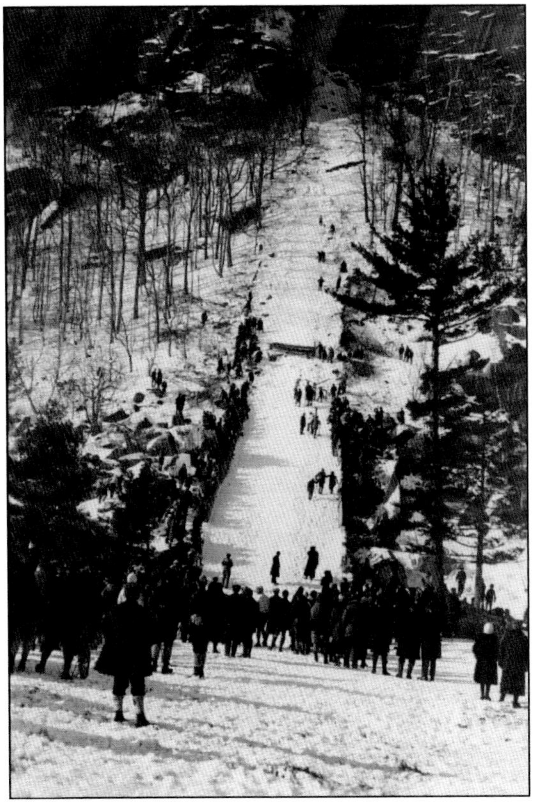

THE CATHEDRAL LEDGE SKI JUMP, NORTH CONWAY. Less well-known than the Kennett High School jump, this facility was located at the base of Cathedral Ledge.

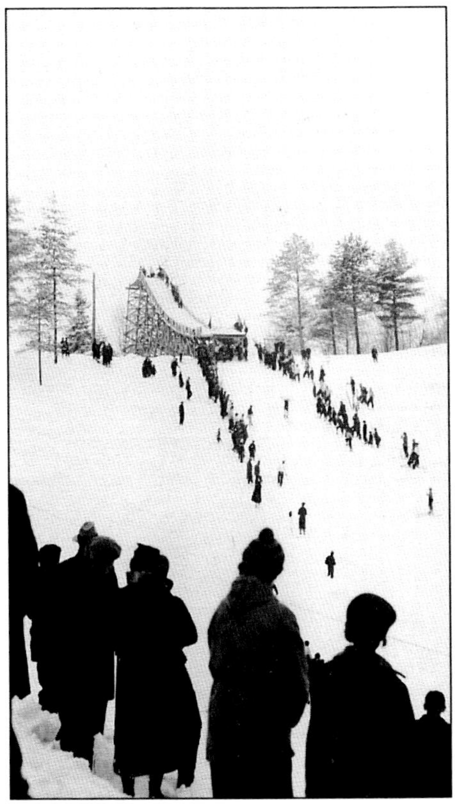

SKI JUMP. Located just across the line in Albany, this jump served as a training center for Conway skiers.

Five

Mill Town, Market Square: Industry and Commerce

The Conways owe much of their cultural diversity to industry. Immigrant workers were drawn to the mills and quarries, bringing the skills and customs of their homelands. Talented stone carvers and gifted craftsmen arrived seeking a better life. The need to feed, house, and clothe a growing population fueled the economy and a service industry evolved to supply the hotels, restaurants, and boarding houses. The rivalry between the villages continued unabated. Earlier the villages had competed for tourists, sometimes shifting stage routes to detour potential guests. As North Conway began to take the lead in the hospitality industry, Conway Village was scorned as a "Mill Town." North Conway, in turn, began its image as a "Tinsel Town."

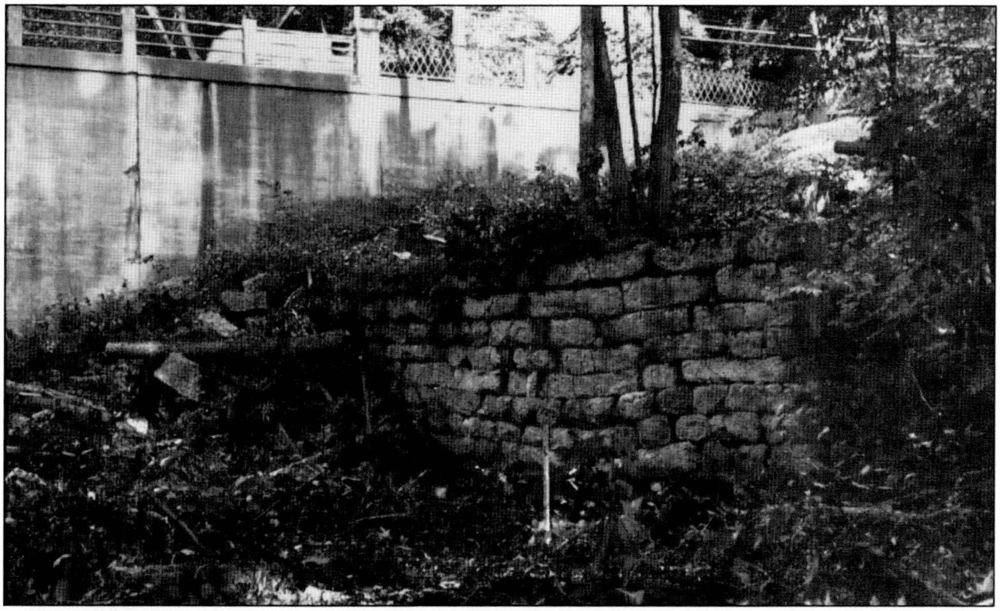

RICHARD AND NOAH EASTMAN'S DAM. Richard Eastman Sr., early settler of North Conway, purchased the mill lot on Kesaugh Brook from Thomas Chadbourne and transferred it to his sons, Richard Jr. and Noah. Above, the remains of the mill dam can be seen.

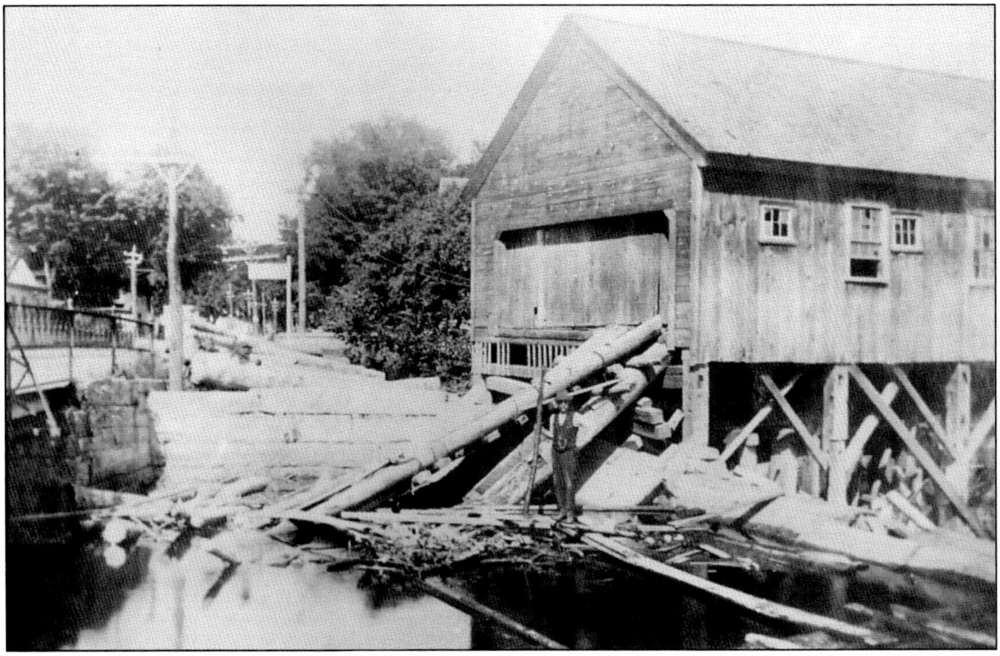

MAIN STREET, CONWAY VILLAGE. The dam in Conway Village was the site of several water-powered mills. Jacob and Horace Berry ran a sawmill and gristmill by the Pequawket Dam on Main Street. Horace became entangled in the equipment and, although badly mangled, lived on for many years. On this site, in 1895, a company founded by B.F. Clark supplied the power for Conway's first electric lights.

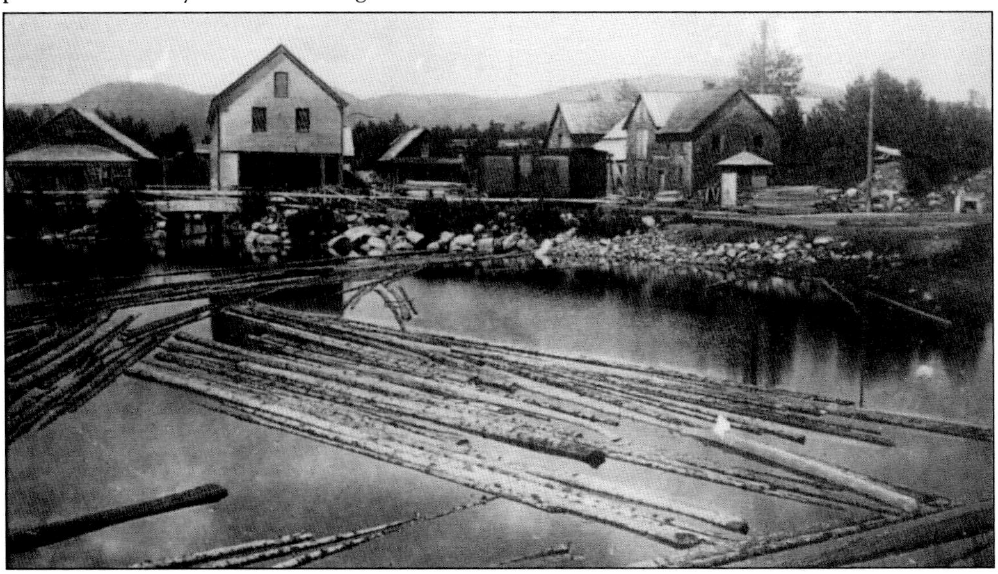

COTTON'S MILLS, CENTER CONWAY, 1909. First called Great Saco Pond and Walker's Pond, Conway Lake supplied power for mills since the arrival of the earliest settlers. Captain Timothy Walker's sawmill supplied lumber for the early houses of Fryeburg and Conway. In 1873, Henry B. Cotton bought one third of the mill property by the dam. He eventually bought the entire property, running a sawmill, gristmill, blacksmith shop, cooper shop, and box factory. Cotton's Mills burned in 1913.

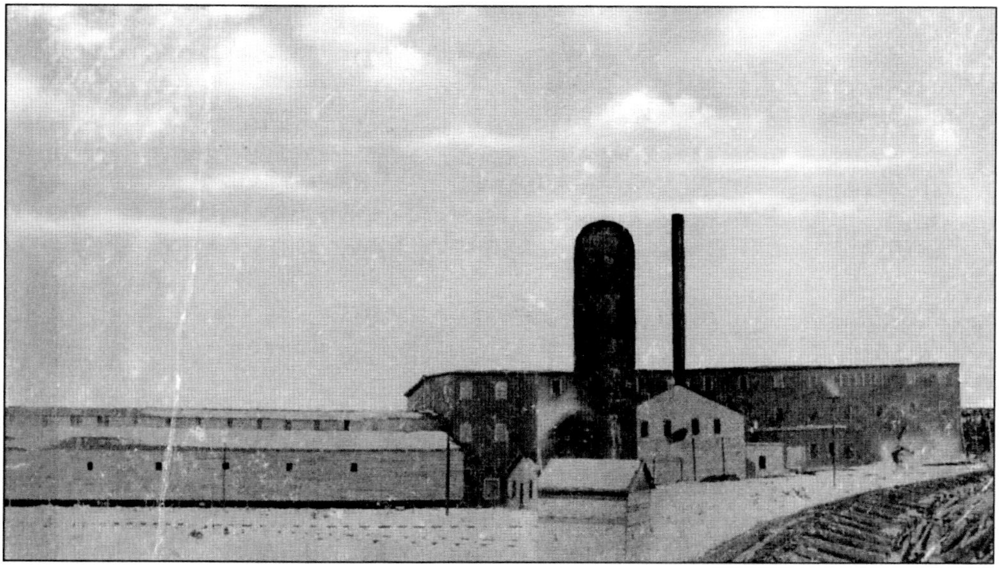

THE CONWAY LUMBER COMPANY'S SAWMILL, 1909. In 1909, the "Big Mill" was boasting a capacity of 125,000 board feet daily. The mill stood on the edge of Pequawket Pond on what is now Hobb's Street. Lumber was brought up from the pond and processed with state-of-the-art machinery. In March 1907, a paper reported two million logs waiting in the Swift River with five million more already in the pond.

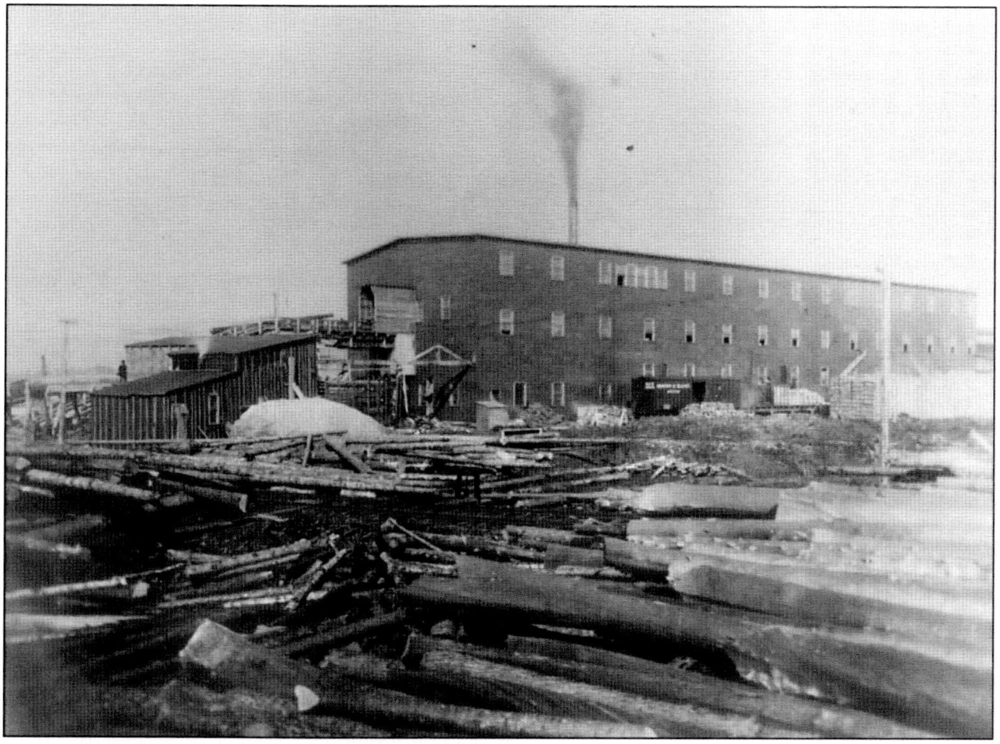

THE CONWAY LUMBER COMPANY. The beginning of the Conway Lumber Company signaled the end of an era in Conway Village. No longer did everyone know everyone else. Many French-Canadian and Polish workers arrived, bringing with them new skills and cultures.

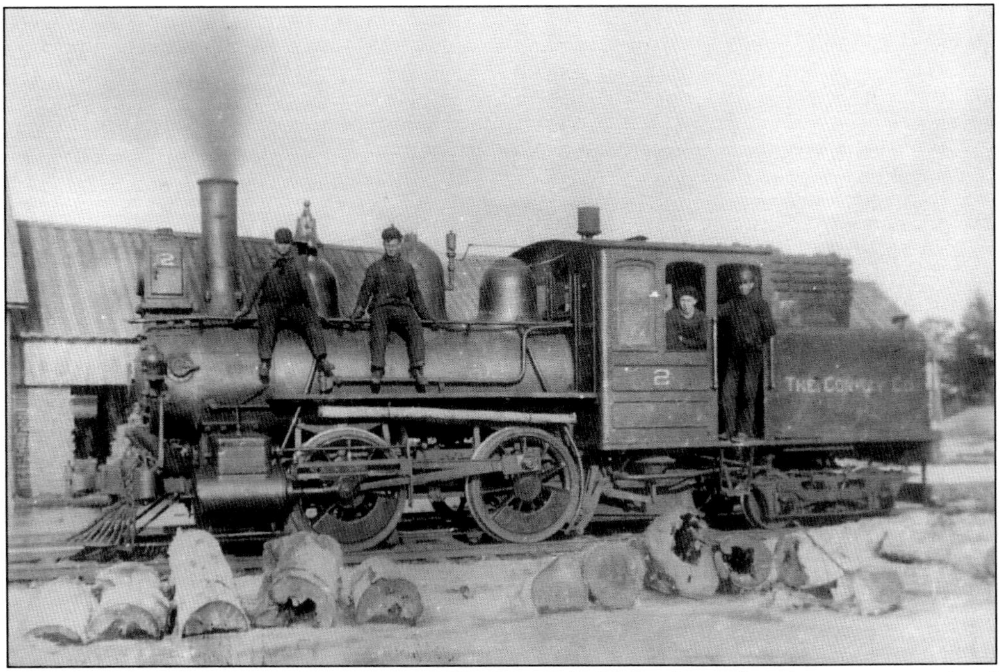

A STEAM SHIFTER, CONWAY LUMBER COMPANY. In the midst of a great many legal maneuvers, the Swift River Railroad was founded to haul timber to the Conway Lumber Company.

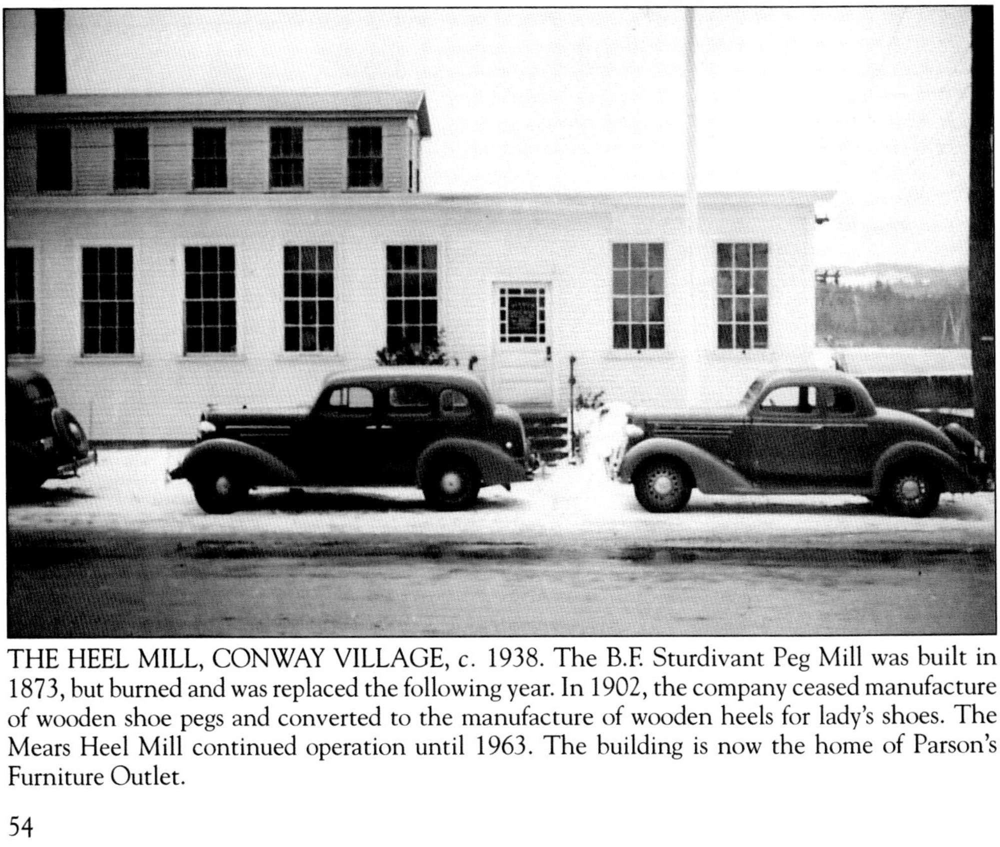

THE HEEL MILL, CONWAY VILLAGE, *c.* 1938. The B.F. Sturdivant Peg Mill was built in 1873, but burned and was replaced the following year. In 1902, the company ceased manufacture of wooden shoe pegs and converted to the manufacture of wooden heels for lady's shoes. The Mears Heel Mill continued operation until 1963. The building is now the home of Parson's Furniture Outlet.

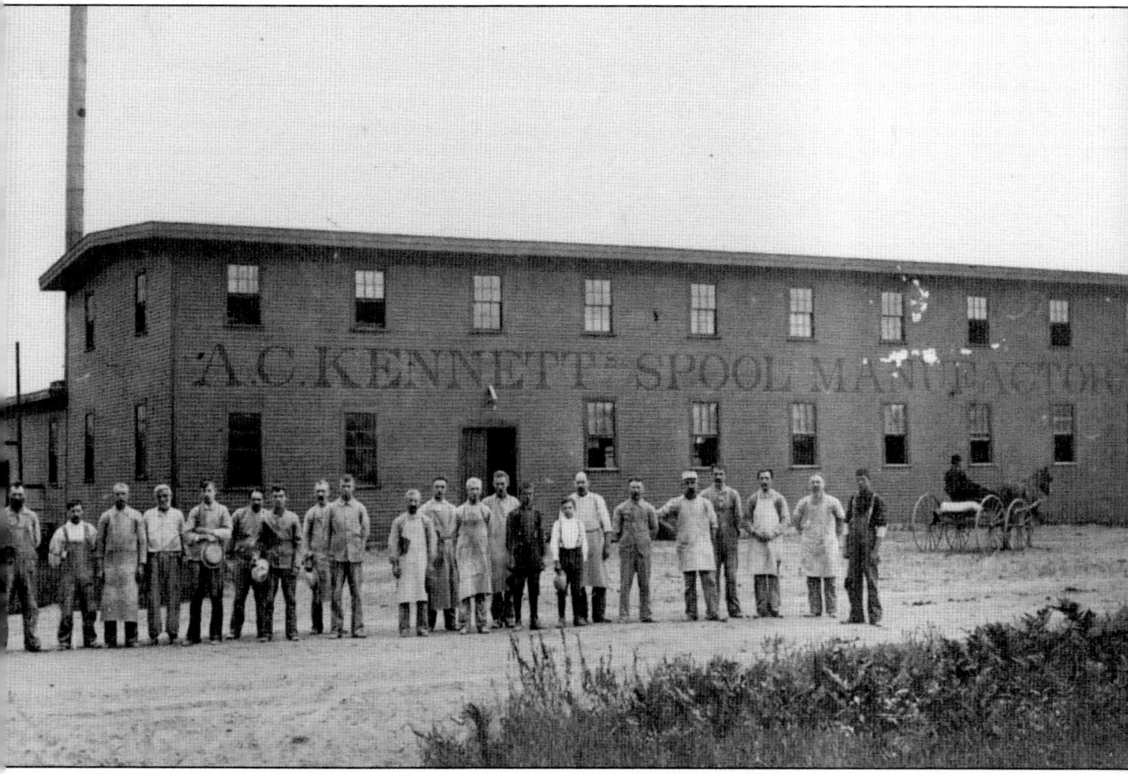

THE A.C. KENNETT SPOOL MILL, WEST MAIN STREET, CONWAY VILLAGE. The Spool Manufactory was begun in Tamworth by Henry Metcalf about 1869, and moved to Conway in 1878. Purchased in 1888 by A. Crosby Kennett, the building capacity was doubled in 1896. By 1905, it was the largest employer in Conway as well as the largest silk spool manufacturer in the world, producing 500,000 gross of spools annually. The mill burned in 1934.

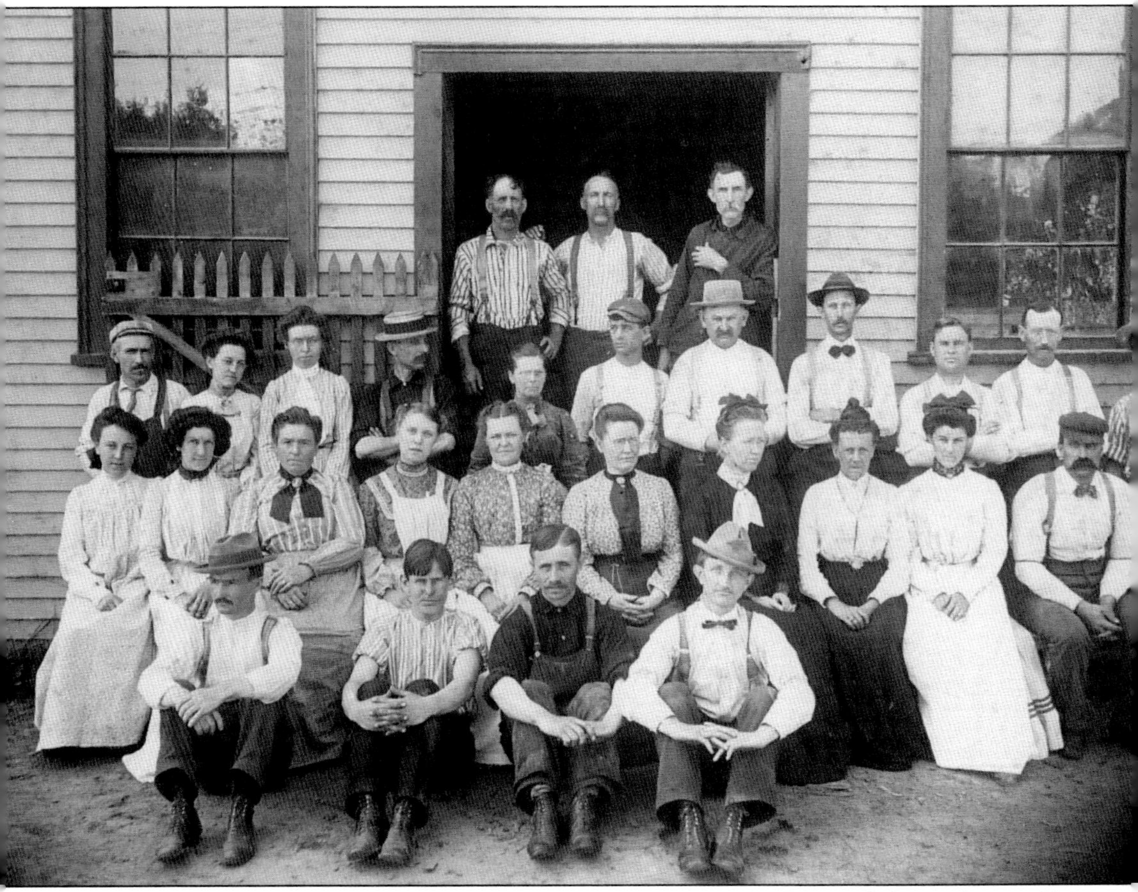

THE PEG MILL CREW, MAIN STREET, CONWAY VILLAGE. From left to right are: (front row) Herbert Lowd, Sam Cole, George Abbott, and T. Durgin; (second row) Agnes Berry, Annie Greenlaw, Alfreda Williams, Miss Hope, Mrs. Hope, Addie Jenness, Sarah Littlefield, Fannie Lowd, Winnie Allard, and Phil Boynton; (third row) Harry Wilder, Beulah Berry, Harriet Sargent, George Heath, Asenath Berry, George Hazelton, Herman Moulton, George Lowd, Bert Coolidge, Charles Fifield, and David Marshal; (standing in door) William Williams, William Sargent, and Ora Hiscock. In 1905, A.C. Kennett was superintendent with long-time employee Ora S. Hiscock as foreman. The monthly payroll during that year totaled $1,500.

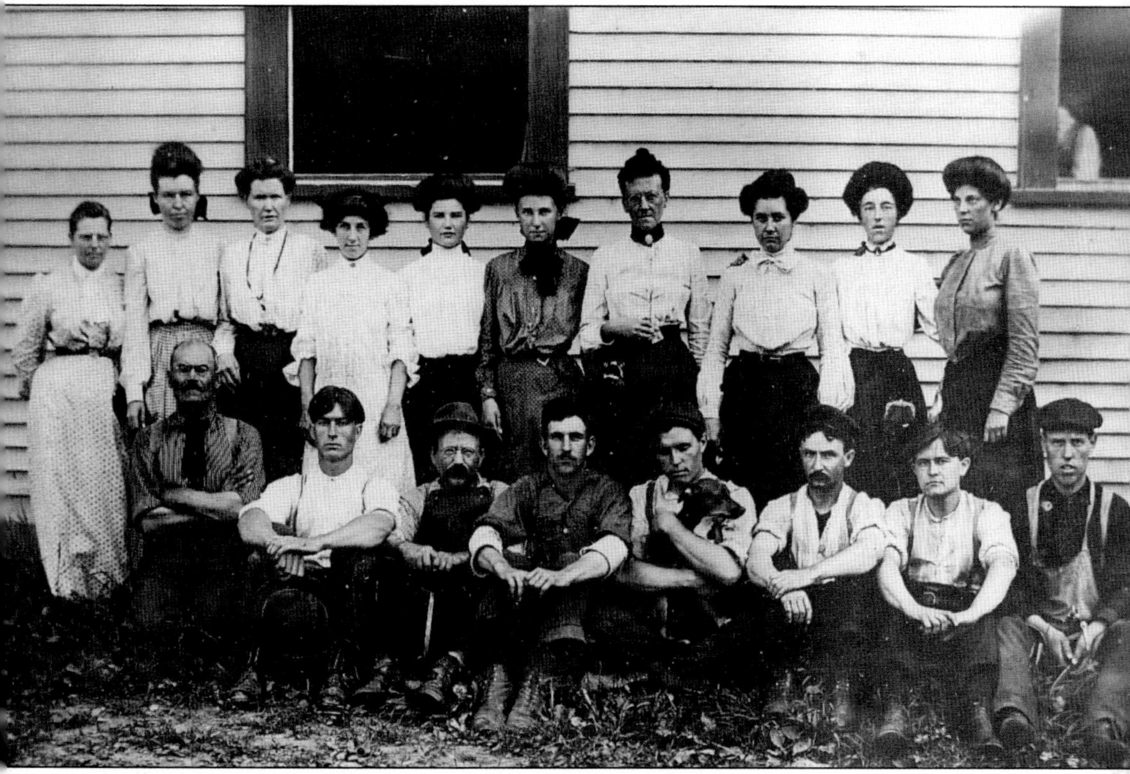

ANOTHER PEG MILL CREW. From left to right are (front row) Alonzo Webster, Neal Thibodeau, F. Keith, Perley Bickford, Phil Robertson, Herbert Lowd, Everett Robertson, and John Moore; (back row) Asenath Berry, Hattie Green, Addie Jenness, Annie Greenlaw, Lena Whitaker, Minnie Cole, Fannie Lowd, Lena Chase, Marcia Durgin, and Maud Hobbs.

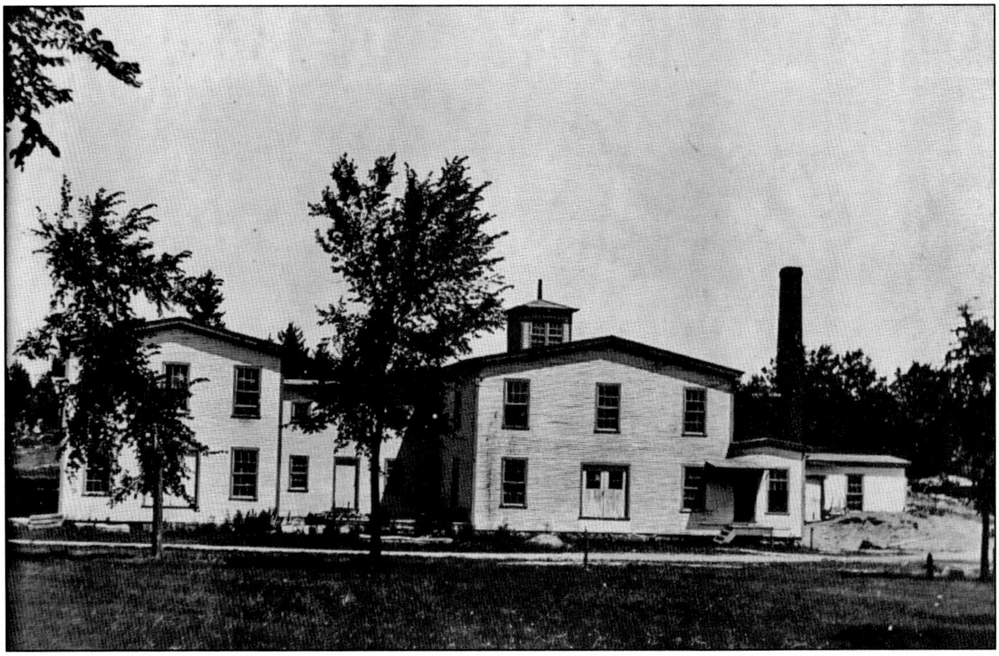

THE CONWAY CHAIR FACTORY, CONWAY VILLAGE. Located near the confluence of the Saco and Swift Rivers, the factory manufactured dining, suite, and reed-seat chairs as well as rockers. The factory burned three times and was rebuilt twice.

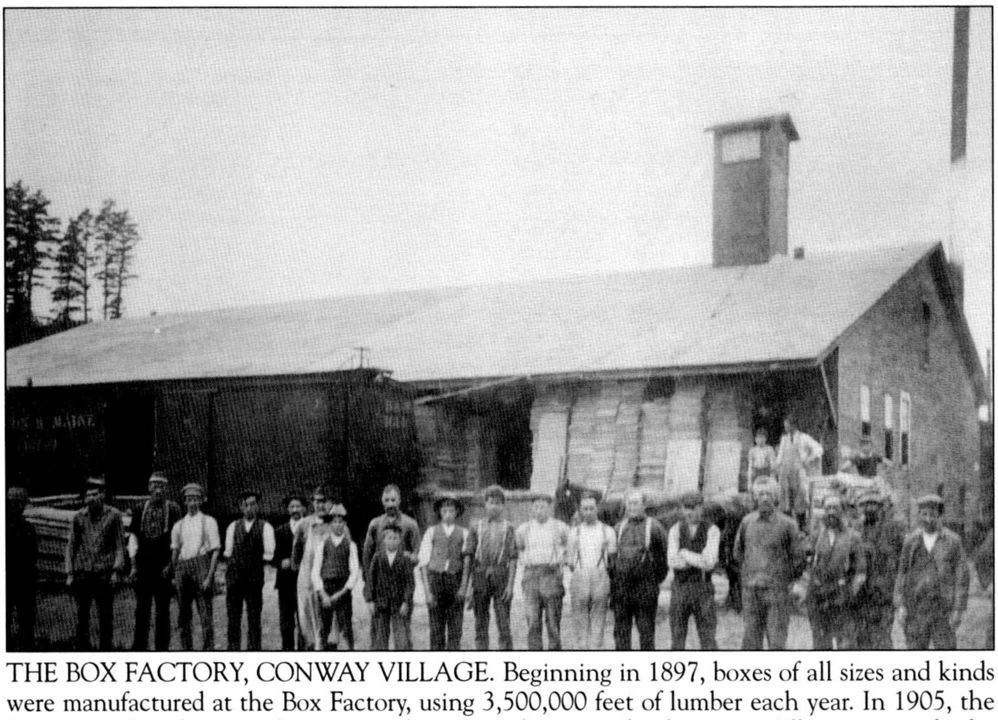

THE BOX FACTORY, CONWAY VILLAGE. Beginning in 1897, boxes of all sizes and kinds were manufactured at the Box Factory, using 3,500,000 feet of lumber each year. In 1905, the factory employed twenty-five men with seventy-five more lumbering in Albany to supply the raw materials. A.C. Kennett, the owner, maintained seven portable sawmills to supply this and other operations.

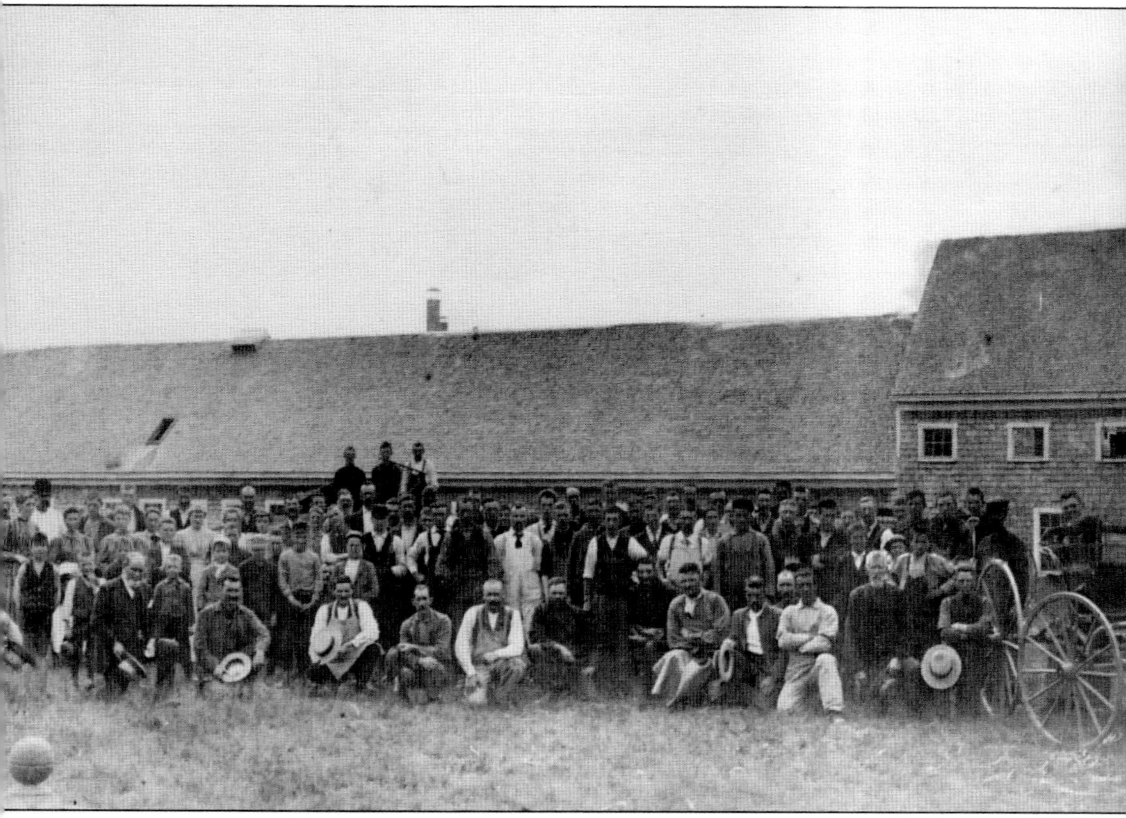

THE CORN SHOP, FARRINGTON AVENUE, CONWAY VILLAGE. Owned by the Baxters of Portland, Maine, the Corn Shop was a seasonal industry employing many of the village young people. At first, the corn was husked by hand; later the factory became fully automated. The building was sold to Fred Merrow and Walter Burnell to house a wood-turning business.

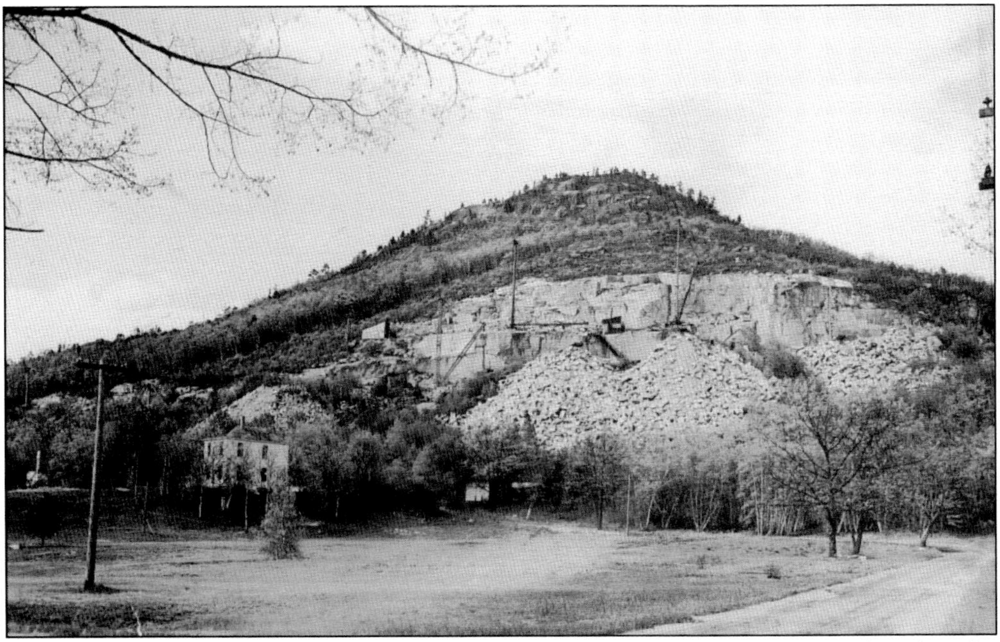

REDSTONE QUARRY. During its heyday, 20 derricks and 350 men were employed at the quarry. Under the auspices of the Maine and New Hampshire Granite Company, Redstone produced both red and green granite. The company supplied white granite from its quarry in Jay, Maine.

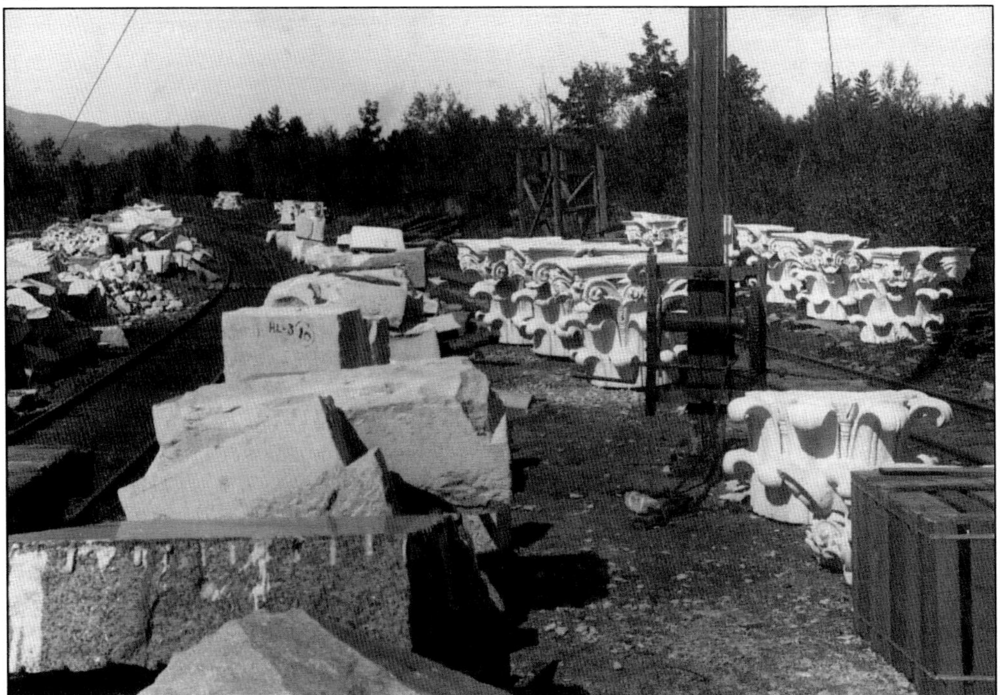

REDSTONE QUARRY. Finely-carved capitals wait by a spur to be shipped. The quarry was known for both the quality of its granite and the skill of its stonecutters.

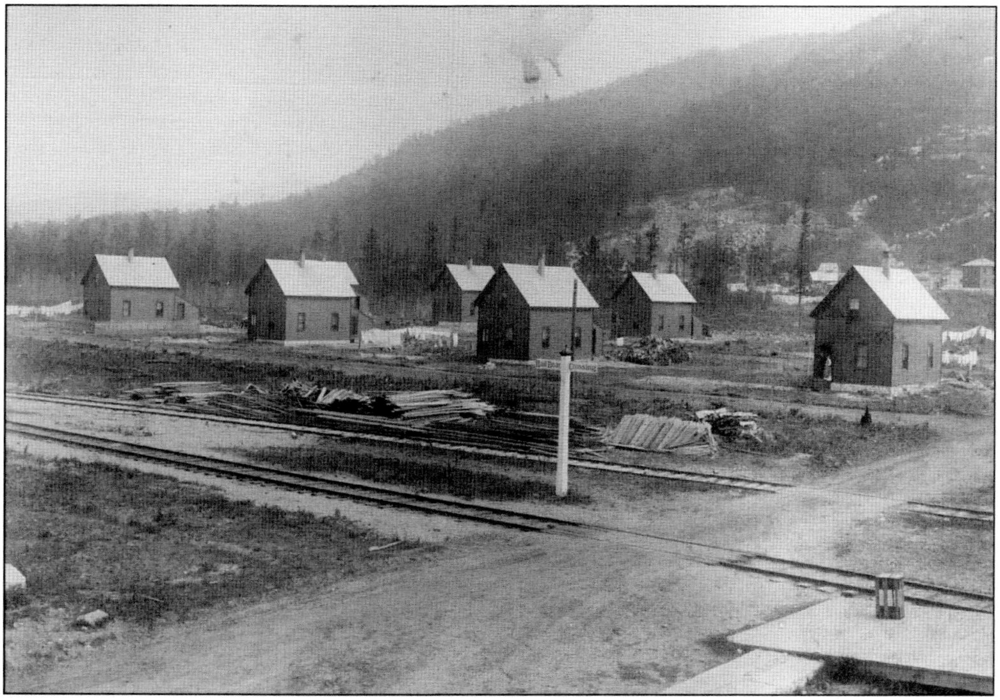

REDSTONE VILLAGE. Originally built as identical company housing, these structures have been greatly modified by their owners to reflect individual tastes and needs. When the houses were put up for auction in 1948, the people living in them had first choice. Some are still owned by the families of quarry men.

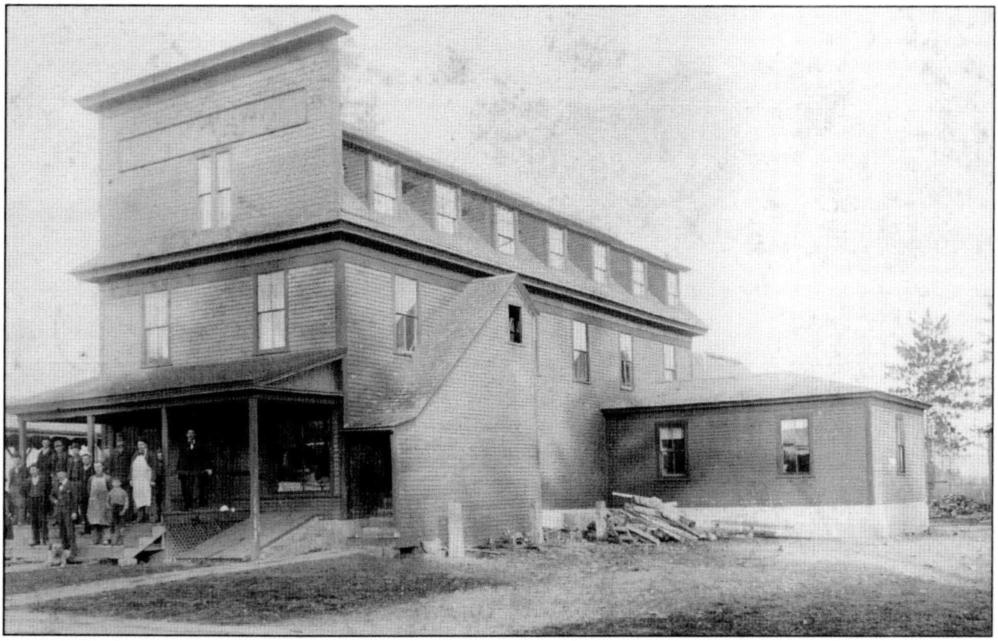

THE FIRST STORE IN REDSTONE, 1893. Edwin T. Emerson was the proprietor of the first store in Redstone. Later proprietors were Craig and Wyman. The second floor of the building housed a dance hall. At one time, the post office was here.

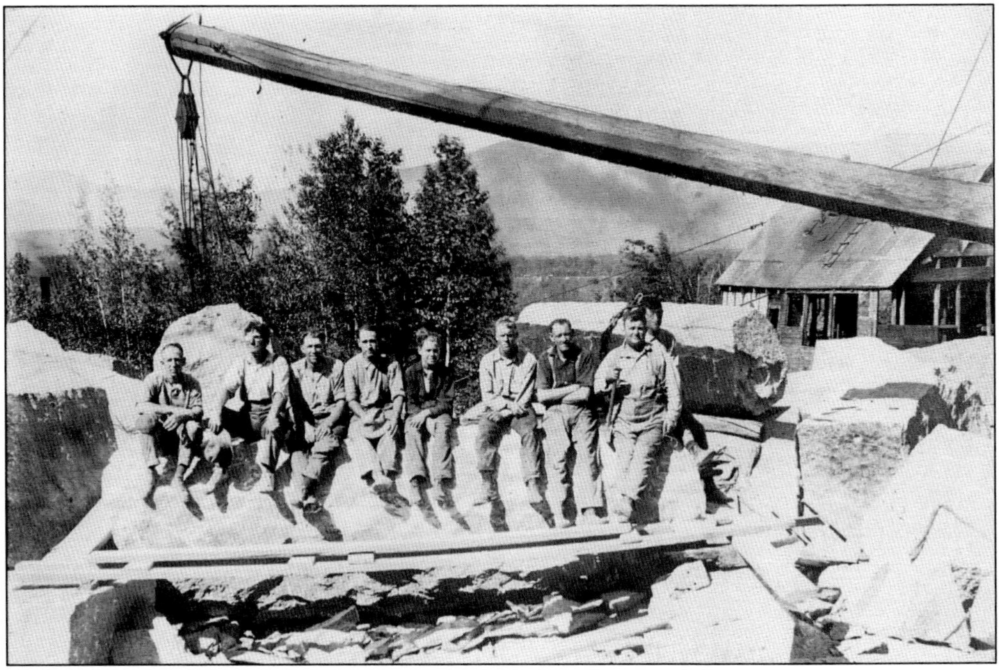

QUARRY WORKERS, REDSTONE. Among other buildings, Redstone granite was used in the construction of the Philadelphia Fidelity Trust building, the Mellon Institute in Pittsburgh, New York City's Curb Exchange building, the Denver Railroad Station, and the Houghton-Dutton Block in Boston. Many talented stone carvers were brought in to work at the quarry.

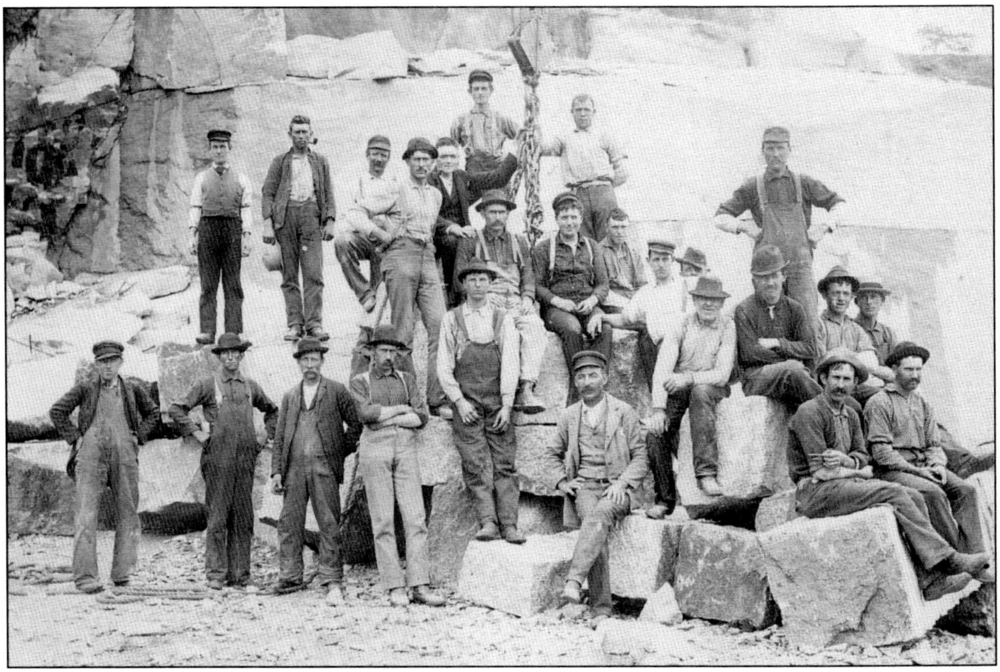

A REDSTONE QUARRY CREW. Many of the quarry workers were drifters moving from job to job. Others made Redstone their permanent home. Salaries for cutters ran about $9 per day, $3 more than for men working in the quarry.

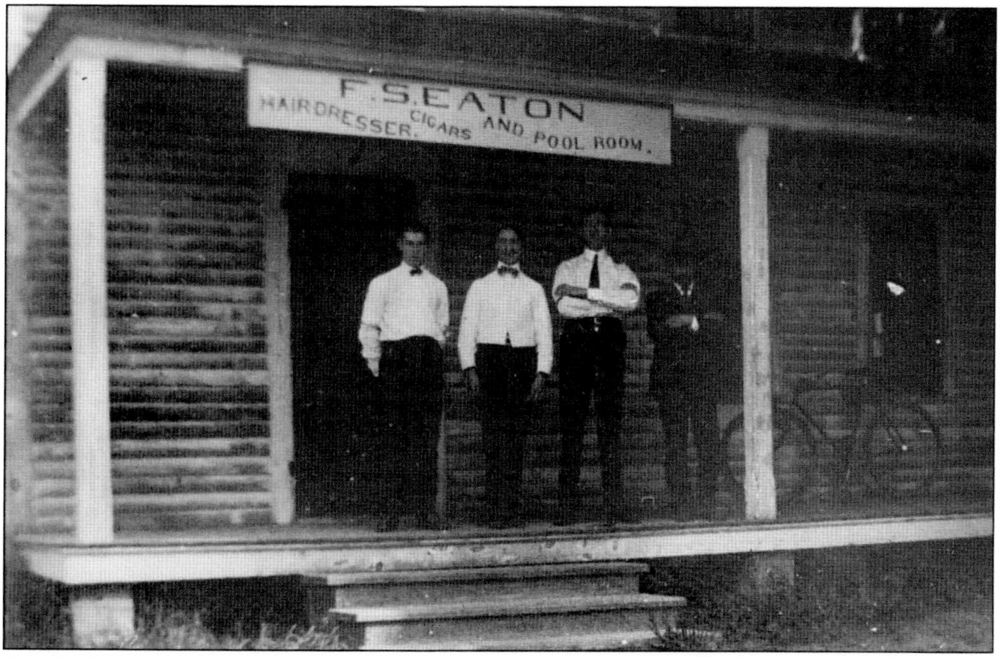

F.S. EATON. Fred Seymour Eaton was a Conway Village entrepreneur at the turn of the century. Another Fred Eaton was an undertaker and carriage maker.

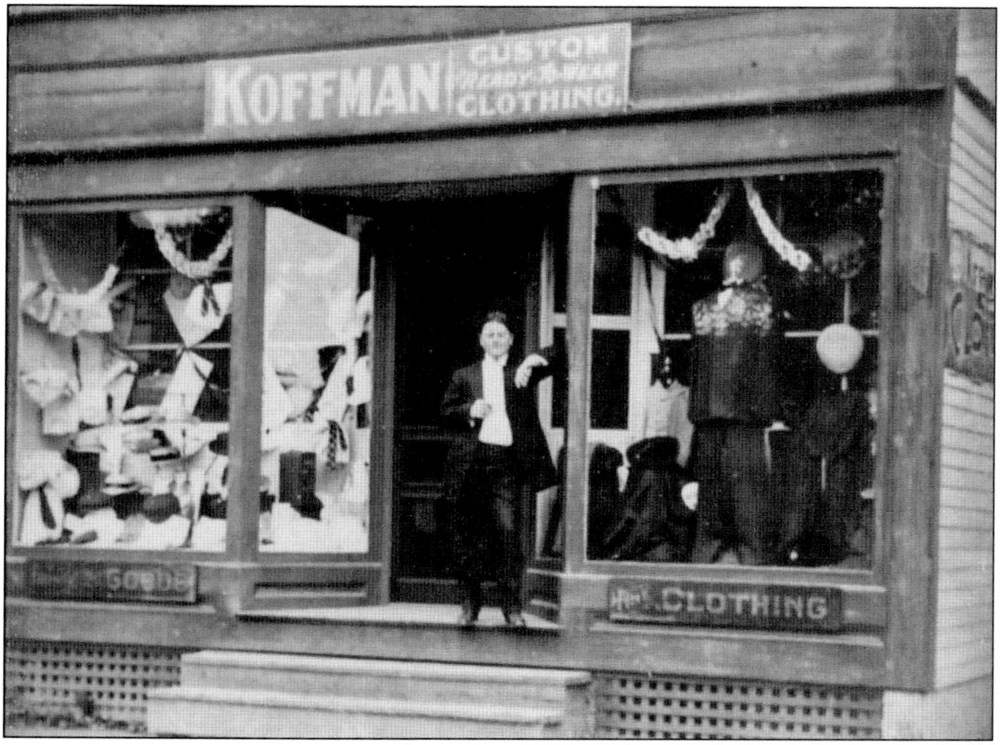

THE KOFFMAN CLOTHING STORE. This store, featuring "ready to wear" clothing, was located in the building later occupied by Stone the Druggist on Main Street across from Kennett High School.

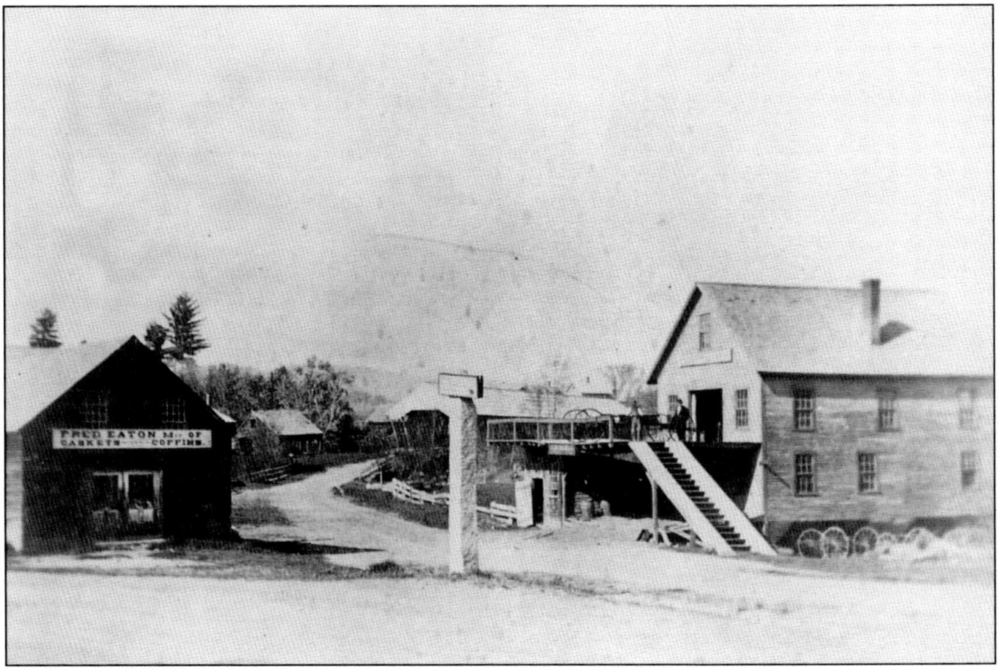

WASHINGTON STREET, CONWAY VILLAGE. The Saco River Bridge is shown flanked by Fred Eaton's Casket Shop and Carriage Shop. Whether you were coming or going, Mr. Eaton was determined to sell you something. A sample of his merchandise can be seen on the deck of the Carriage Shop.

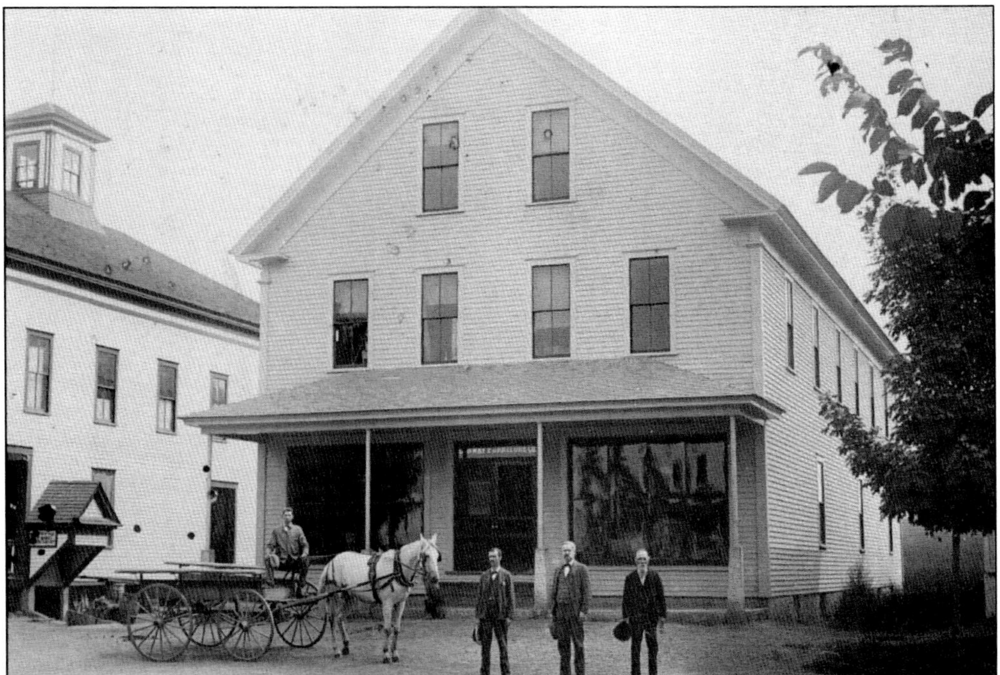

THE CONWAY FURNITURE COMPANY. This Washington Street landmark later housed Davis's Store. The "Conway Opera House" is on the left.

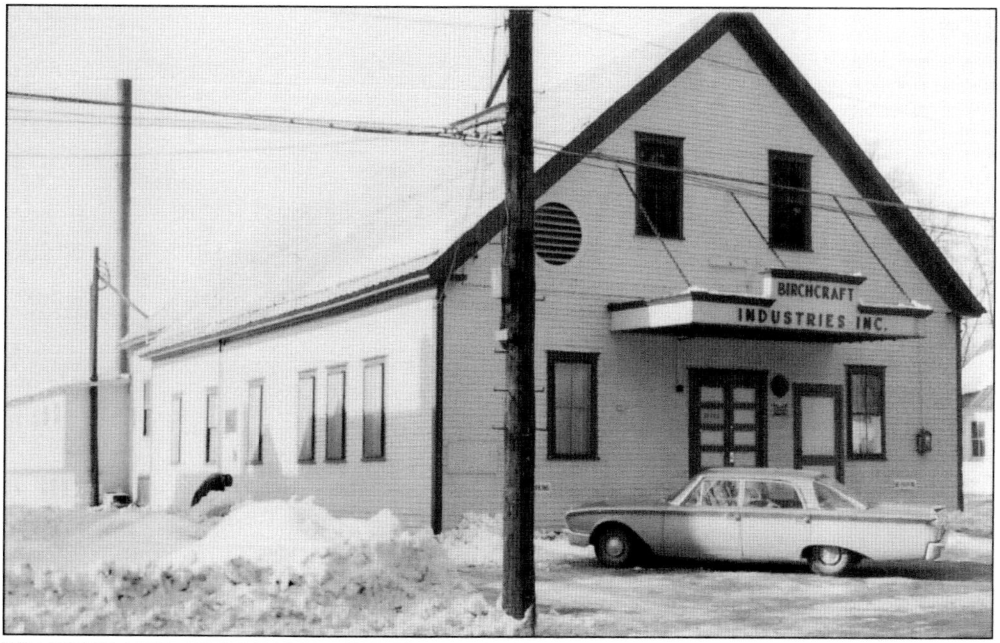

BIRCHCRAFT, PLEASANT STREET, CONWAY VILLAGE. Walter Straw built this building as a music hall and movie theater (The Bijou). It was sold to Leon Bolduc who later built the Majestic Theater Block and opened a wood-working factory in the former Bijou.

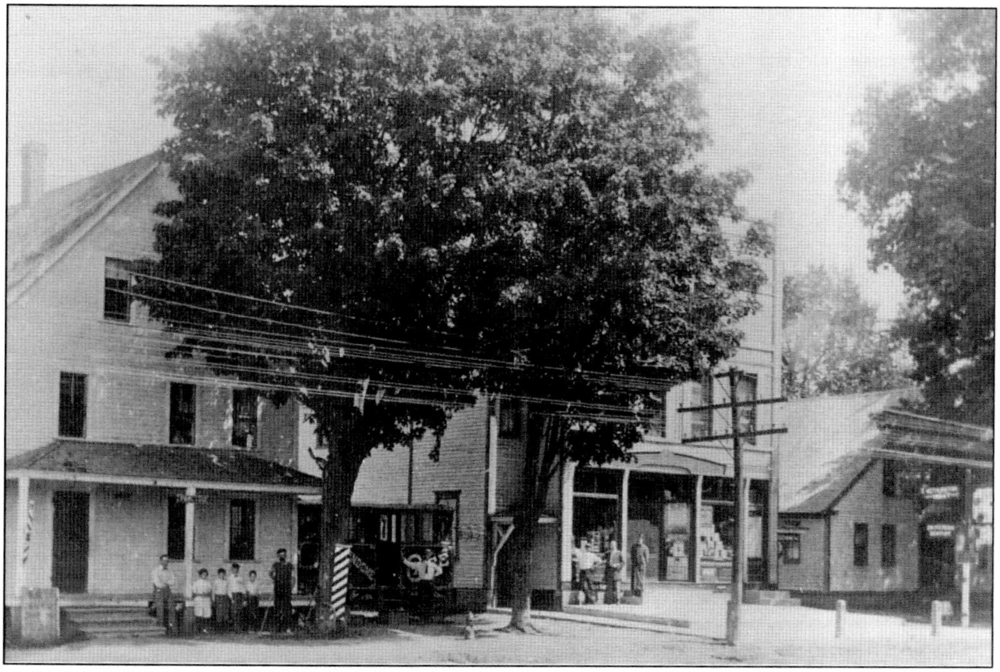

MAIN STREET, CONWAY VILLAGE, c. 1909. On the site of the present Majestic Theater, these buildings burned in 1923. From left to right are Towle's Barber Shop, Shaw's Pharmacy, and Mrs. Ford's house. The Barber Shop also boasted a pool hall. Thurston's Meat Market, housed in the rear of the drugstore, later moved further down Main Street. Note the cafe wagon parked between the buildings. Alton Shorey, manager, is shown in front of Shaw's (center).

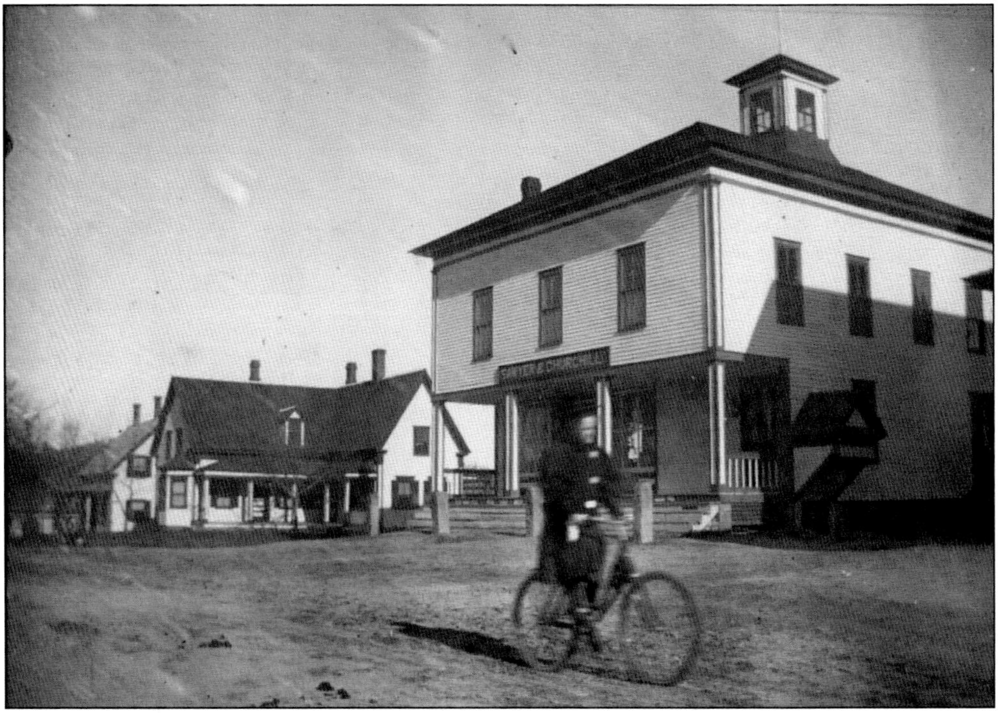

THE CONWAY OPERA HOUSE. Moved from this site on Washington Street in 1919, the "Opera House" was once the only hall in town. With a dining room on the third floor and stores on the first, the second floor was used for plays, musicals, and meetings.

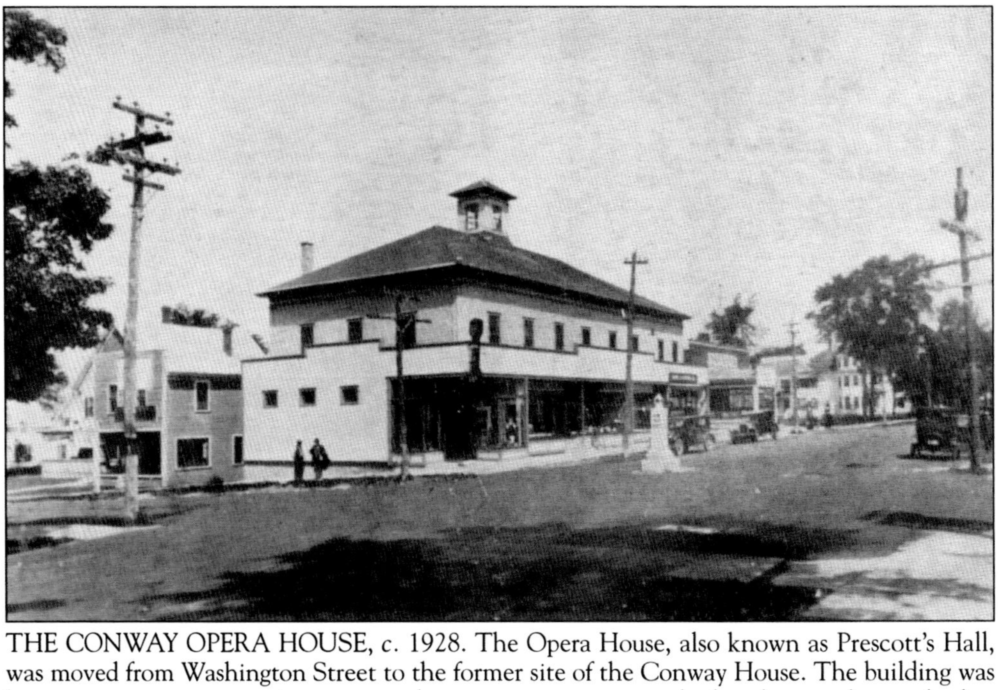

THE CONWAY OPERA HOUSE, *c.* 1928. The Opera House, also known as Prescott's Hall, was moved from Washington Street to the former site of the Conway House. The building was host to a grocery store, an ice cream parlor, an auto parts store, a barber shop, and several other businesses. It last housed the Western Auto Store which burned in February 1976.

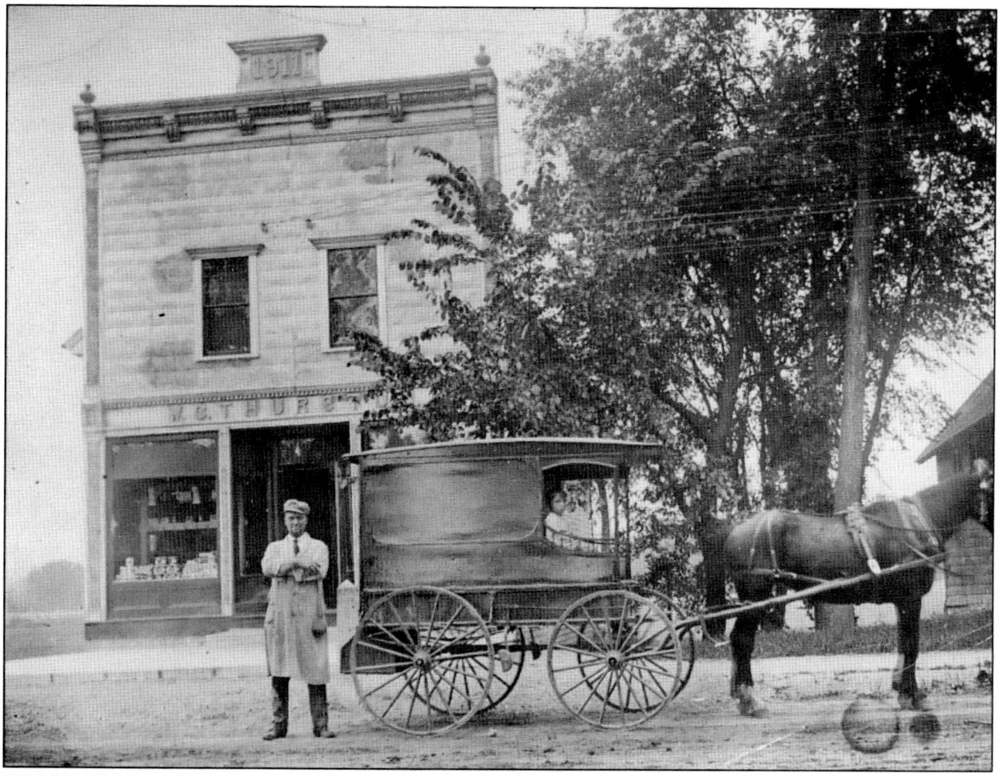

THURSTON'S MEAT MARKET, MAIN STREET, CONWAY VILLAGE. W.C. Thurston stands before the 1911 building that he built to house his market.

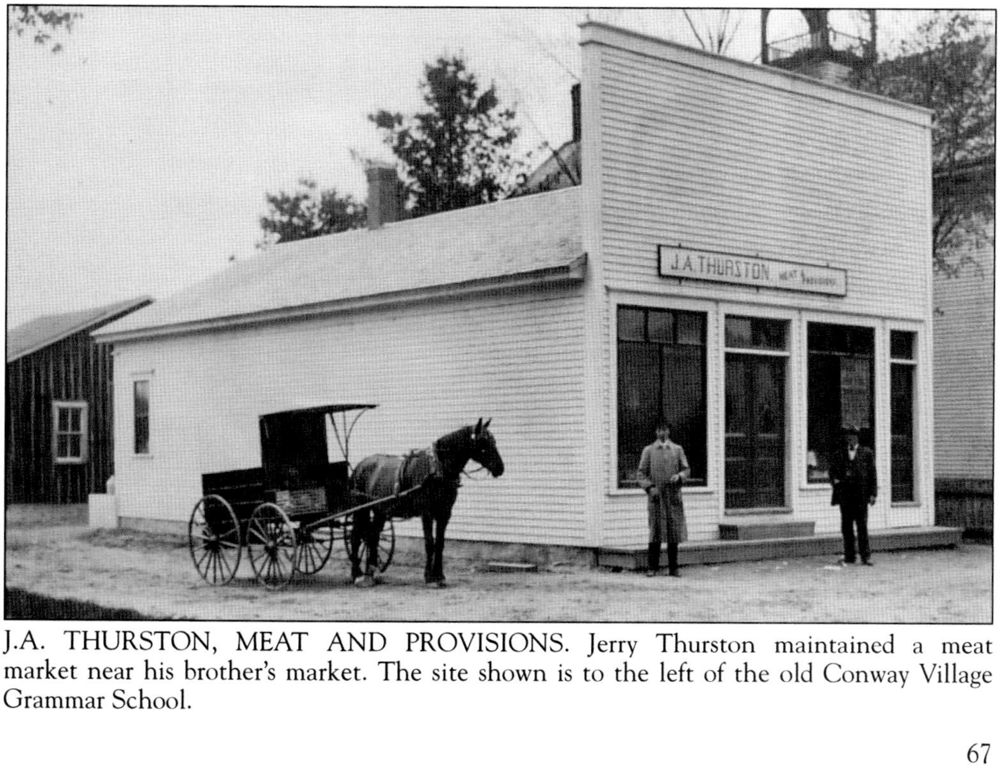

J.A. THURSTON, MEAT AND PROVISIONS. Jerry Thurston maintained a meat market near his brother's market. The site shown is to the left of the old Conway Village Grammar School.

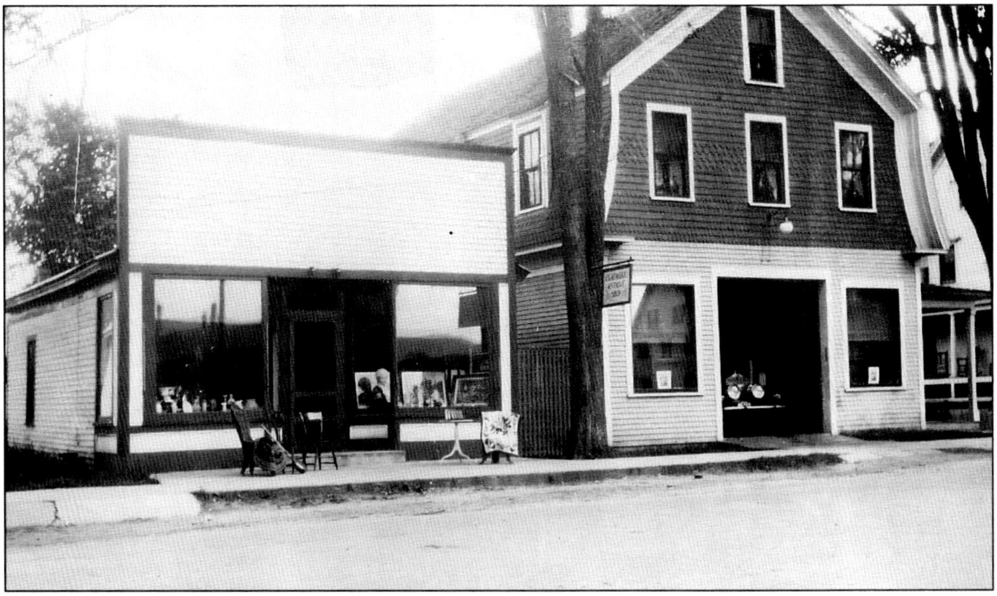

LORA KENNETT'S ANTIQUE SHOP, CONWAY VILLAGE, AUGUST 31, 1928. Mrs. A.C. Kennett dabbled in antiques from this building beside the Kennett Garage on West Main Street. The garage is now the Kennett Company Office.

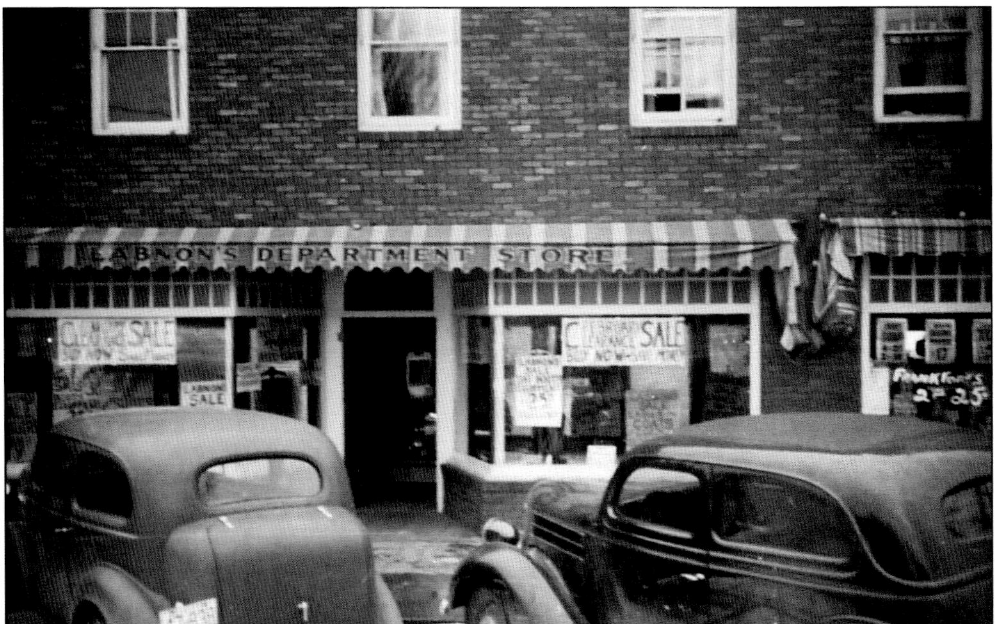

LABNON'S DEPARTMENT STORE, *c.* 1938. For many years, Labnon's Department Store sold clothing from this Bolduc Block storefront.

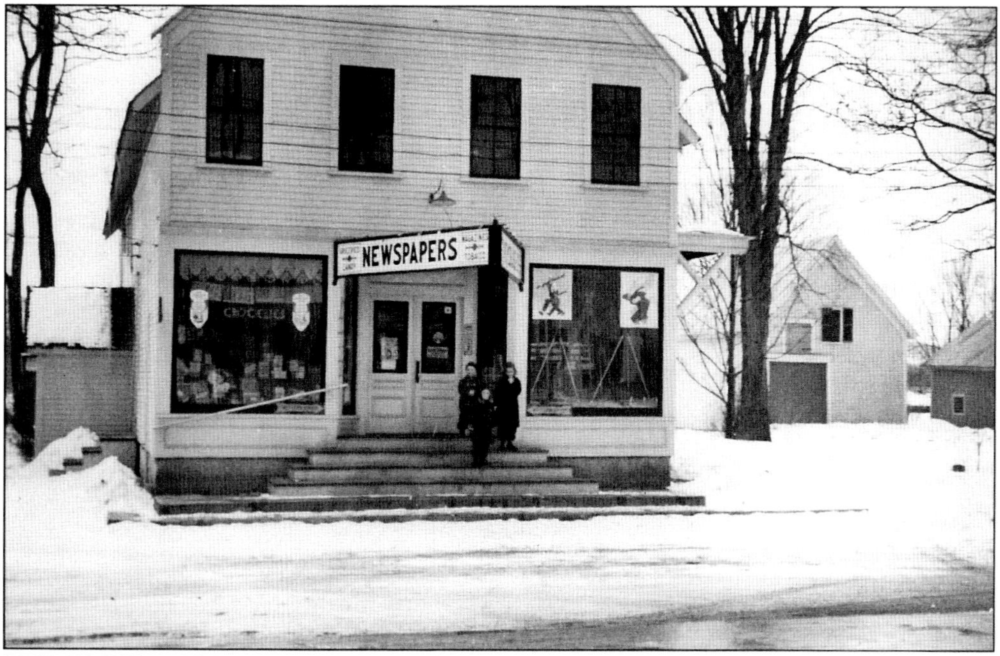

THE PAPER STORE, *c.* 1938. Formerly Shackford's Store, the Paper Store flourished on Conway Village's Main Street for many years. The site has also been the home of Terri's Sweet Shop, Pumpernickles, and Grammy McIntosh's. In 1995, this building houses Cafe Noche. It was moved from a site near Kennett High School.

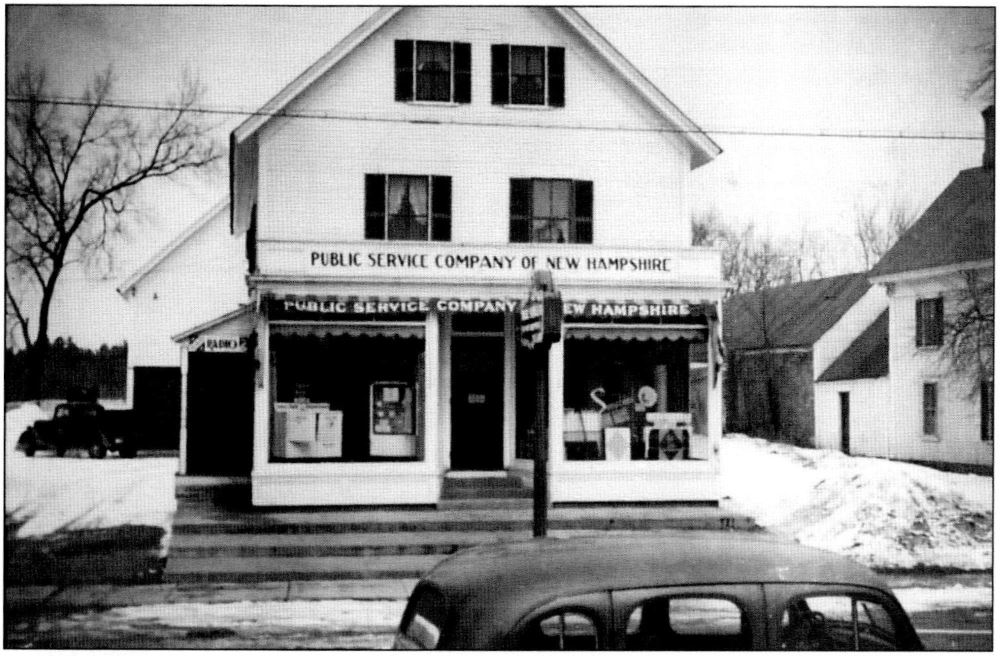

THE PUBLIC SERVICE COMPANY, *c.* 1938. The Public Service Company of New Hampshire office was located in this Main Street, Conway Village building, now Bailey Auto Supply. The Landry house is shown on the right.

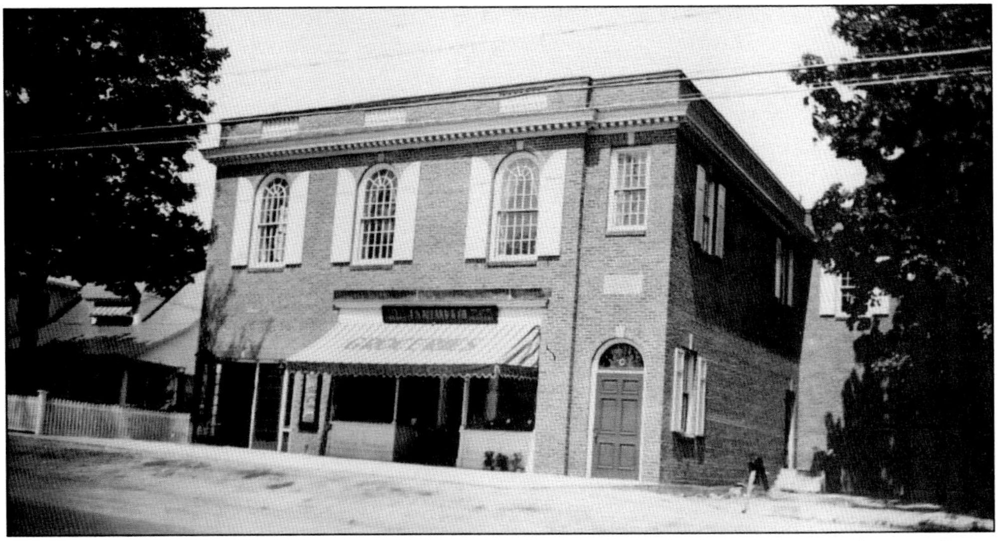

THE MASONIC TEMPLE, NORTH CONWAY. The present building was built in 1931 to replace an earlier structure destroyed by fire. The ground floor houses a storefront and theater.

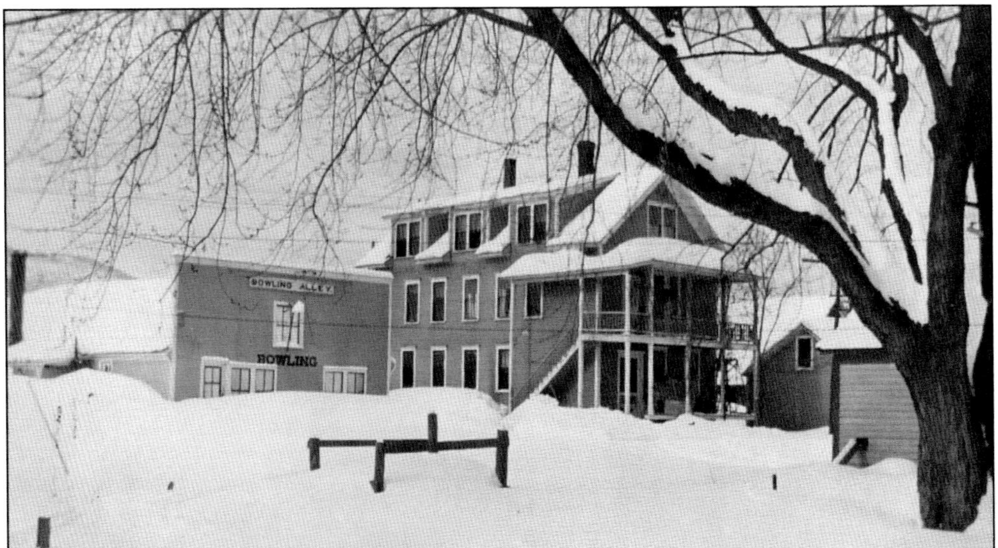

THE REPORTER OFFICE, FEBRUARY 10, 1918. Located in a North Conway alley known as Reporter Court, this building housed the valley's longest running newspaper. *The Reporter* began in 1883 as *The Sandwich Reporter* and was published until 1992. Publication in North Conway began in 1893.

Six

You Can Get There from Here: Highways and Transportation

The first trails into the Conways followed the lake and stream systems, taking advantage of water travel wherever possible. Travel by sled and snowshoe was preferable on trails not designed for wheeled vehicles. Even after roads were improved, tourists endured rough stage rides, punctuated by steamship travel across Lake Winnipesaukee. It was the advent of the railroad that first made travel fast and comfortable. Later, automobiles provided a freedom of travel that changed the valley forever.

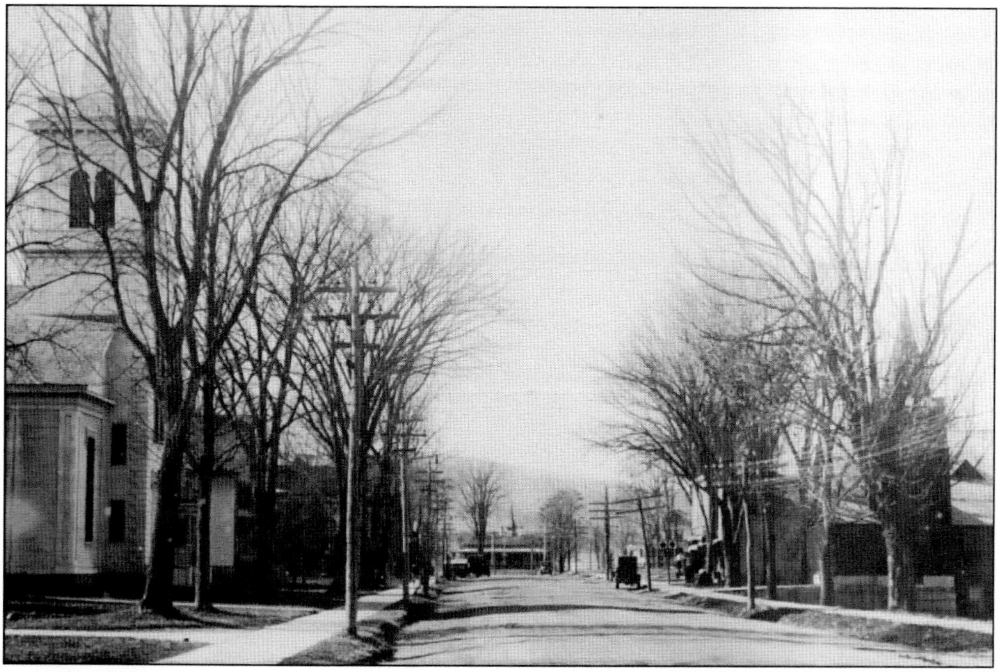

MAIN STREET, CONWAY VILLAGE, *c.* 1920. The Conway Methodist Church is shown on the left, with the Congregational Church on the right. The Conway Station is at the far end of the street.

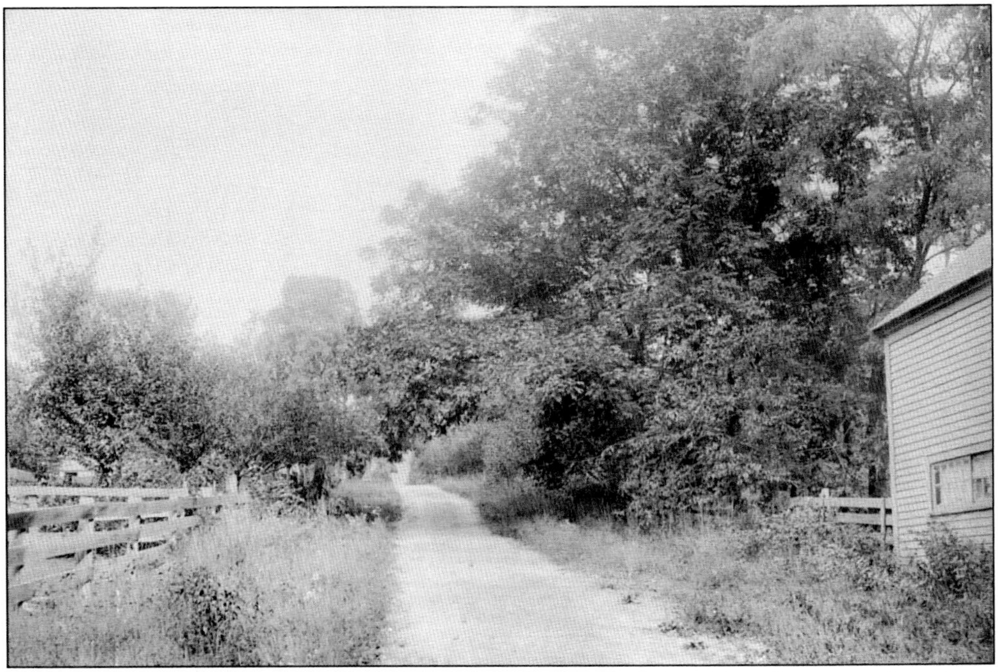

LOCUST LANE. Benjamin Champney's Studio is shown on the right. Champney, founder of the White Mountain School of Art, brought many artists to North Conway.

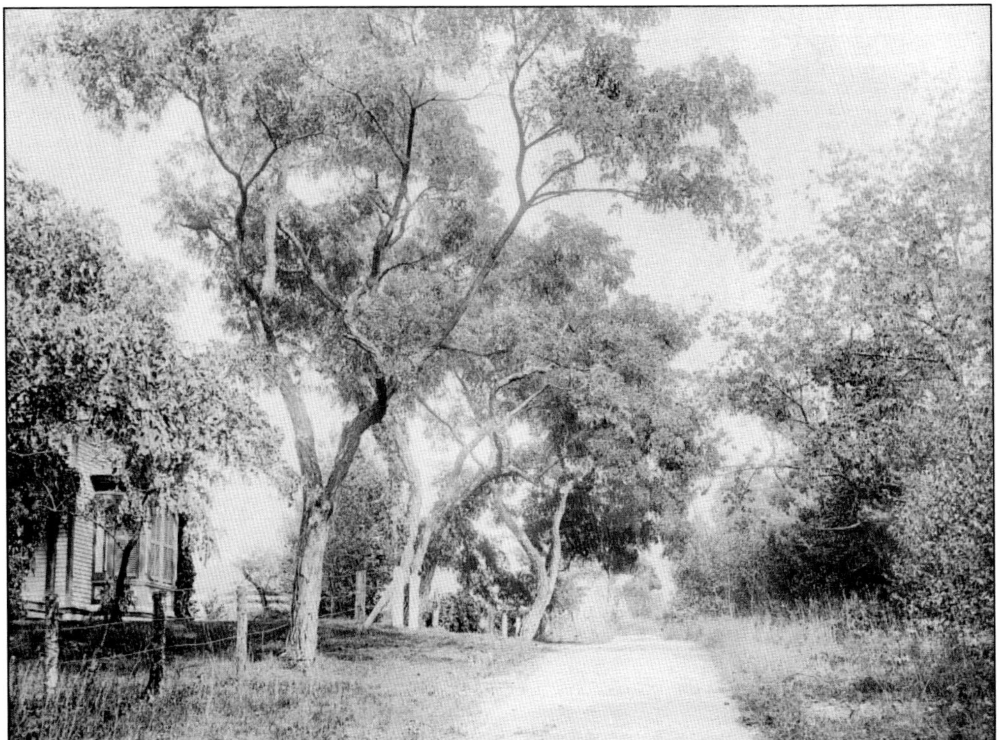

LOCUST LANE, NORTH CONWAY. Once known as Hansen's Lane, this side street is now the exit from the Red Jacket Inn. The Alpheus Furber house is shown on the left.

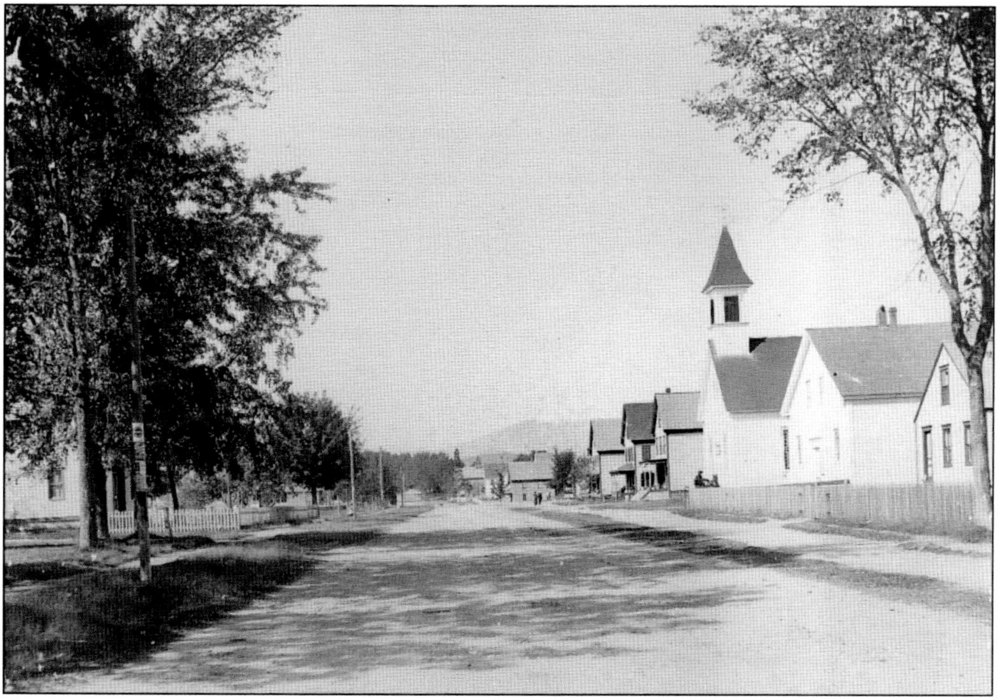

MAIN STREET, CENTER CONWAY. This road, built in 1766, passes through the geographic center of the Conways. Notice the Town Hall (to the right of the church). This building was renovated in 1905. A contemporary newspaper article reports that there was no cussing or spitting on the floor to mar the first meeting in the new hall.

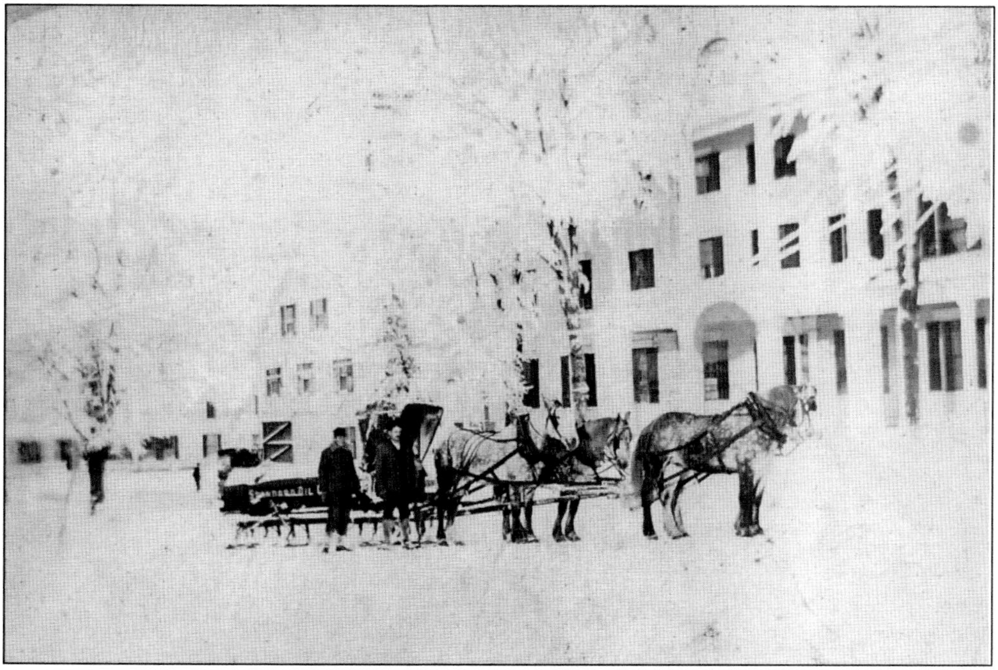

A STANDARD OIL COMPANY TEAM. The Standard Oil tank mounted on a sled is pictured in front of the Conway House at the Four Corners in Conway Village.

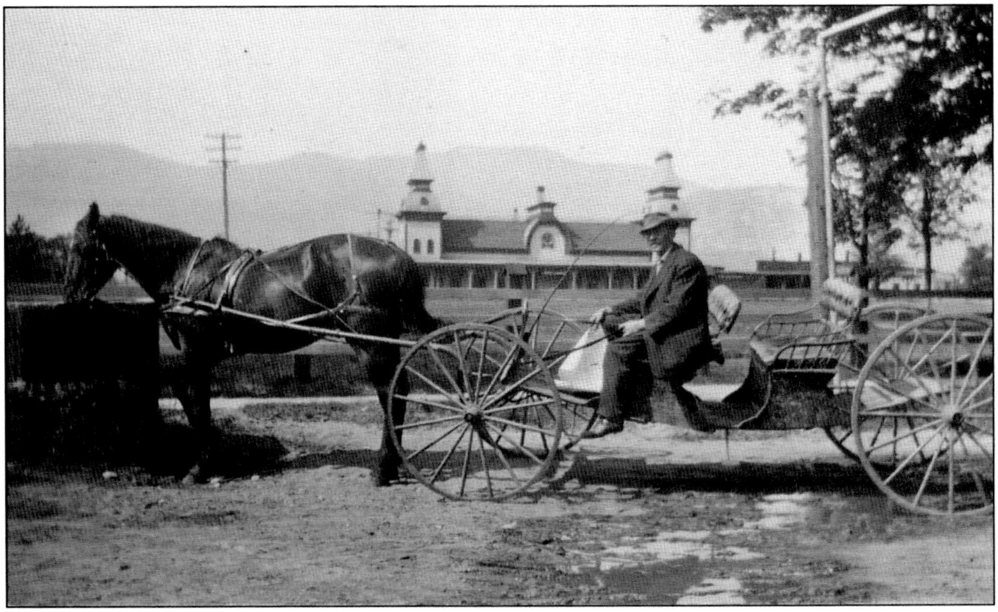

LEVI RICKER, *c.* 1920. Mr. Ricker is pictured in front of the B&M Station, North Conway, with the horse and buggy in which he carried mail from the station to the post office.

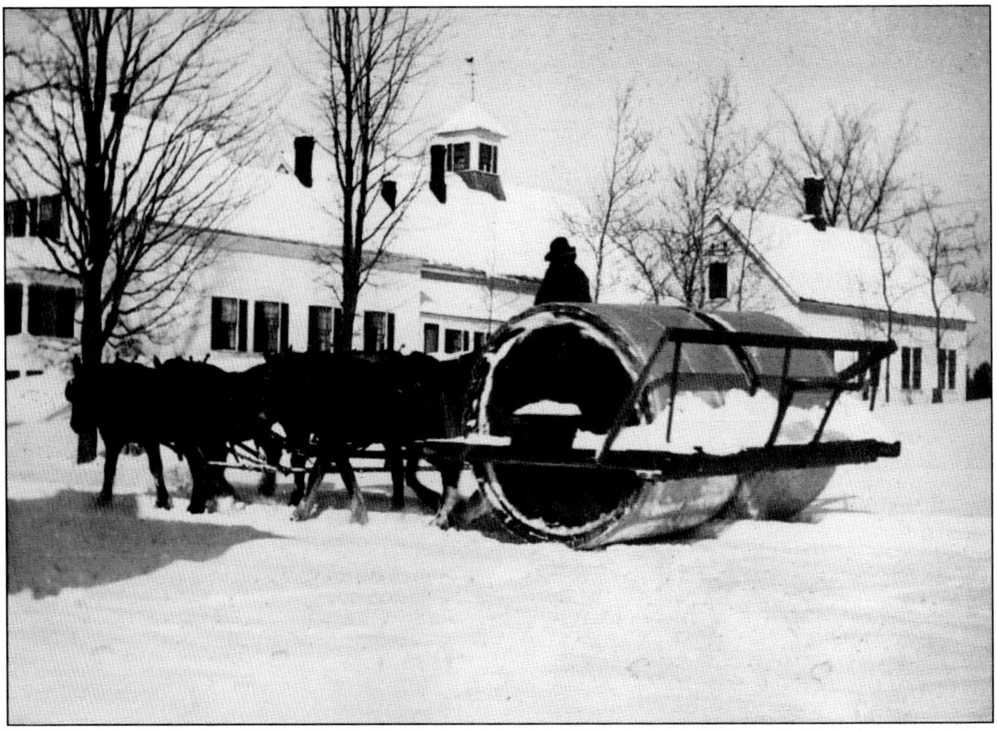

SNOW ROLLER. Earl McLellan is shown driving this roller in front of the Chester Potter house. During very heavy storms, multiple teams could be hooked to the roller.

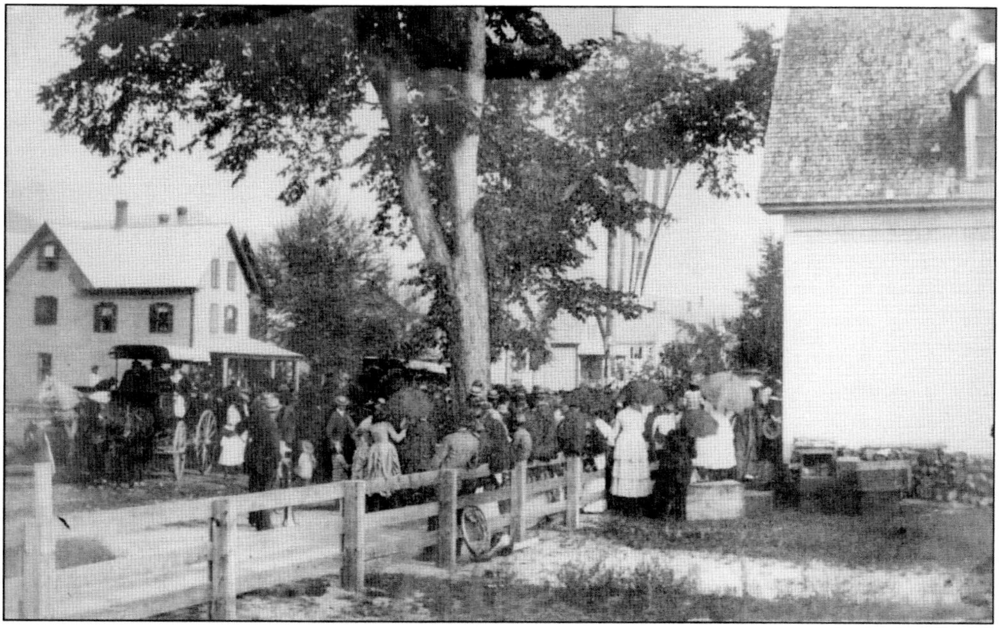

FLAG RAISING. A flag was being raised in conjunction with the Blaine H. Logan political campaign in front of the Woodbury home in North Conway Village. Mr. Logan lost to Grover Cleveland.

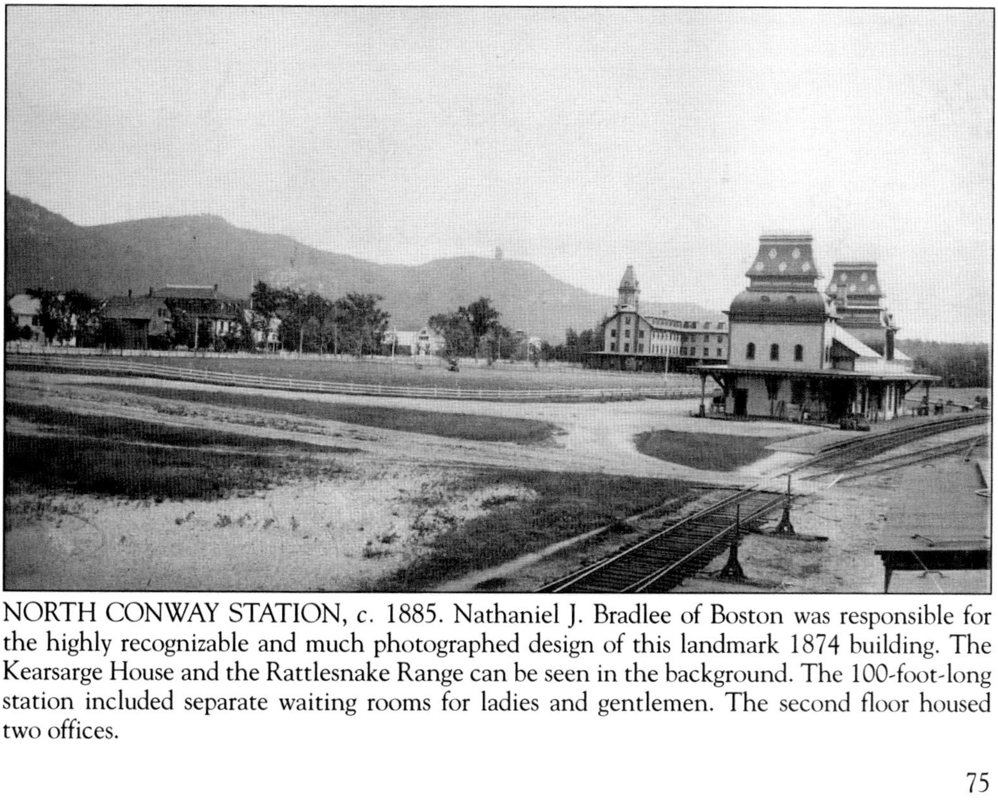

NORTH CONWAY STATION, *c.* 1885. Nathaniel J. Bradlee of Boston was responsible for the highly recognizable and much photographed design of this landmark 1874 building. The Kearsarge House and the Rattlesnake Range can be seen in the background. The 100-foot-long station included separate waiting rooms for ladies and gentlemen. The second floor housed two offices.

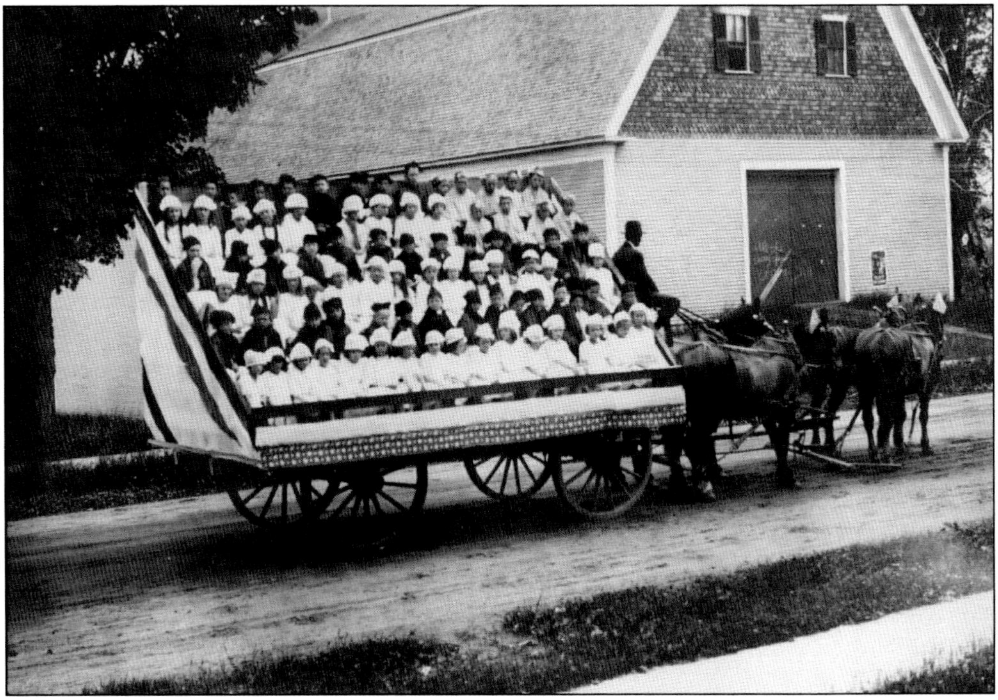

A HORSE-DRAWN FLOAT, MAIN STREET, CONWAY VILLAGE. Looking like a crate of chicks ready for shipping, this parade entry is passing in front of the Kennett barn.

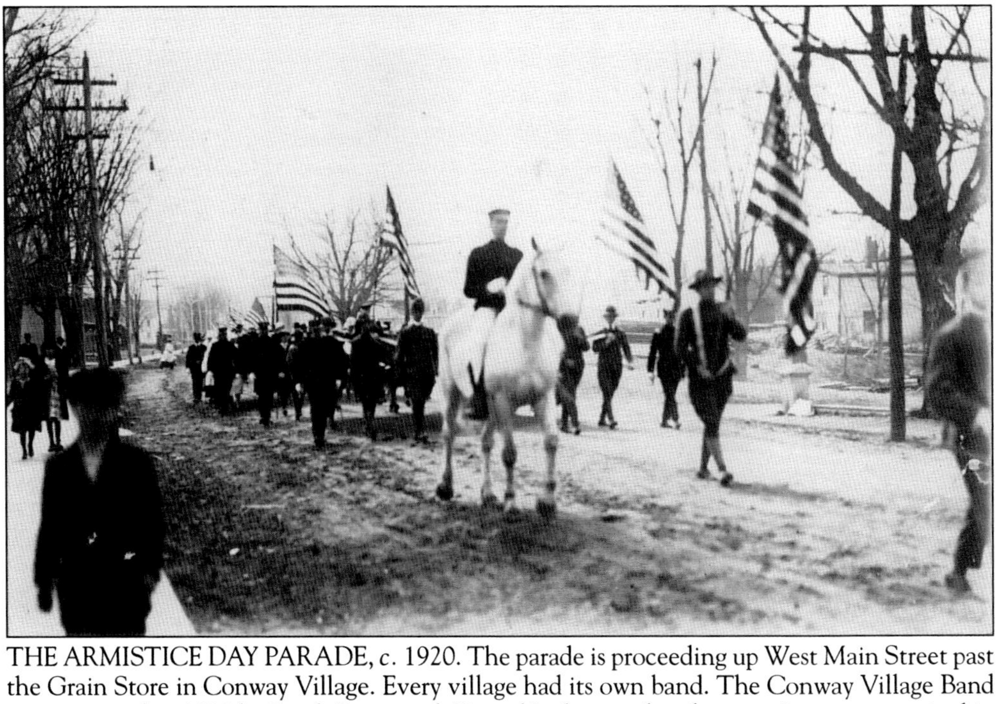

THE ARMISTICE DAY PARADE, *c.* 1920. The parade is proceeding up West Main Street past the Grain Store in Conway Village. Every village had its own band. The Conway Village Band was organized in 1880 by Frank Davis with Daniel Jackson as bandmaster. It was reorganized in 1915 with Dana Farrington becoming bandmaster in 1933. In 1900, Frank Davis mustered an all girl band.

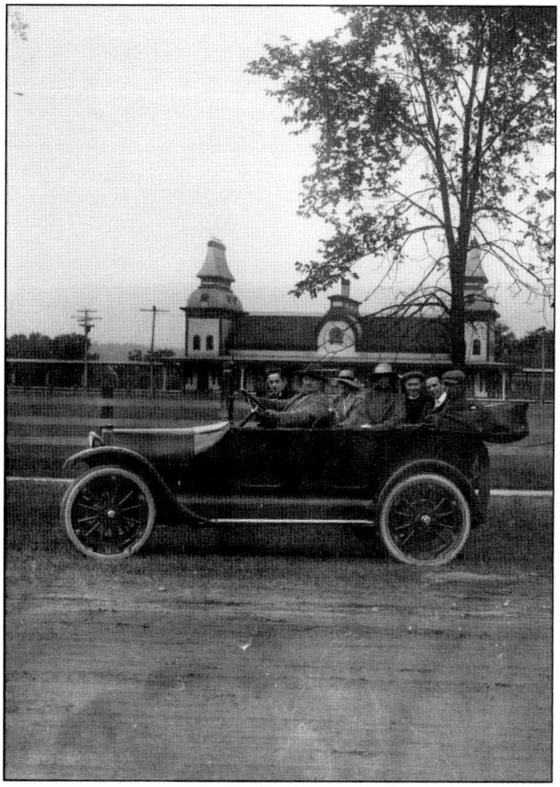

SCHOULER PARK, NORTH CONWAY. The advent of automobiles spelled the final death knell for the grand hotel era. The population was more mobile and families no longer spent weeks and months in one spot. Motels and overnight cabins appeared throughout the valley.

AUTOMOBILE CLUB, *c.* 1912. This group of New Hampshire motorists, touring the White Mountains in identical automobiles, posed before the Kearsarge House, North Conway.

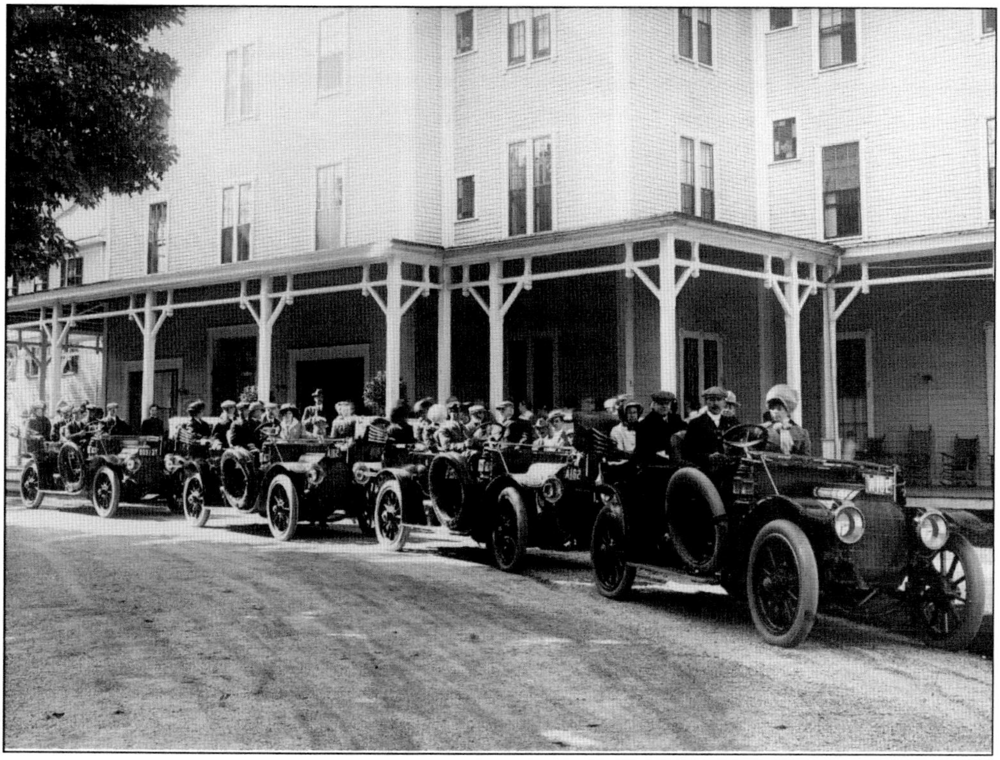

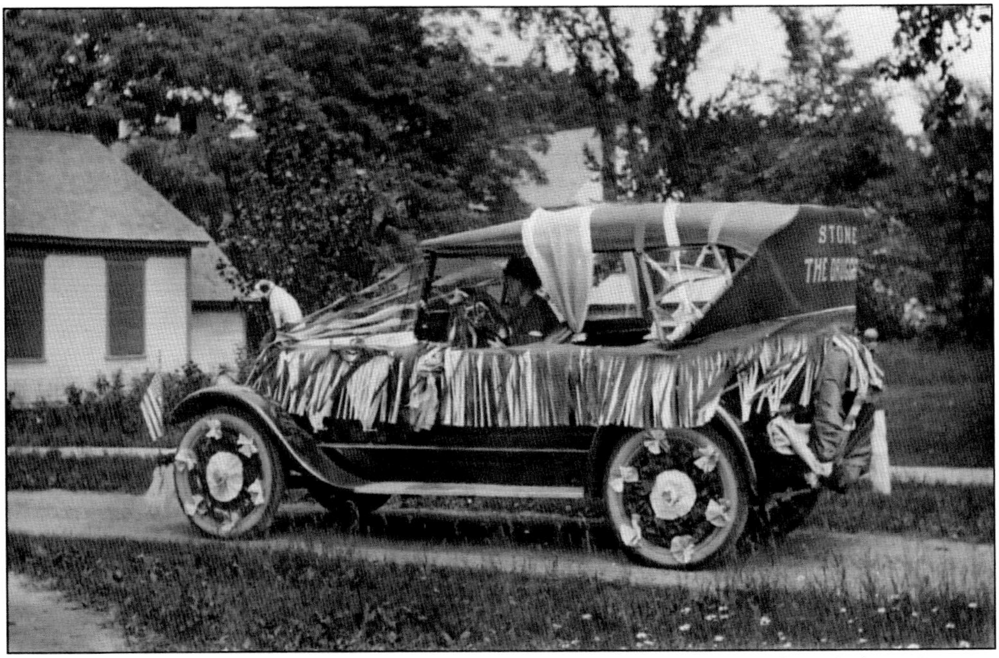

READY FOR A PARADE, *c*. 1925. Stone the Druggist was decorated and ready for a Conway Village parade. Note "Nipper," the RCA Victor dog, mounted on the hood.

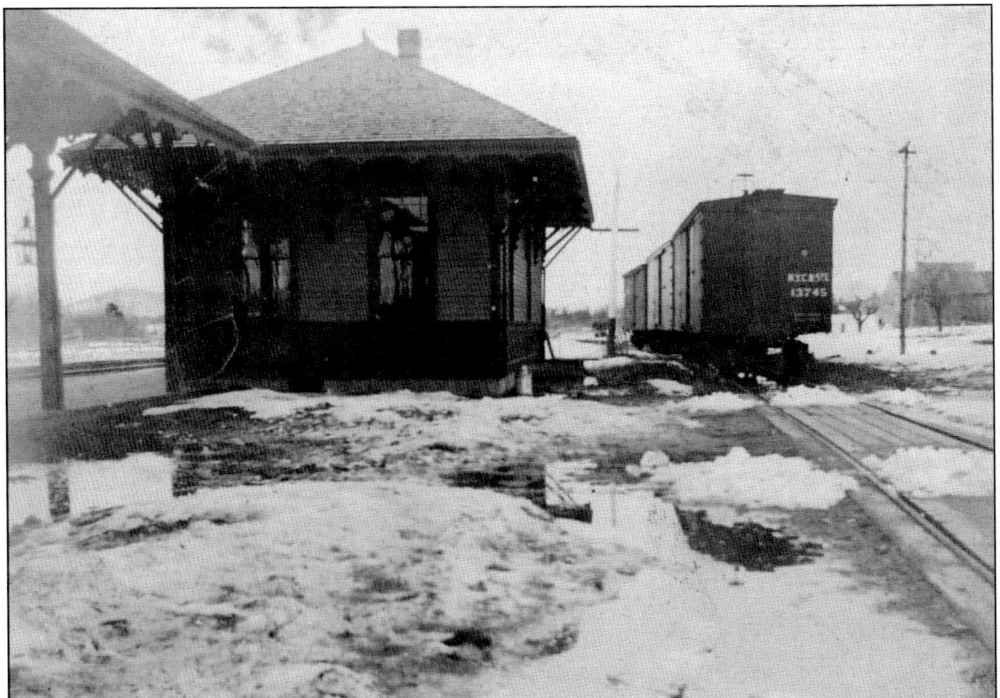

THE MAINE CENTRAL RAILROAD STATION, CENTER CONWAY. Although the Maine Central provided passenger service to Conway for several decades, the line was primarily used to haul freight from Maine to Canada. All service stopped through the Conways in the early 1980s. The station was moved to Conway and renovated as a private home.

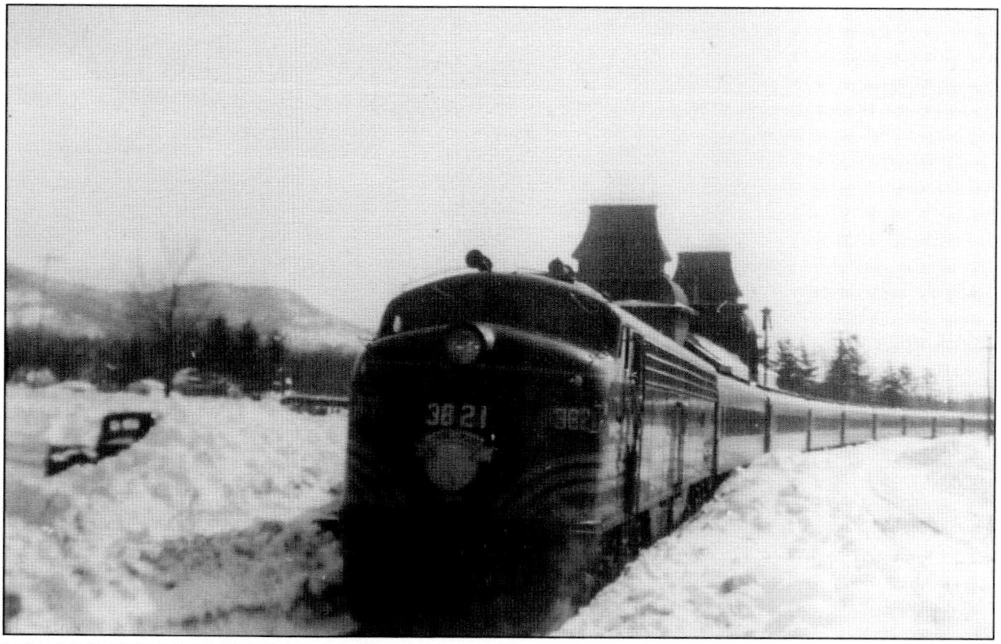

B&M LEAVING NORTH CONWAY STATION. During the 1930s and '40s, "snow trains" brought hundreds of skiers to North Conway. Skis could be rented on the equipment car and guides were available with the latest ski conditions.

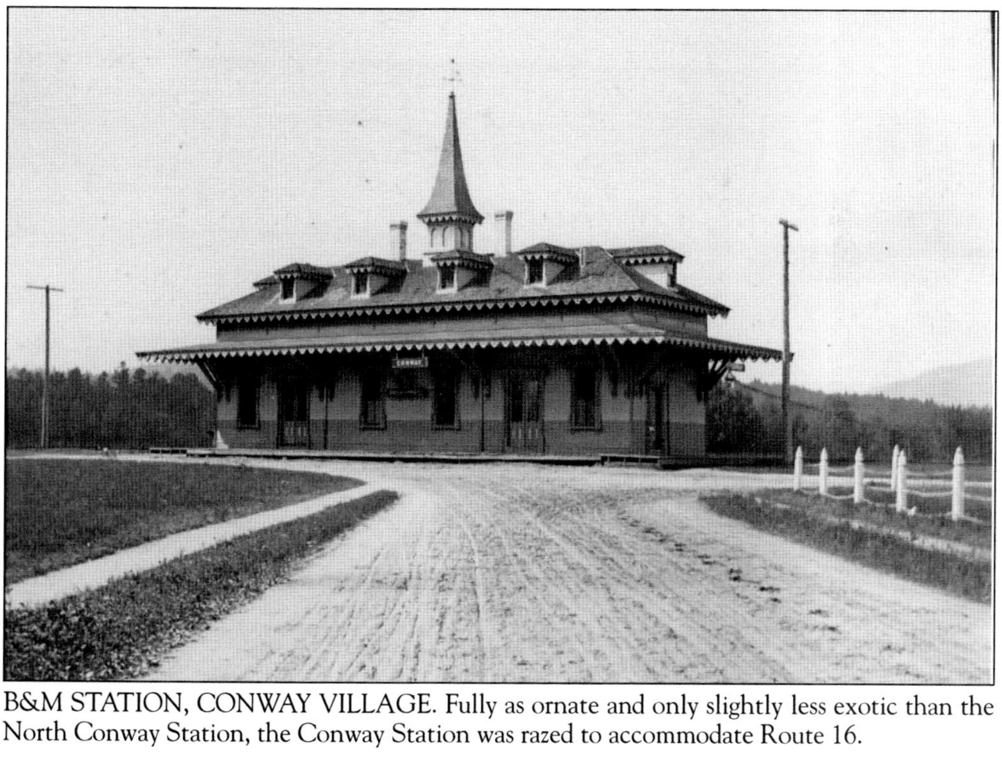

B&M STATION, CONWAY VILLAGE. Fully as ornate and only slightly less exotic than the North Conway Station, the Conway Station was razed to accommodate Route 16.

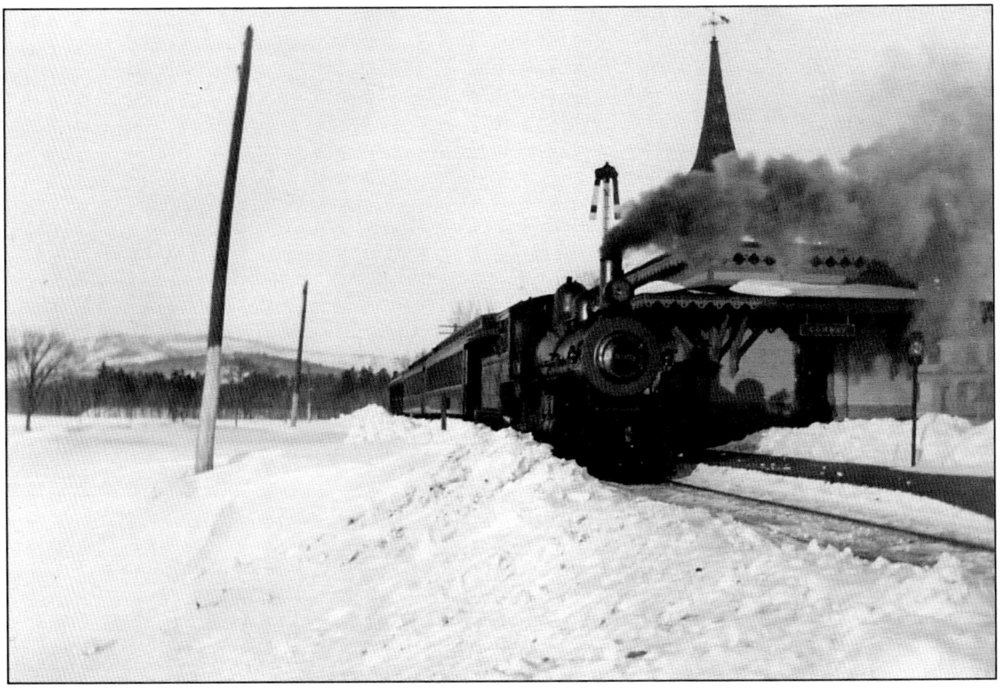

B&M LEAVING CONWAY. Frank Davis was the first station agent and telegrapher at the Conway Station. Passenger service from Dover was discontinued in 1961.

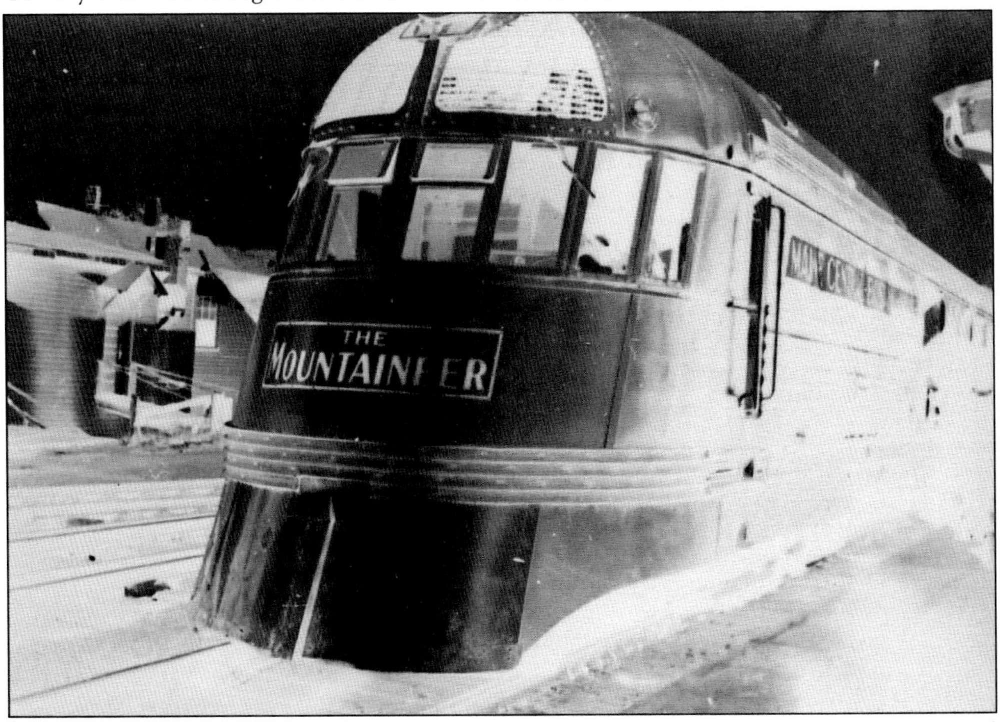

THE FIRST STREAMLINER INTO CONWAY. The Mountaineer, which ran for several years between Boston and Littleton, also saw service as The Flying Yankee, The Chesire, and The Minute Man.

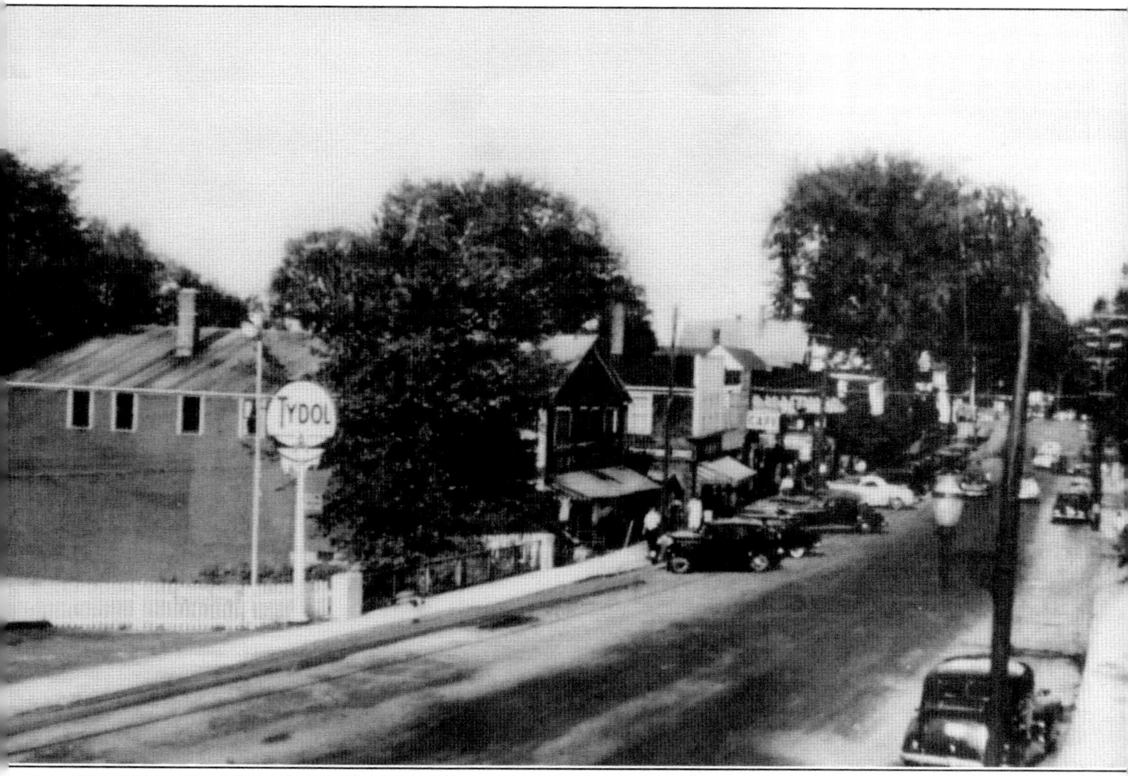

MAIN STREET, CONWAY VILLAGE, *c.* 1950. Diagonal parking was still allowed when this view was taken looking east from the bridge.

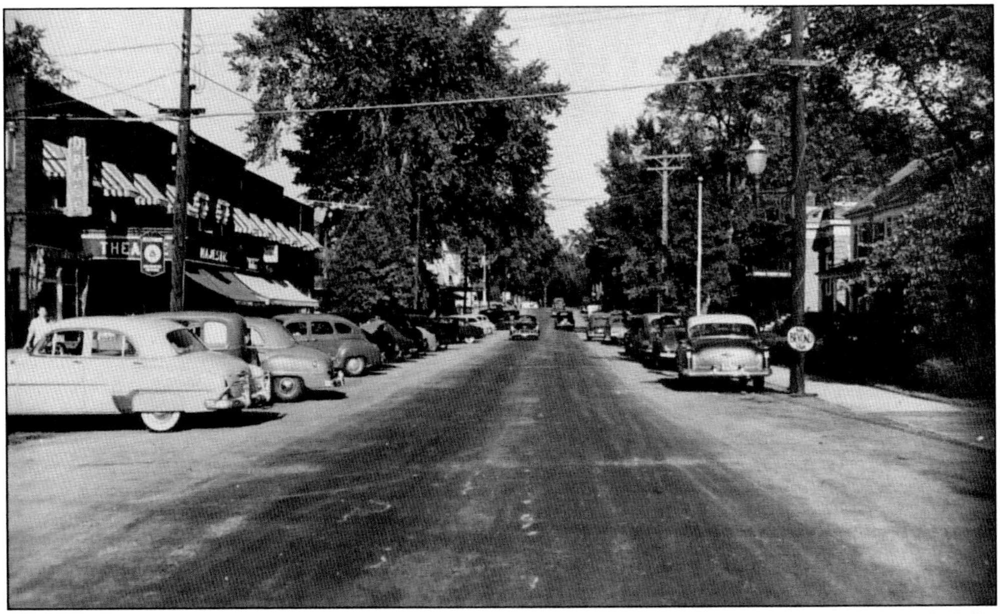

MAIN STREET, CONWAY VILLAGE, *c.* 1952. Conway's Main Street was shaded by picturesque elms until Dutch Elm disease decimated them during the 1960s and '70s. The "Dr. Wiggin House" can be seen at the far right.

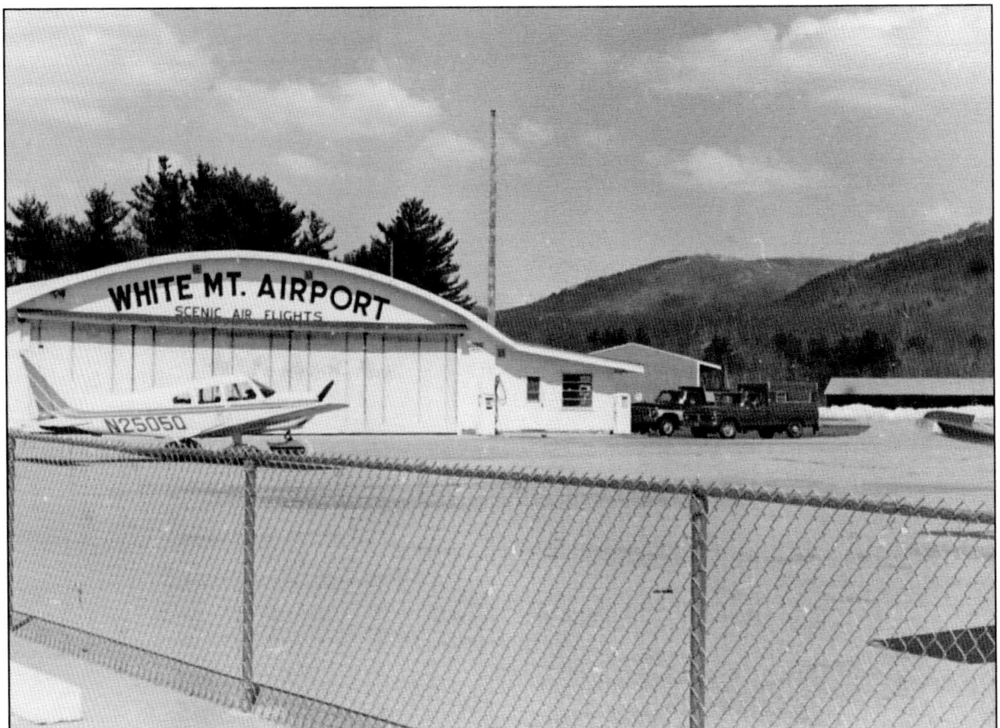

WHITE MOUNTAIN AIRPORT. On the site of a former race track, Wylie Apte Sr. built the White Mountain Airport, pulling stumps and raking by night, flying by day. The site is now occupied by Settler's Green.

Seven

Death and Taxes: Religion, Politics, and Education

As was the custom, the first meetinghouse was located in the geographic center of the town. It became apparent that this was not the easiest location for the majority of townspeople. The meetinghouse, which served as both church and town hall, was relocated to North Conway. Before mandatory attendance was introduced, education often came second to farm work. Many students were kept out of school during planting and harvest. It should not be inferred from this that education was unimportant to the early settlers; the establishment of a school in each neighborhood was a high priority. Itinerant ministers traveled to remote neighborhoods where planks were stretched between chairs for makeshift pews.

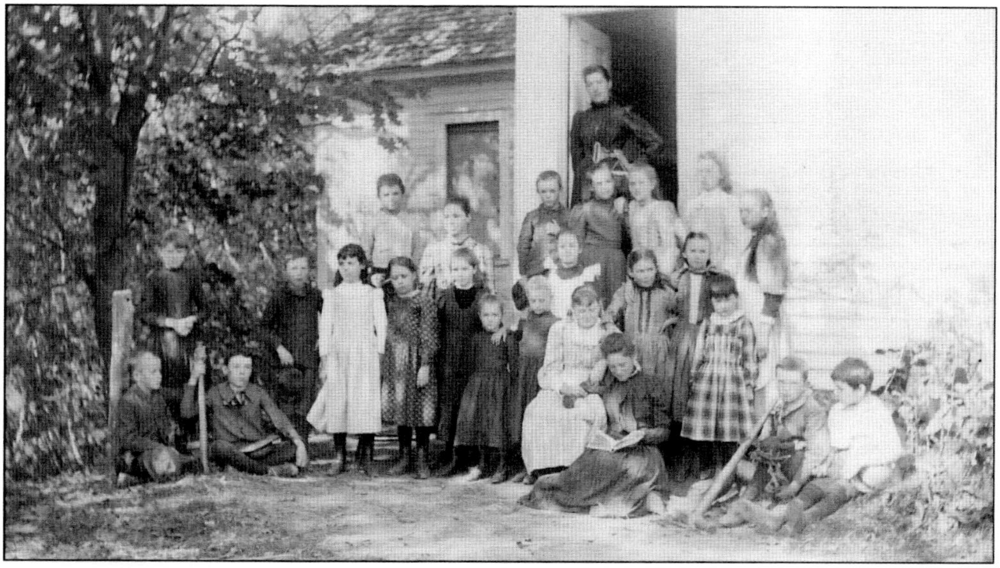

ECHO LAKE SCHOOLHOUSE. The teacher, Edna Eastman, had to deal with eight grades in one room as well as the duties of cleaning, heating, and otherwise maintaining the school. After graduating from the eighth grade, young ladies often became teachers until marriage set them on a more domestic course. Discipline problems were likely to arise from students only a year or two younger than the teacher.

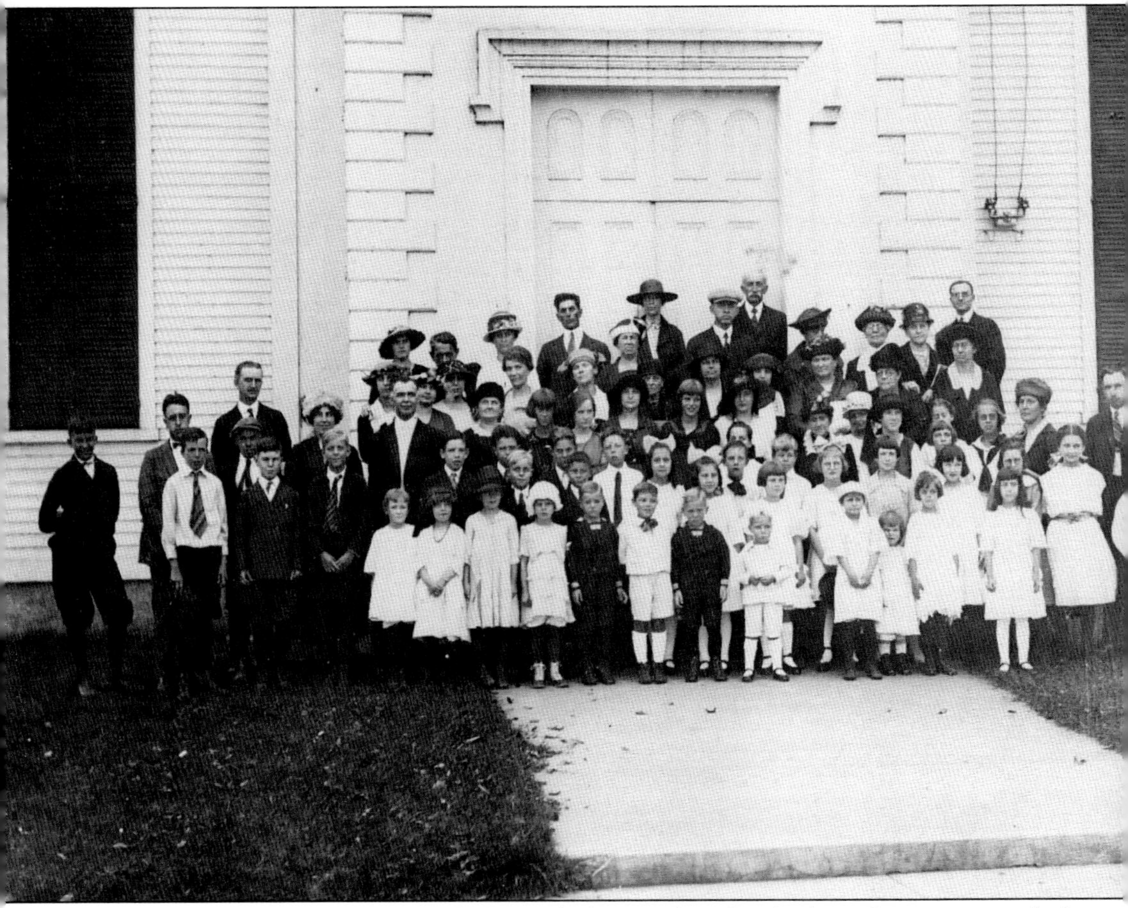

A METHODIST CHURCH GROUP. Decked out in their Sunday best, this group poses before the Methodist Church in Conway Village. The church was built in 1826, financed by the selling of pews. The congregation shared a minister with the First Church in North Conway until 1866, when a Methodist Society was organized in the Village.

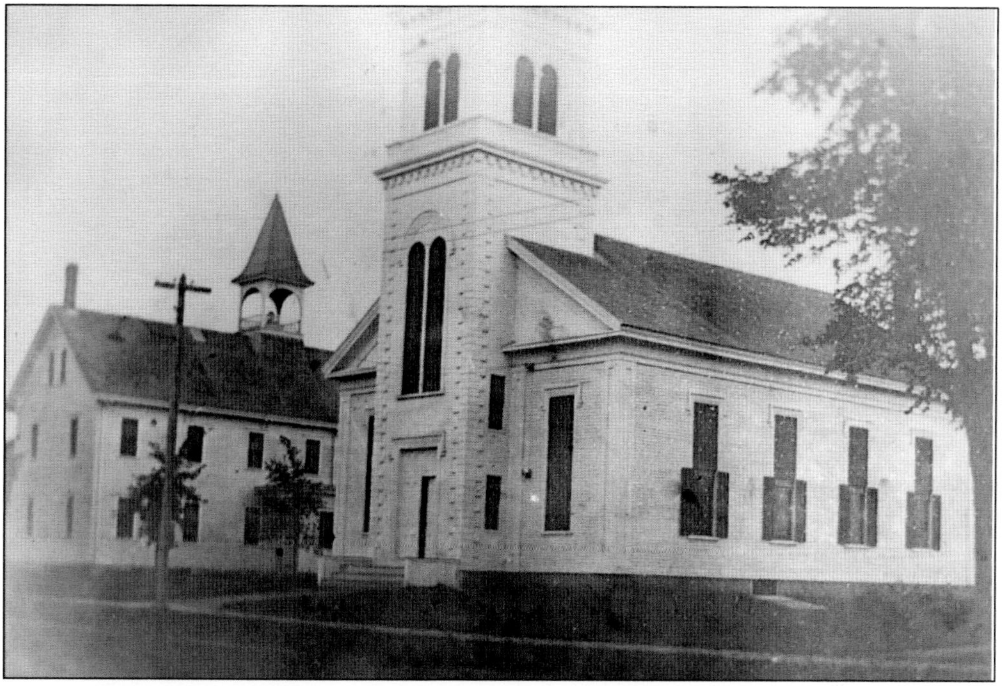

THE METHODIST CHURCH AND GRAMMAR SCHOOL, CONWAY VILLAGE. One of the grandest edifices in the Village, this 1883 grammar school was replaced in 1957. Classes were still held intermittently in the old building through the 1970s. It was last used as the Conway Recreation Center. In 1911, the Grammar School was rotated 180 degrees, moved back on the lot, and doubled in size. Here it is seen in its original position.

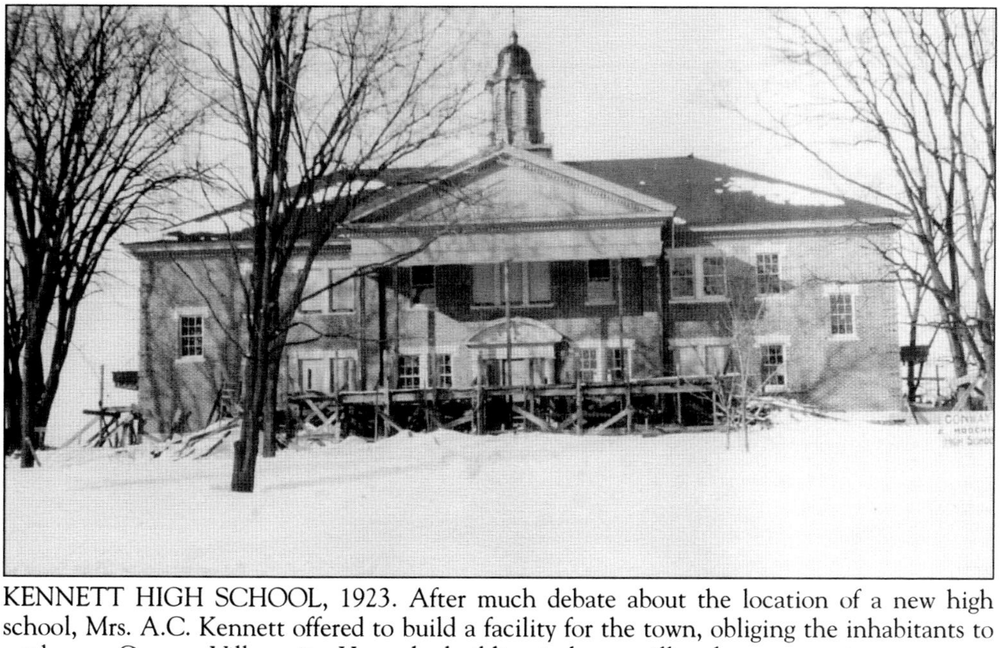

KENNETT HIGH SCHOOL, 1923. After much debate about the location of a new high school, Mrs. A.C. Kennett offered to build a facility for the town, obliging the inhabitants to settle on a Conway Village site. Here, the building is shown still under construction.

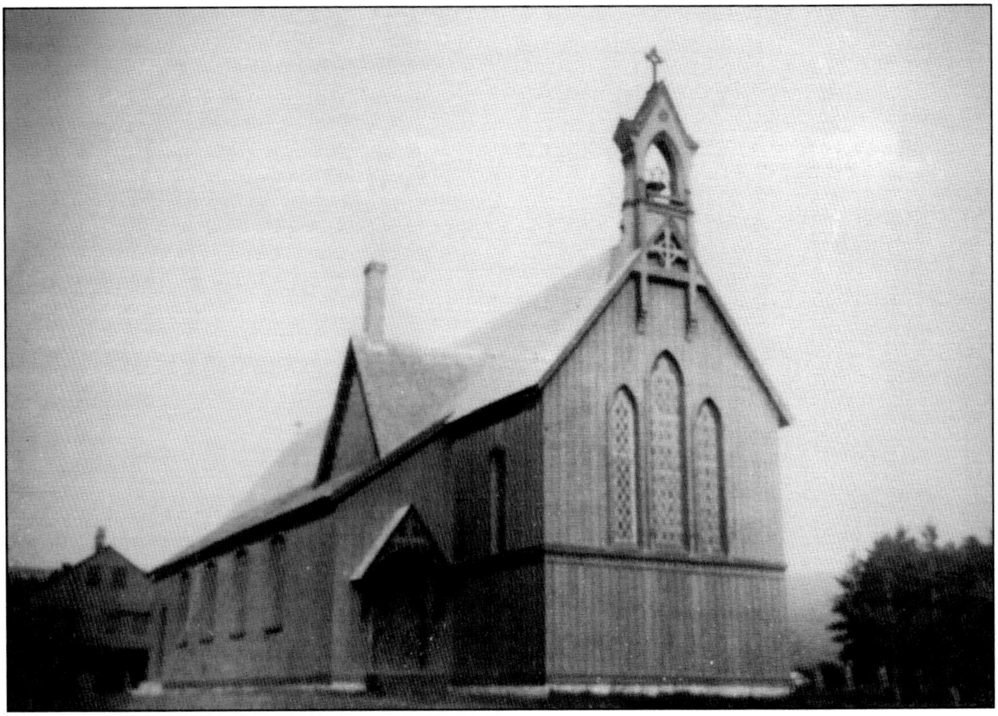

THE CHRIST CHURCH, EPISCOPAL, NORTH CONWAY. Samuel Thompson, of the Copperhead political persuasion and unhappy with the Congregational minister's views on the Civil War, offered to help finance the establishment of the Episcopal Church.

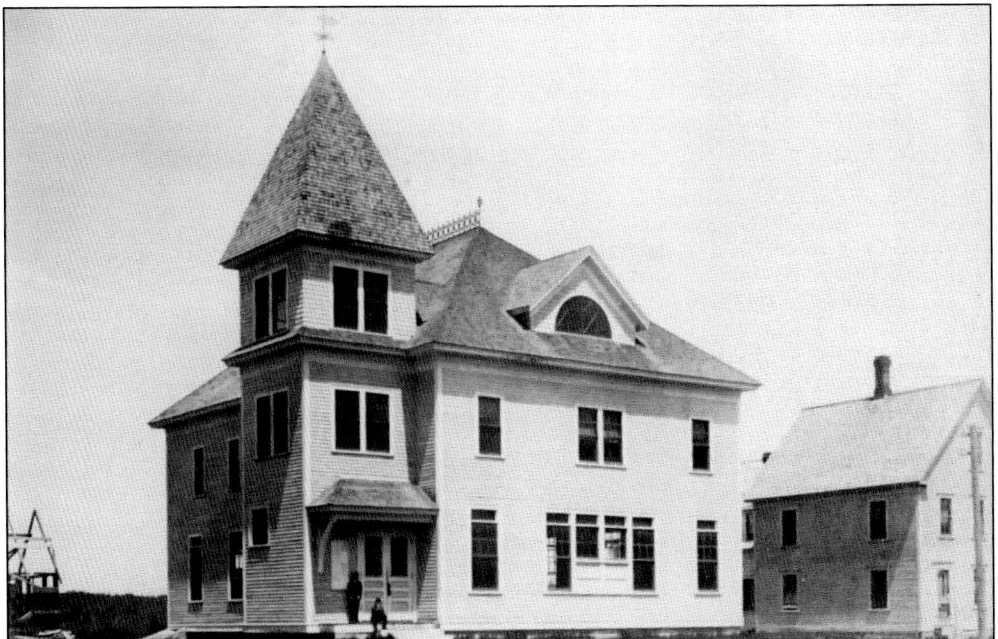

CONWAY TOWN HALL, CENTER CONWAY. Renovated in 1903, the Town Hall boasted good ventilation and ample seating. This was the main battlefield for sniping between the villages.

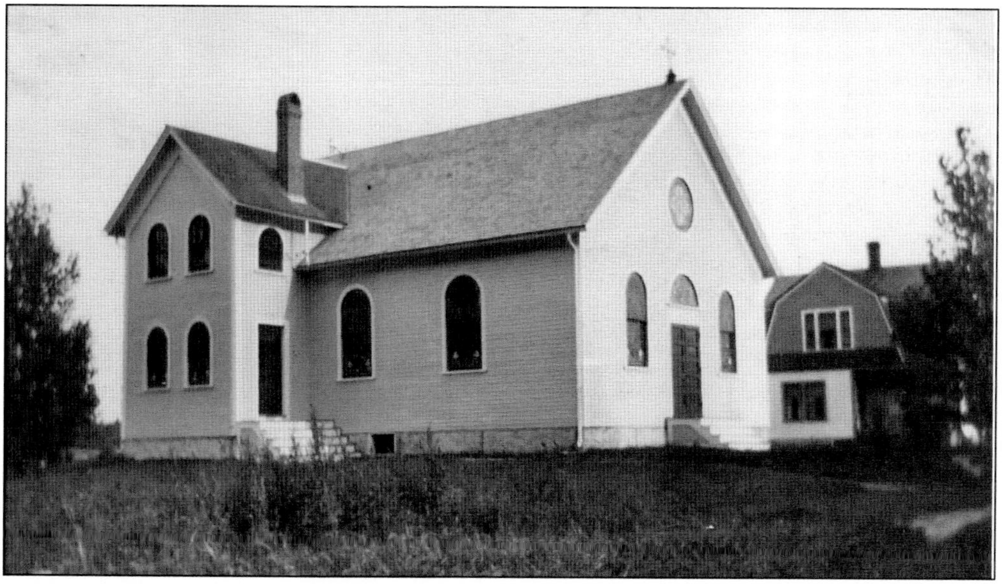

THE SAINT CHARLES CHURCH. The first Catholic church in Conway Village is shown here on Lake Street. This building became an apartment house when the new Saint Charles was built in 1950.

THE DISTRICT #3 SCHOOLHOUSE, SOUTH CONWAY. The 1875 school report listed twenty-six teachers in the Conways, twenty-four females and two males. Two were listed as deficient, five just endurable, seven fair, eight good, and four excellent.

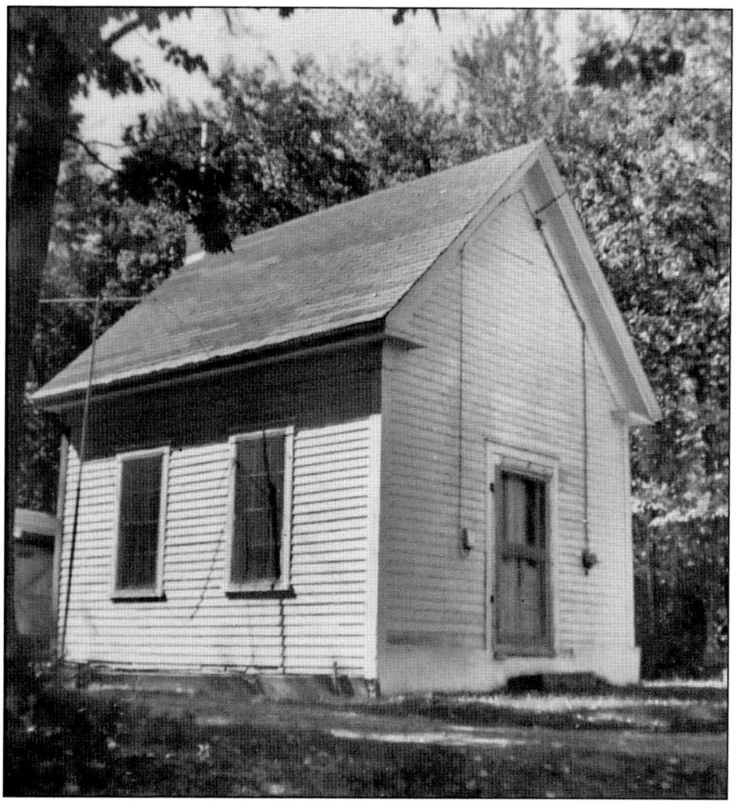

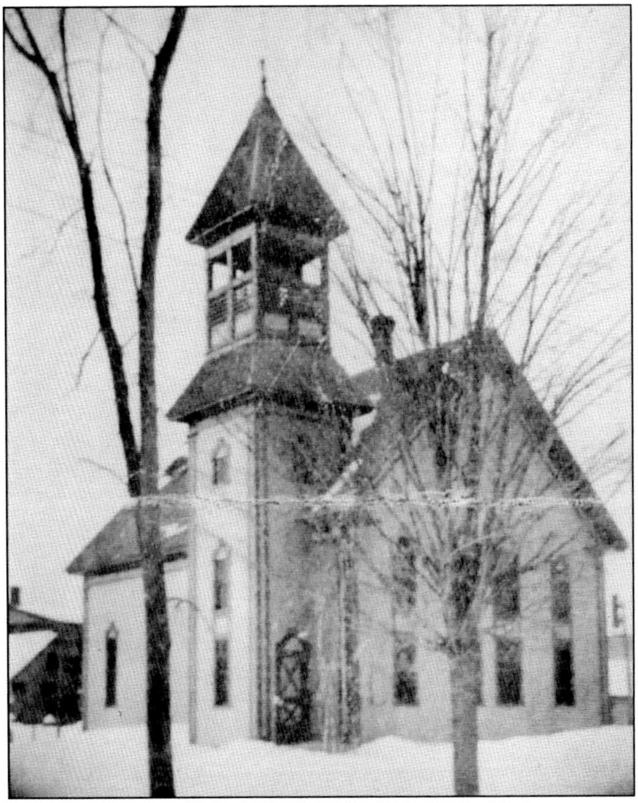

THE NORTH CONWAY METHODIST CHURCH. Under the leadership of David Pratt, a Methodist church was built on Kearsarge Street in 1882. In 1930, the final service was held and the building was turned over to the Carroll County Telephone Company. New England Telephone tore down the church in 1931.

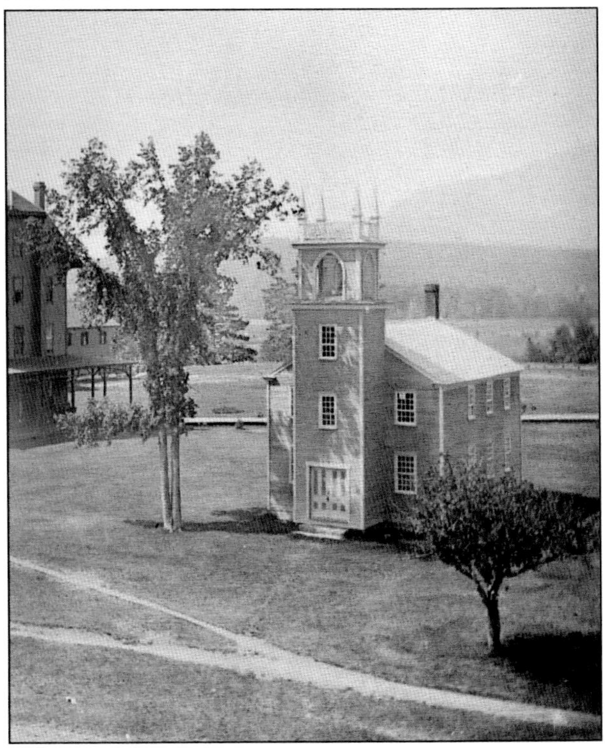

NORTH CONWAY ACADEMY. Organized in 1828, the Conway Academic School continued until 1874 (some sources say 1885) on a site south of the North Conway Railway Station. The building, standing on land coveted by the Kearsarge Hotel, was torn down under the cover of darkness.

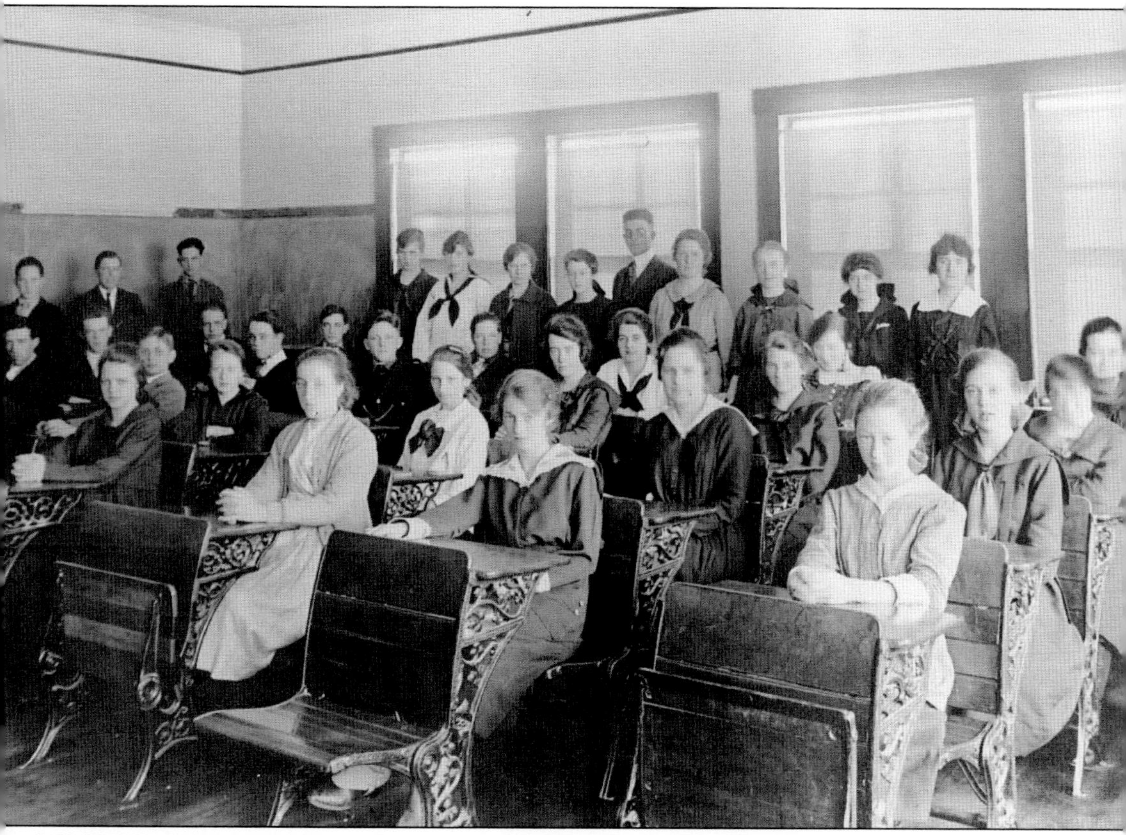

CONWAY HIGH SCHOOL, 1919. Shown standing from left to right are Ray Doe, Randolph Churchill, Harold Whitaker, Helen Lovejoy, Emma Smith, Mildred Hewey, Alice Lowd, Ray Morrill Prine, ? French, Florida King, Margaret Headley, and Miss Clarkins (teacher). Beginning at the far left, from front to back are: (first row) Ralph Berry, Russell Snow, and Horace Giddings; (second row) Rupert Hobson, Winston Prescott, George Levoy, and Herbert Whitaker; (third row) Carrie Campbell, Melba Abbott, Phil Davis, and Walter Allard; (fourth row) Elizabeth Hounsell, Sadie Tasker, Vivian Witham, and Lurene Carlton; (fifth row) Ann Carson, Alberta Taylor, Lillian Demeritt, and Blanche Purdy; (sixth row) ? Ward, Helen Snow, Laura Batchelor, and Halcyne Cloutman.

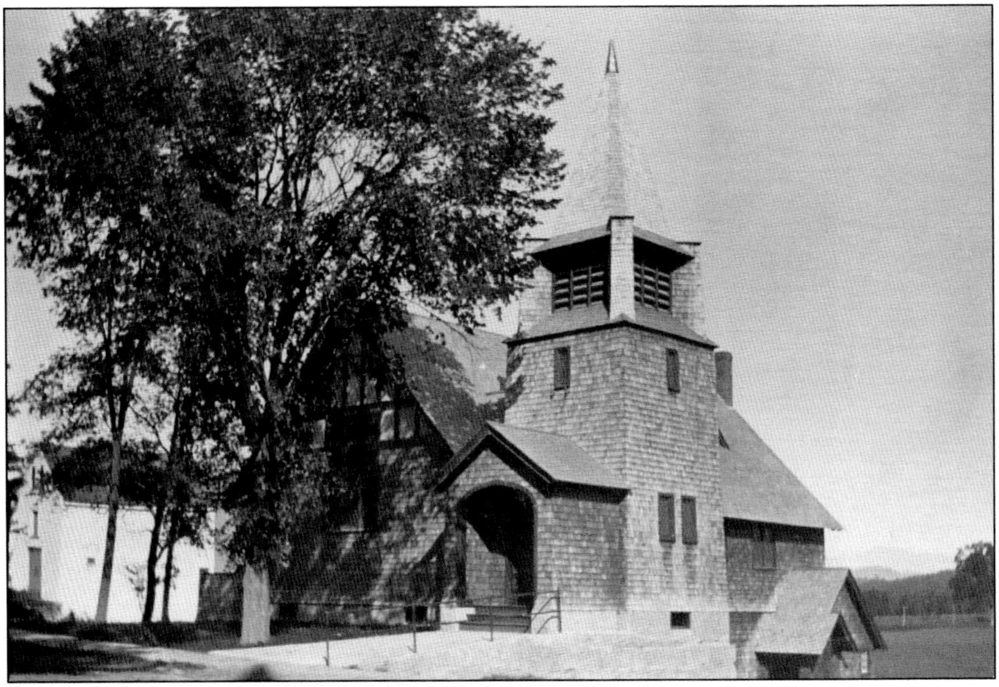

CONWAY VILLAGE CONGREGATIONAL CHURCH. The Congregational Church met in the Methodist building on Sunday evenings until 1906, when a Congregational Church was built across the street. A large addition was dedicated in 1956.

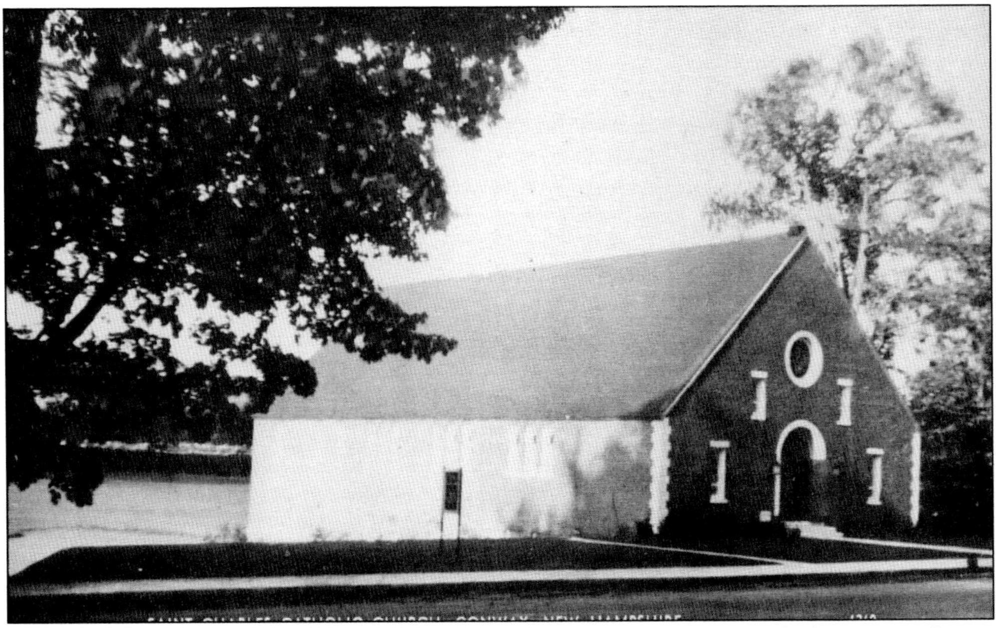

SAINT CHARLES CATHOLIC CHURCH, CONWAY VILLAGE. Catholic services began in the Conway Grammar School in 1907. Soon, immigrants flocking to the Conway Lumber Company increased the Catholic population and made possible the building of a church on Lake Street. In 1951, this larger church was dedicated on Main Street on the former site of the Kennett barn.

Eight

A Lamp in the Window: Houses

Besides a house and barn, farmers constructed a wide range of buildings including carriage sheds, chicken houses, ice houses, spring houses, sap houses, and back houses. In New England, the farmhouse often evolved into a set of extended buildings with characteristic features. If a farmer was out past dark, his wife would leave a lamp burning in the window to guide his way home. Many farmhouses were enlarged to accommodate boarders as a source of added income. Some of these boarding houses took on lives of their own and became hotels. In town, houses were sometimes grand, with merchants wishing to show off the fruits of their prosperity.

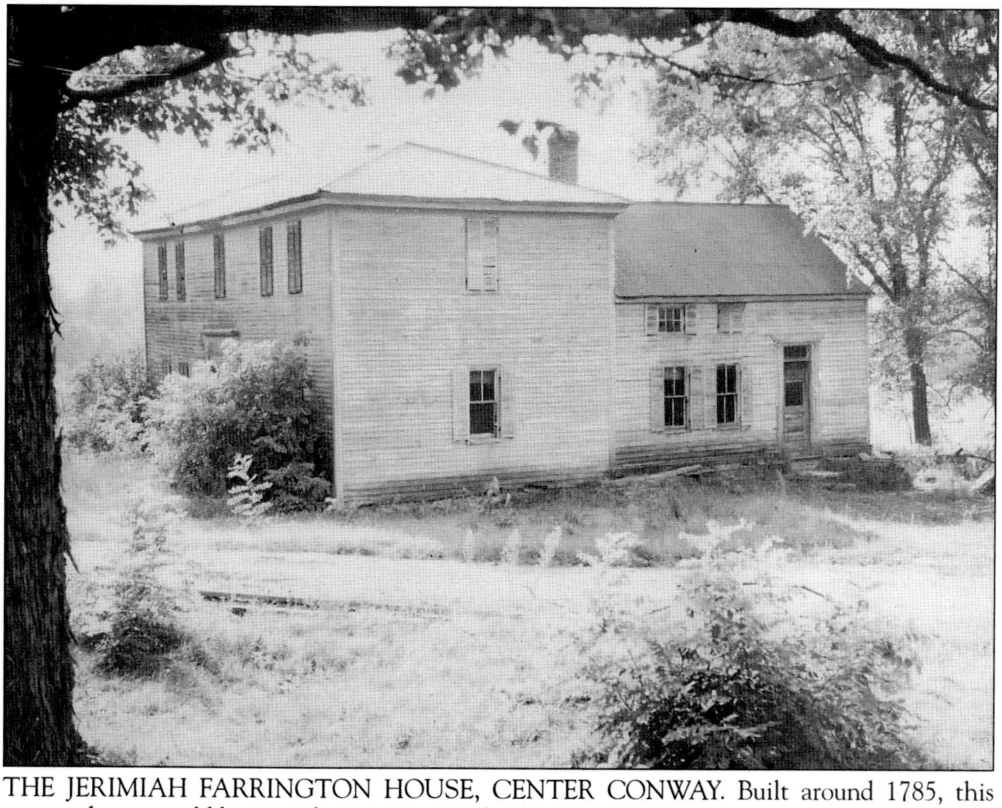

THE JERIMIAH FARRINGTON HOUSE, CENTER CONWAY. Built around 1785, this ancient house could be seen, for many years, slowly decaying by the side of the highway.

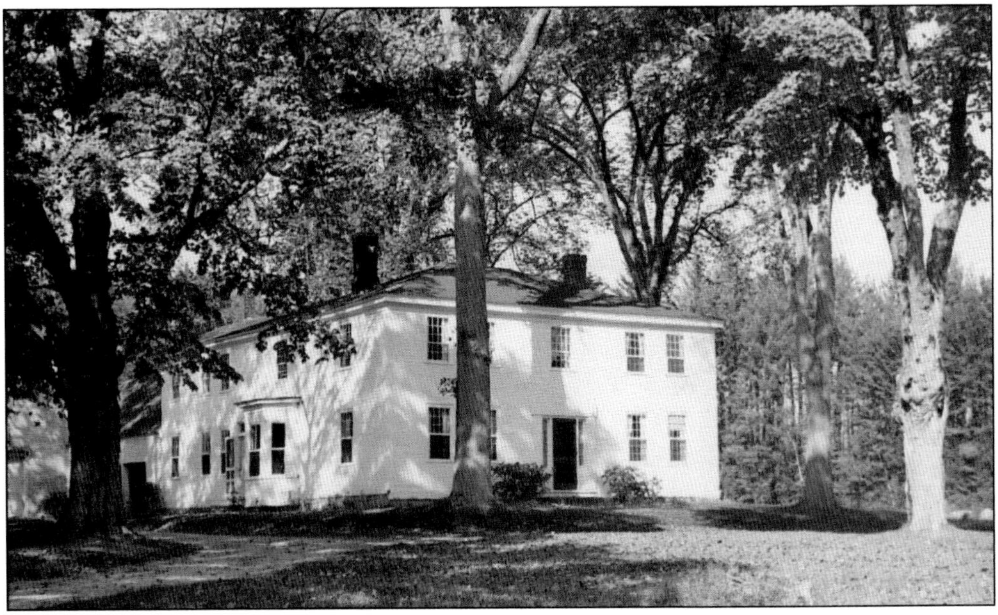

THE MERRILL HOUSE, WEST SIDE ROAD. Amos Merrill, son of Thomas Merrill, Esquire, of Concord, erected this classic home in about 1800. The bay window and ell were added during the Civil War. Merrill descendants still own the house.

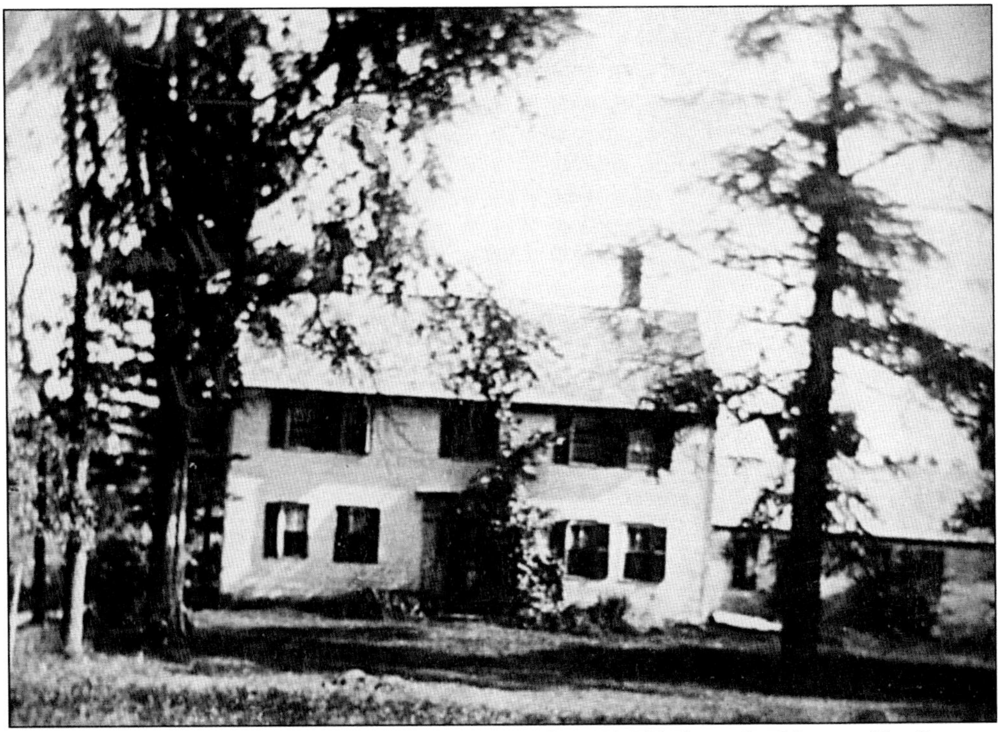

THE RICHARD EASTMAN HOUSE, NORTH CONWAY. Early settler Thomas Chadbourne built this house in about 1768 on the comer of Artist Falls Road and Main Street. The house and mill rights were soon sold to Richard Eastman. This building is considered the oldest existing house in North Conway.

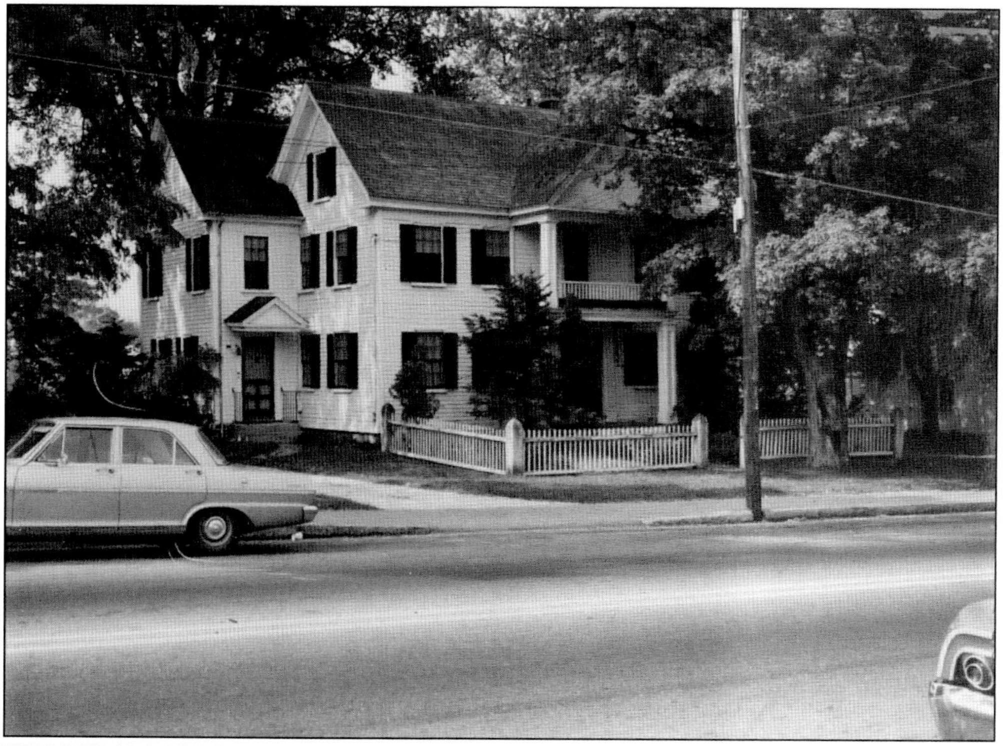

THE HIRAM ABBOTT HOUSE, 1964. Later known as the Dr. Reynolds house, this beautiful structure stood on Main Street in Conway Village. It was razed to make room for a filling station.

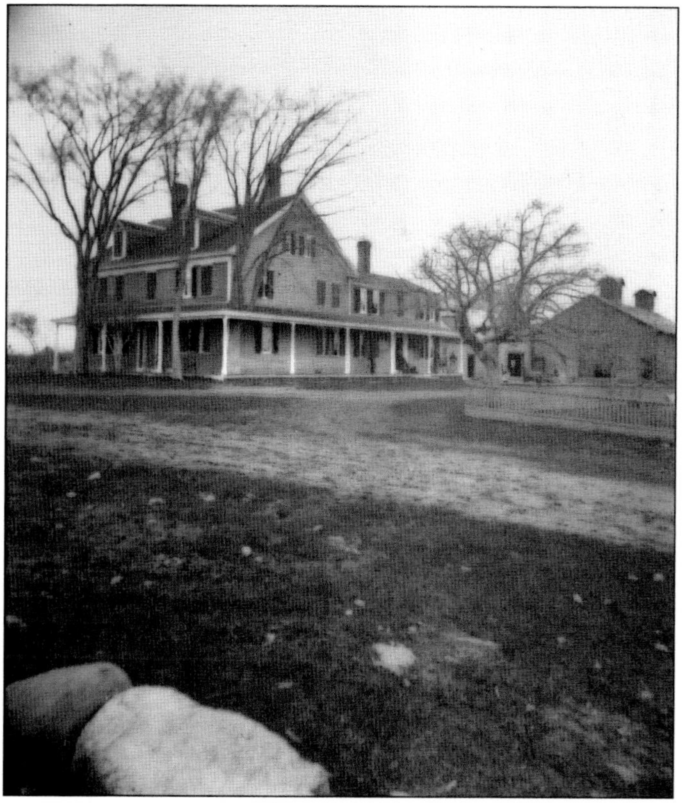

THE RED BARN, NORTH CONWAY. Once part of the Moat Mountain House, this building saw many uses before becoming the core of the Red Barn Outlet Center. This early photograph was intended to be used as a stereograph.

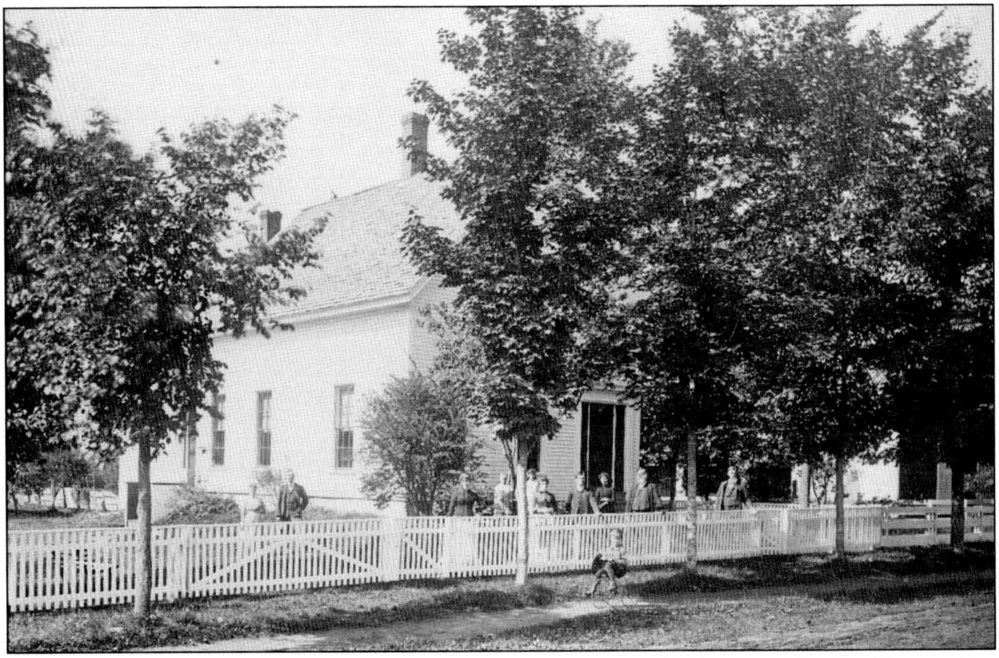

THE WILDER HOUSE, MAIN STREET, CONWAY VILLAGE. Occupied first by Christopher Wilder and later by Peg Mill manager B.F. Clark, this building became run down and was eventually demolished.

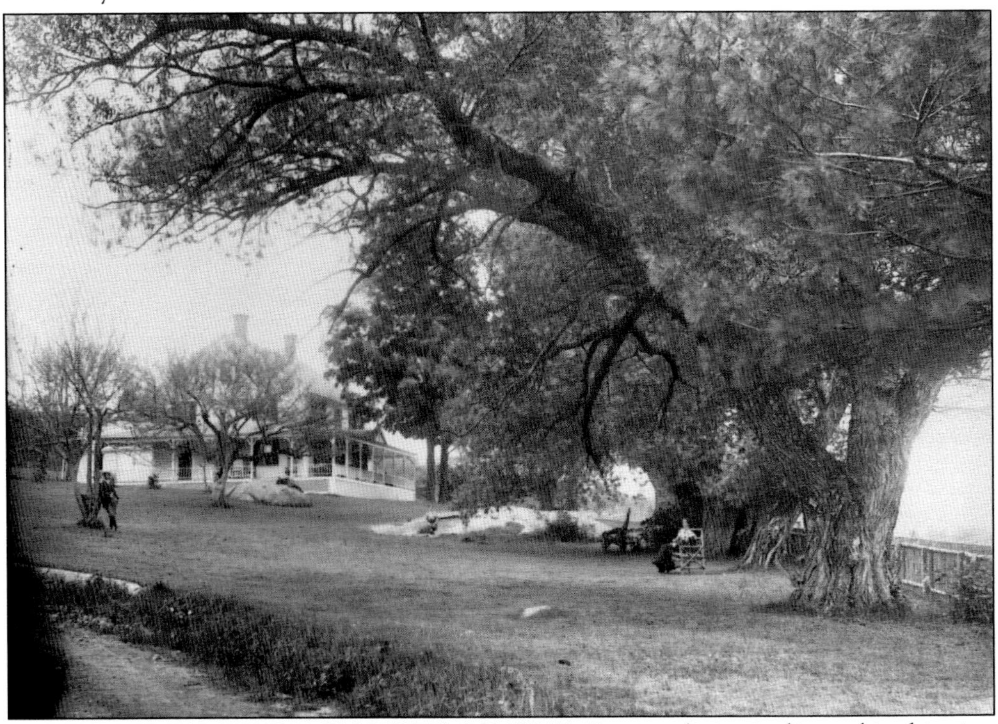

THE FURBER FAMILY HOME, NORTH CONWAY. Gracious living is glimpsed in this view of the Arthur Furber home near Sunset Hill. The sweeping verandah offered elegant living and panoramic views.

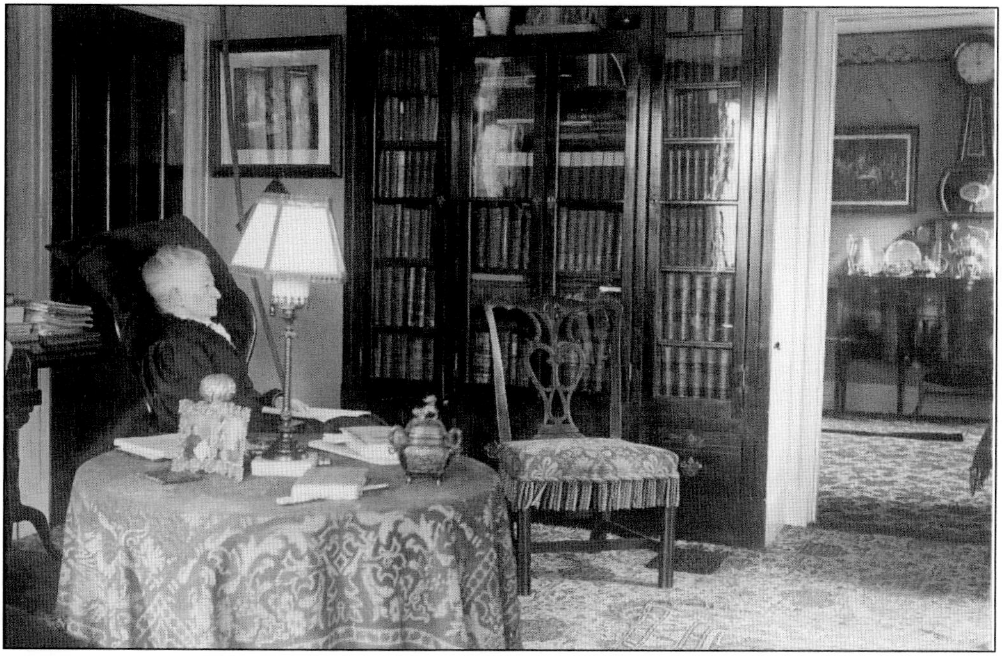

THE THOM RESIDENCE, CONWAY VILLAGE. Built in 1826, the Thom house became the core of the Presidential Inn in 1917. This interior view shows the elegance of the furnishings. Note that the country Chippendale chair has been updated with Victorian tassels. The lady, shown seated, was probably Martha Susan (Shackford) Thom.

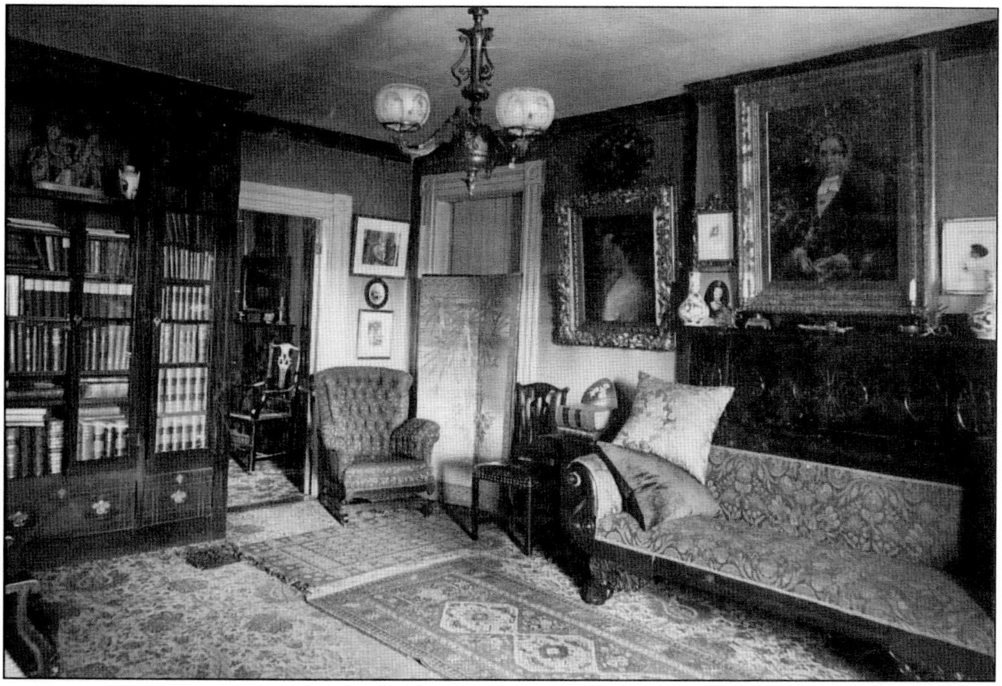

THE THOM RESIDENCE. Victorian appointments in this stylish room include a platform rocker, antique Empire sofa, and family portraits. The platform rocker was invented to save carpets from the ravages of standard rockers.

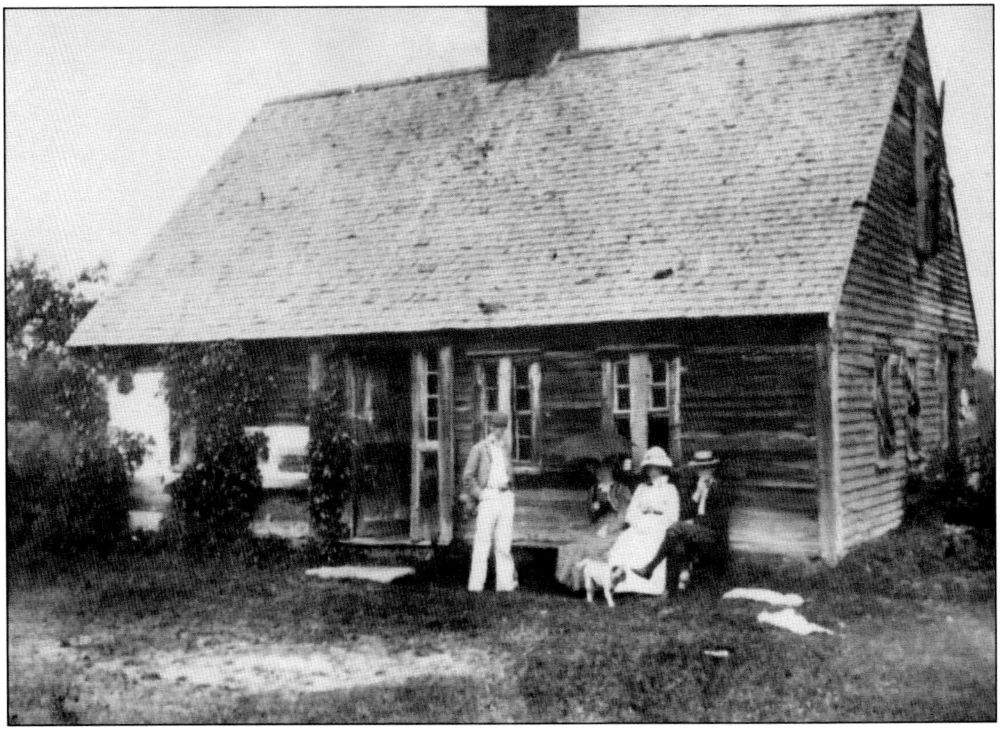

THE WILLIAM PALMER HOUSE. Built in the early nineteenth century by William Palmer, this South Conway home is a classic example of a center chimney cape.

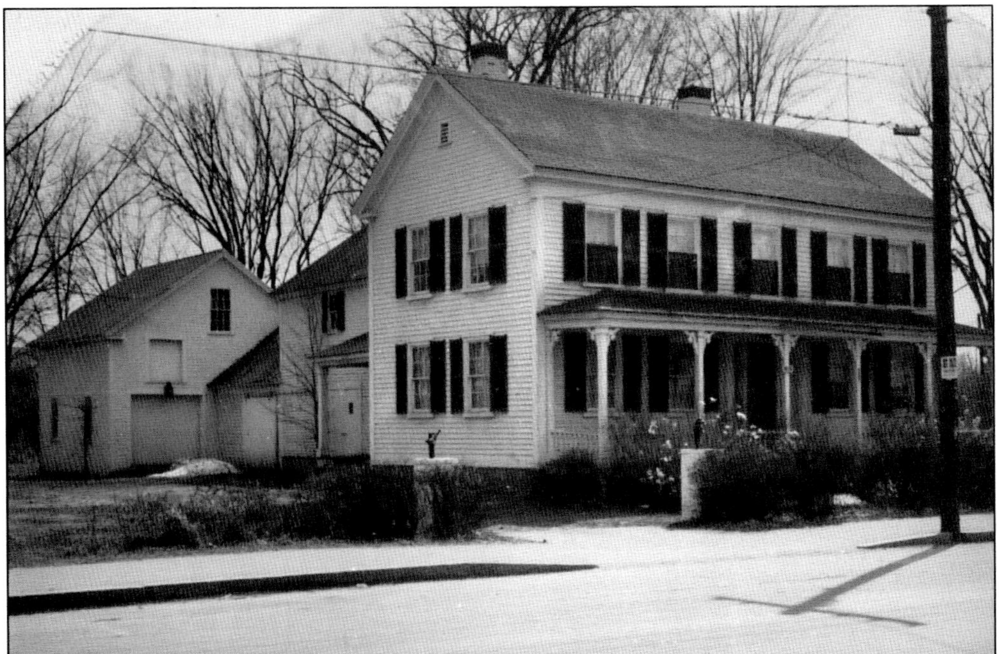

THE "DR. WIGGIN HOUSE." Residents of Conway Village still lament the loss of this Main Street home. Built c. 1818, the building was razed to make room for the new Conway Post Office.

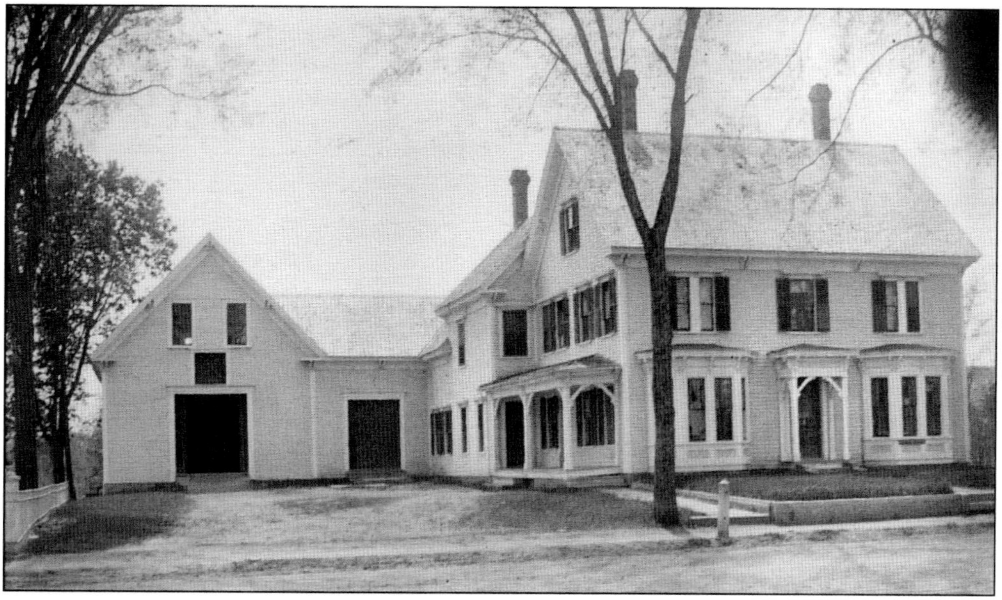

THE METCALF HOUSE, WEST MAIN STREET, CONWAY VILLAGE. Henry Metcalf moved his spool manufacturing business to Conway in 1878. Ten years later, he sold the company and this house to A.C. Kennett. It became the home of Robert Kennett and later the offices of Carroll County Mental Health.

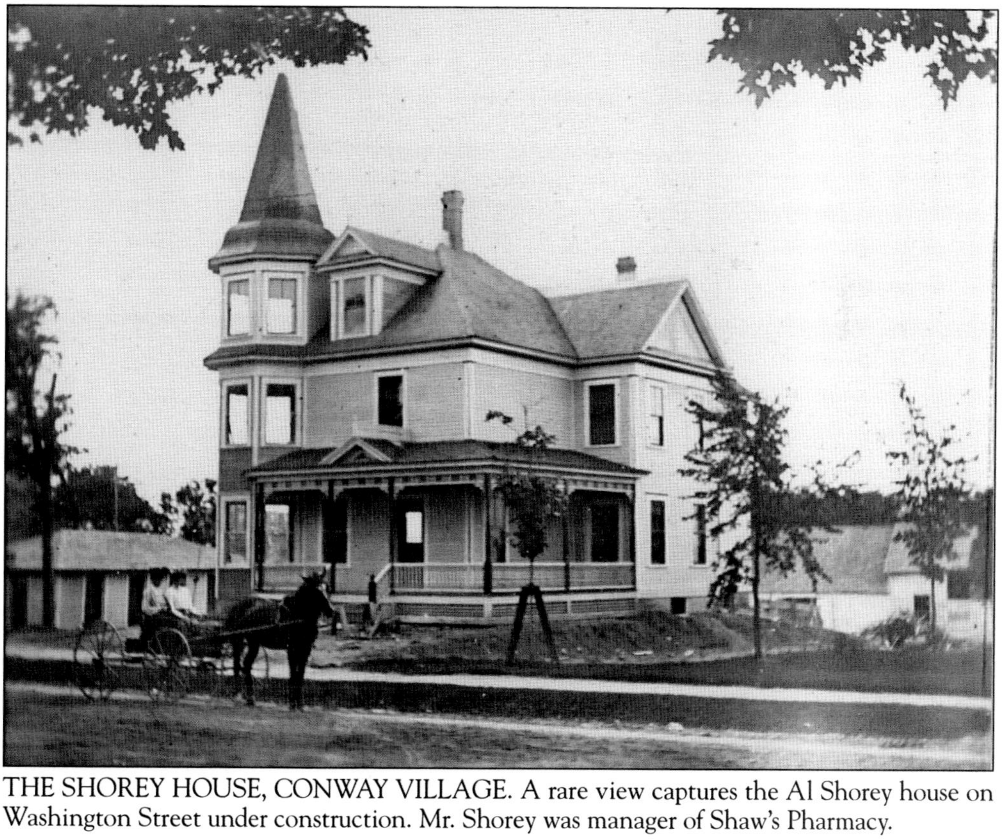

THE SHOREY HOUSE, CONWAY VILLAGE. A rare view captures the Al Shorey house on Washington Street under construction. Mr. Shorey was manager of Shaw's Pharmacy.

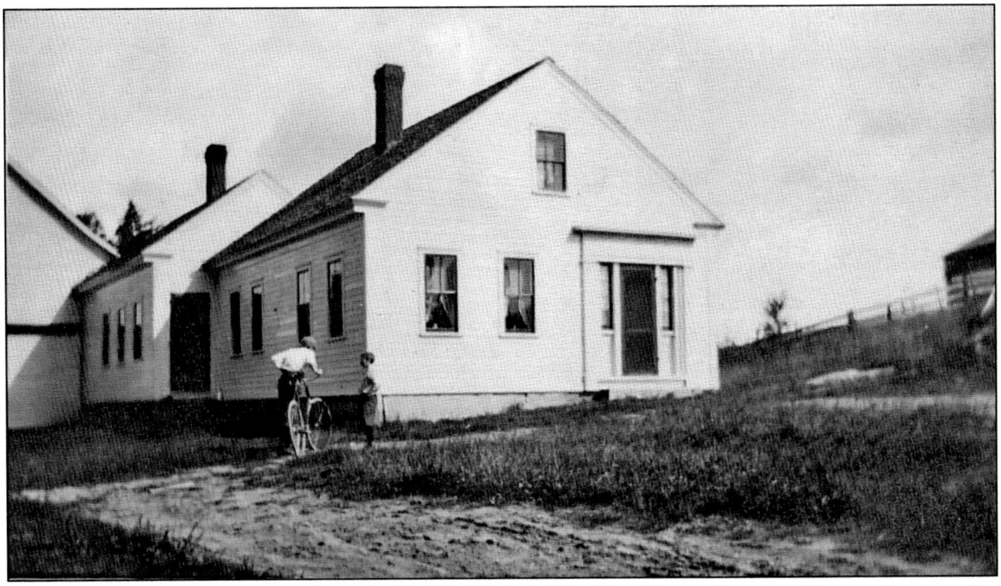

THE OZEN DAVIS HOUSE, CONWAY VILLAGE. The Davis house still stands near the Saco River Covered Bridge. Note the granite foundation and wood-shingled roof.

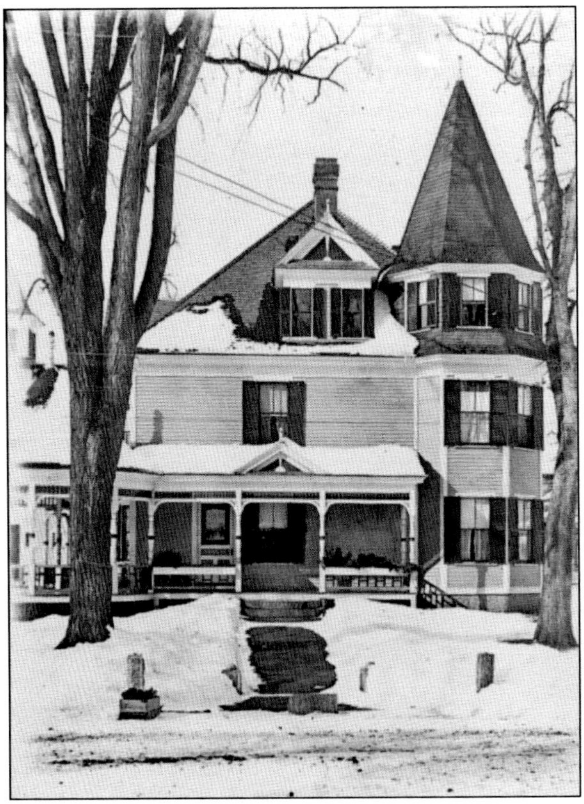

THE A.C. KENNETT HOUSE, WEST MAIN STREET, FEBRUARY 2, 1920. Prominent Conway Village businessman Alpheus Crosby Kennett owned this gracious Victorian home near the B&M Station. It was torn down in 1961.

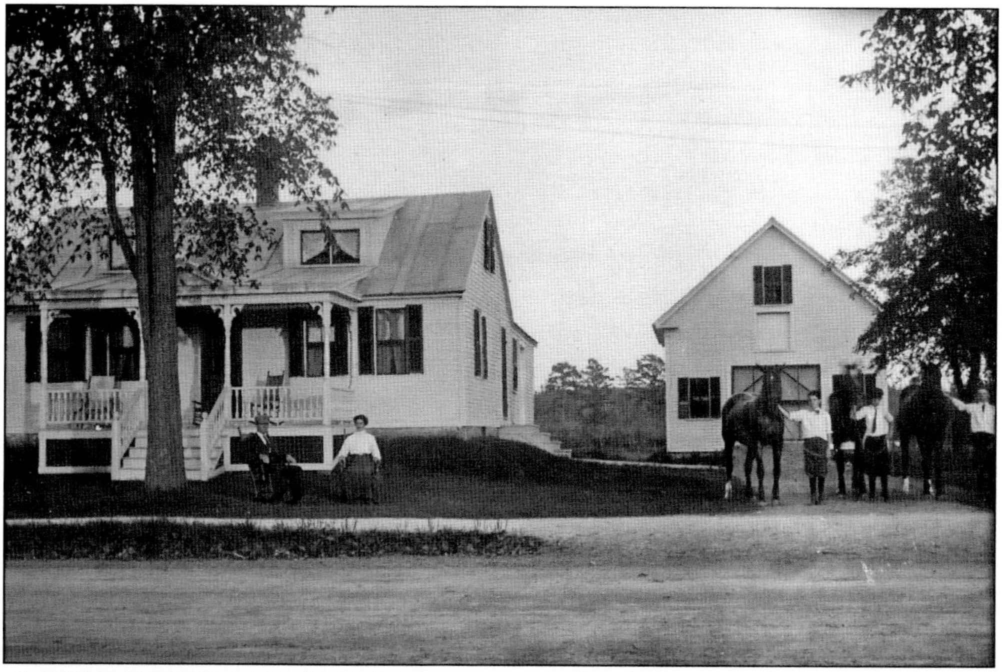

THE ELVAH THURSTON HOUSE. This Conway Village home can still be recognized on the south side of West Main Street.

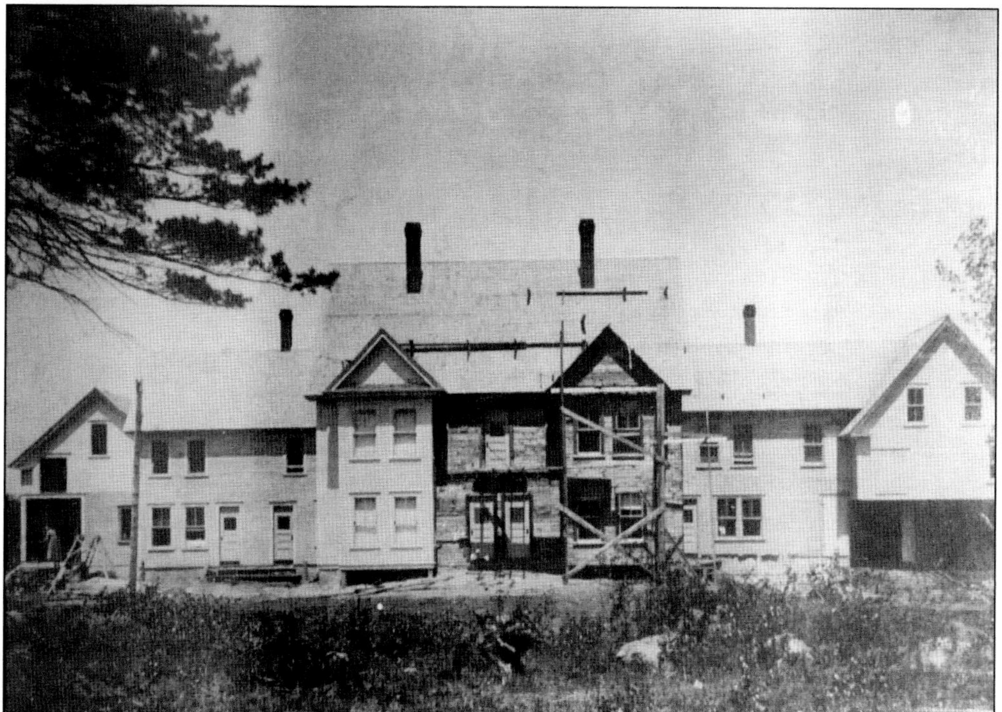

THE SHACKFORD AND CHASE PLACE, EAST MAIN STREET, CONWAY VILLAGE. Now the home of WBNC and WMWV Radio, the Orren Chase house is shown during the throes of renovation.

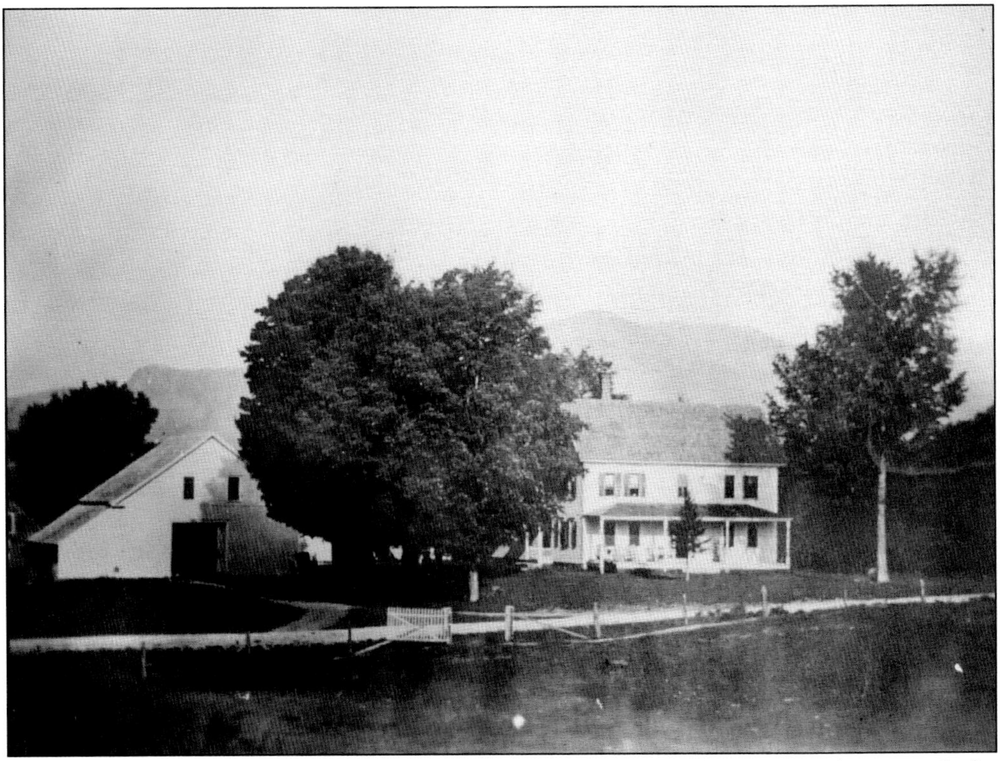

THE MERRILL FARM, CONWAY VILLAGE. Once a thrifty and prosperous homestead, the Merrill Farm is now run as an inn.

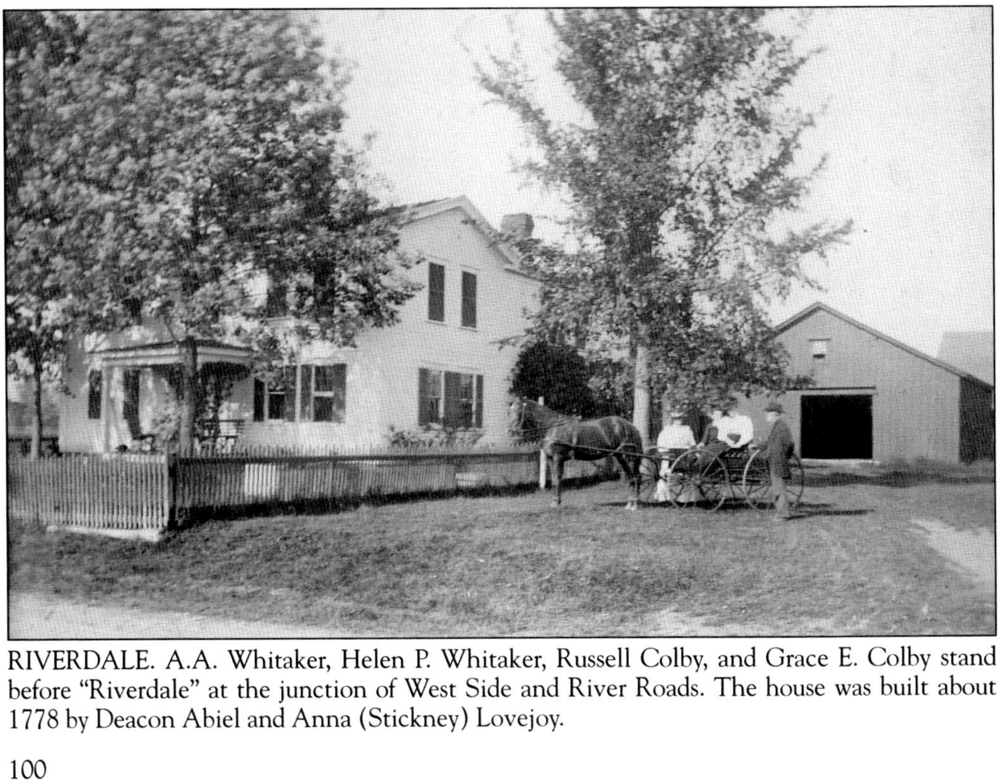

RIVERDALE. A.A. Whitaker, Helen P. Whitaker, Russell Colby, and Grace E. Colby stand before "Riverdale" at the junction of West Side and River Roads. The house was built about 1778 by Deacon Abiel and Anna (Stickney) Lovejoy.

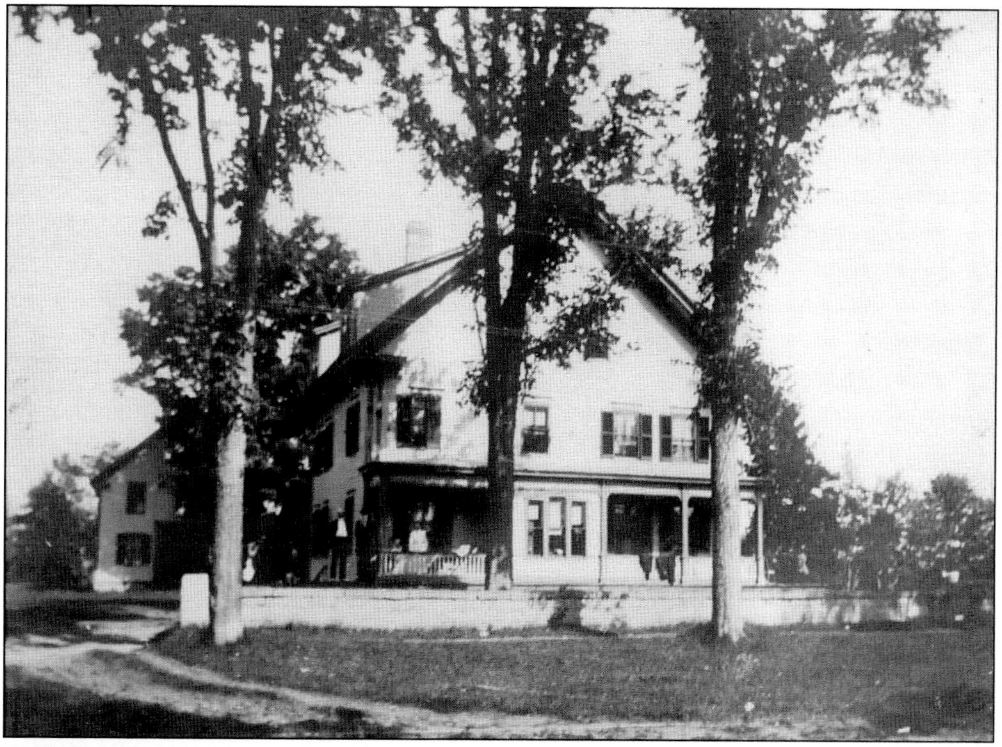

THE FRANK DAVIS HOME, CONWAY VILLAGE. Conway Station agent, livery man, and drygoods dealer, Frank Davis lived in this stately Washington Street residence.

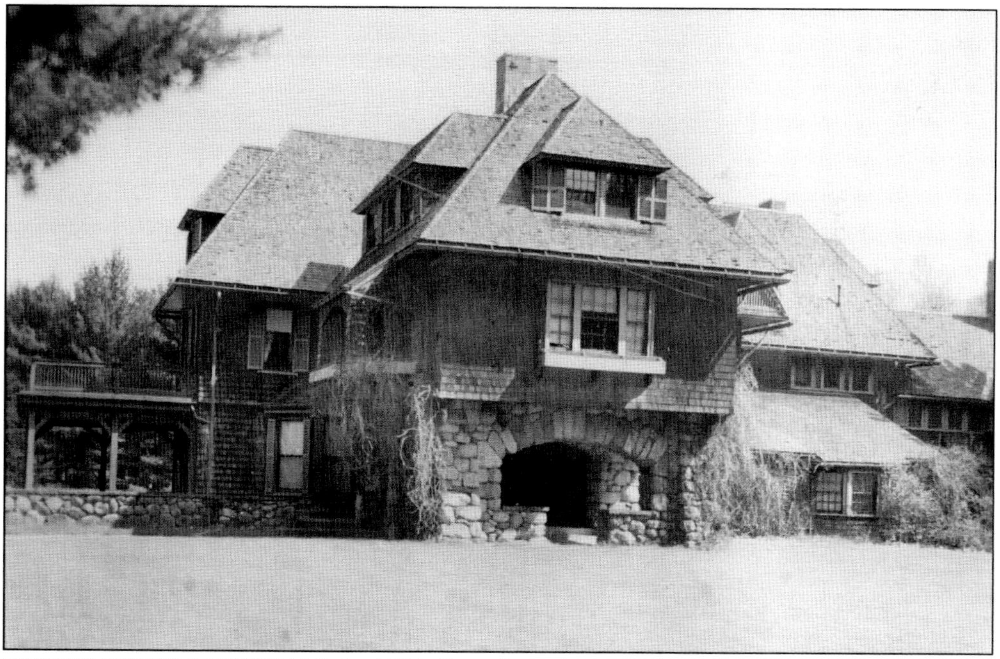

STONEHURST, INTERVALE. In 1874, Stonehurst became the summer retreat of the Erastus Bigelows, owners of Bigelow Carpet. Their daughter, Mrs. Daniel Merriman, turned the estate into the center of North Conway Society. In 1946, Stonehurst became a hotel and resort.

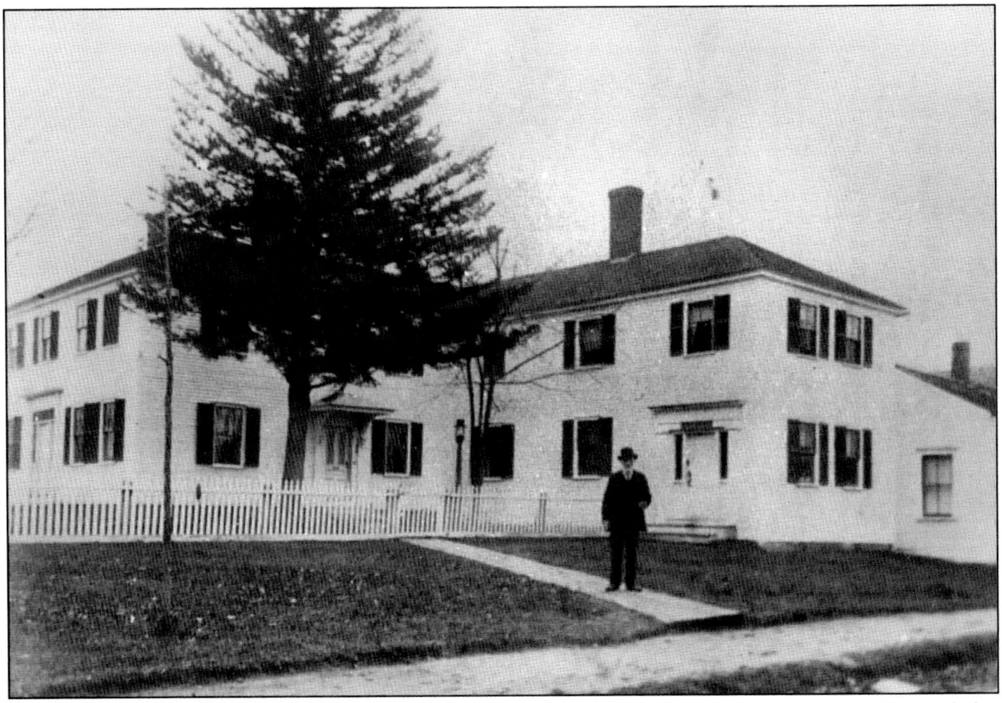

THE WILDER HOUSE, FOUR CORNERS, CONWAY VILLAGE. Once the office of the Conway Savings Bank, the rear portion of this house was divided and moved to become the basis for a Wilder Street home and a Greenwood Avenue home. In later years the remaining section became the home and office of Dr. Charles Smith.

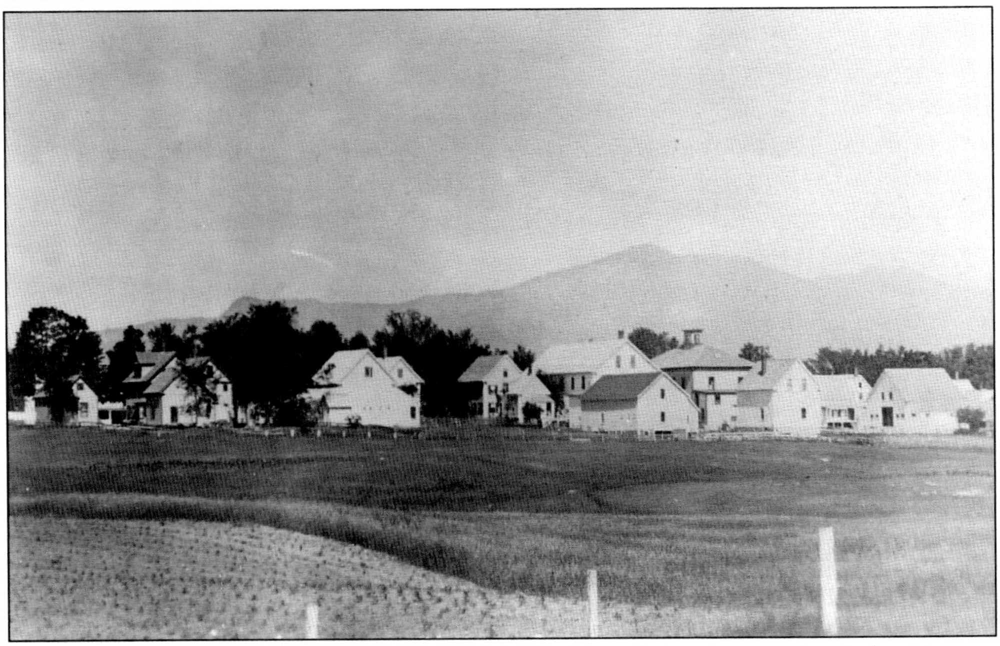

WASHINGTON STREET, CONWAY VILLAGE. The distinctive cupola of the Conway Opera House can be seen in this photograph of Washington Street. Shown beside the Opera House is the rear of the Davis Block. Moat Mountain is in the background.

Nine

The Natives Ain't Restless: People

The New Hampshire tradition of fierce independence and self-reliance has always been alive and well in the Conways, complimented by the influx of immigrant workers, artists, and entrepreneurs. In the final account, it is the people that define a community.

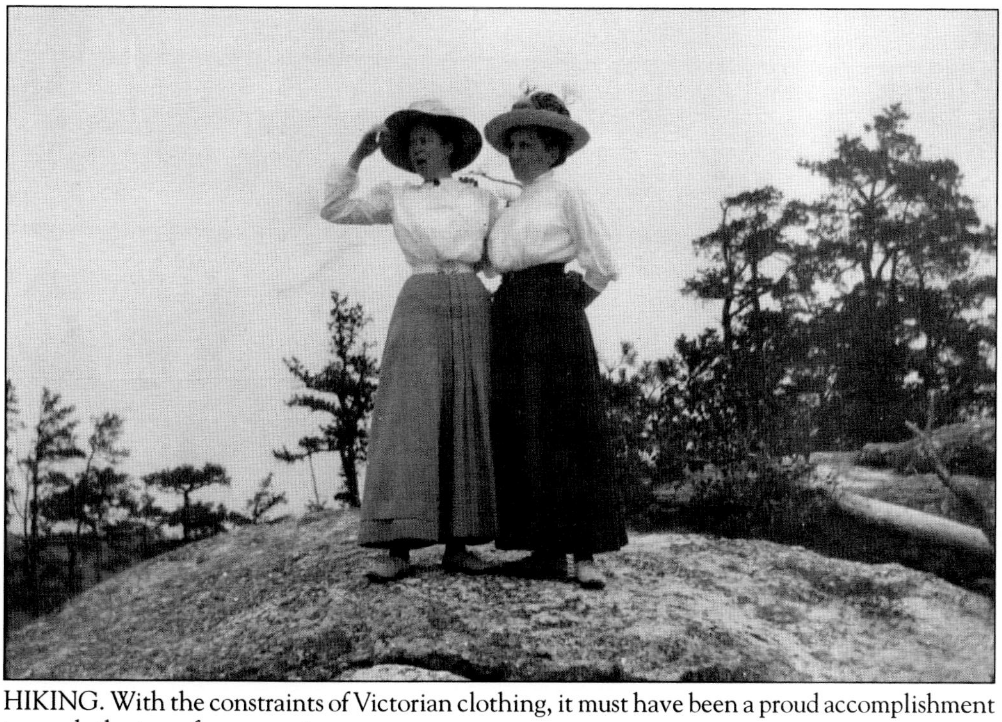

HIKING. With the constraints of Victorian clothing, it must have been a proud accomplishment to reach the top of a mountain.

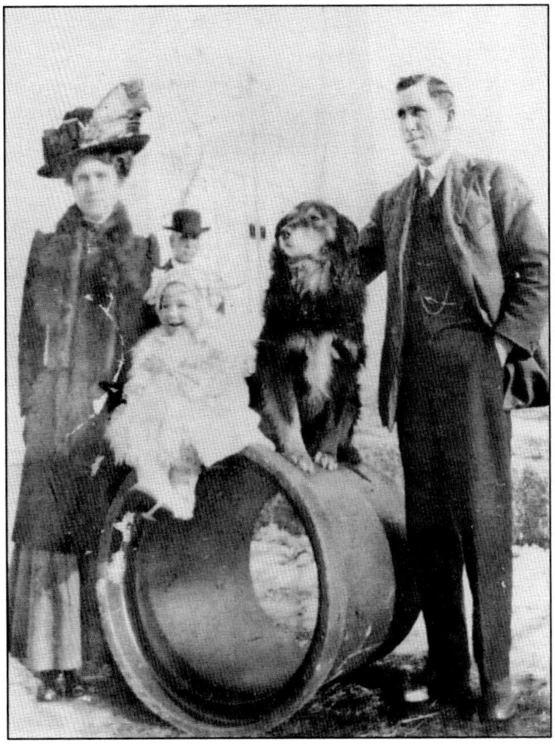

THE POTTERS, 1910. Ethel, Harry, and Robert Jefferson Potter pose with their dog, Prince.

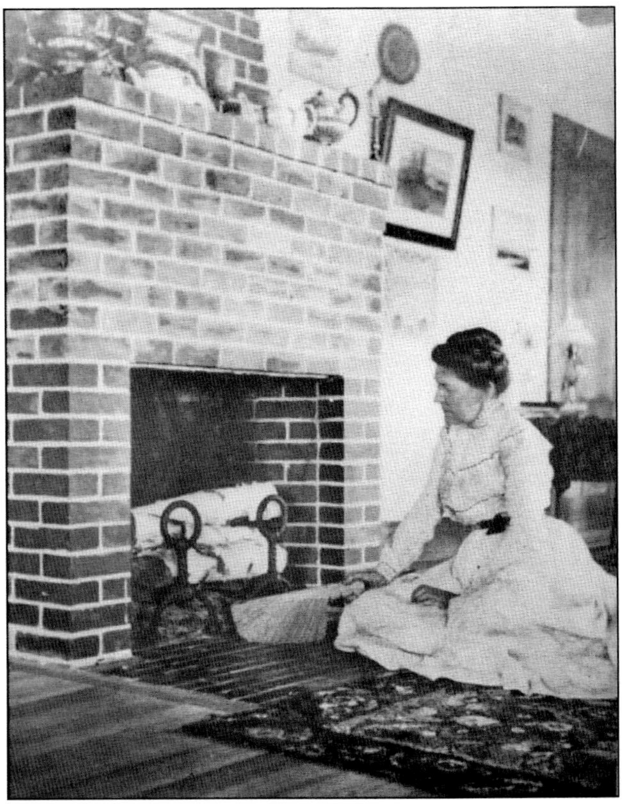

LUCY ATHERTON. Lucy Atherton sits before the fireplace in her South Conway farm.

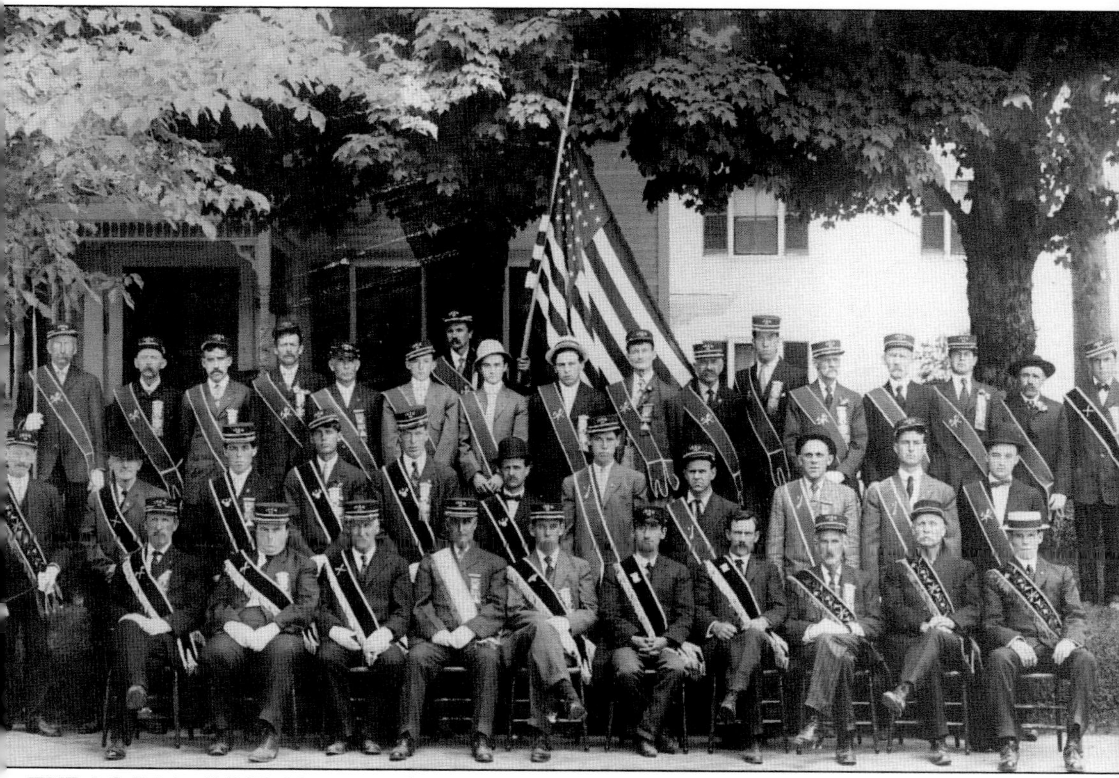

THE I.O.R.M., JUNE 26, 1910. The International Order of Red Men is shown posing in full regalia.

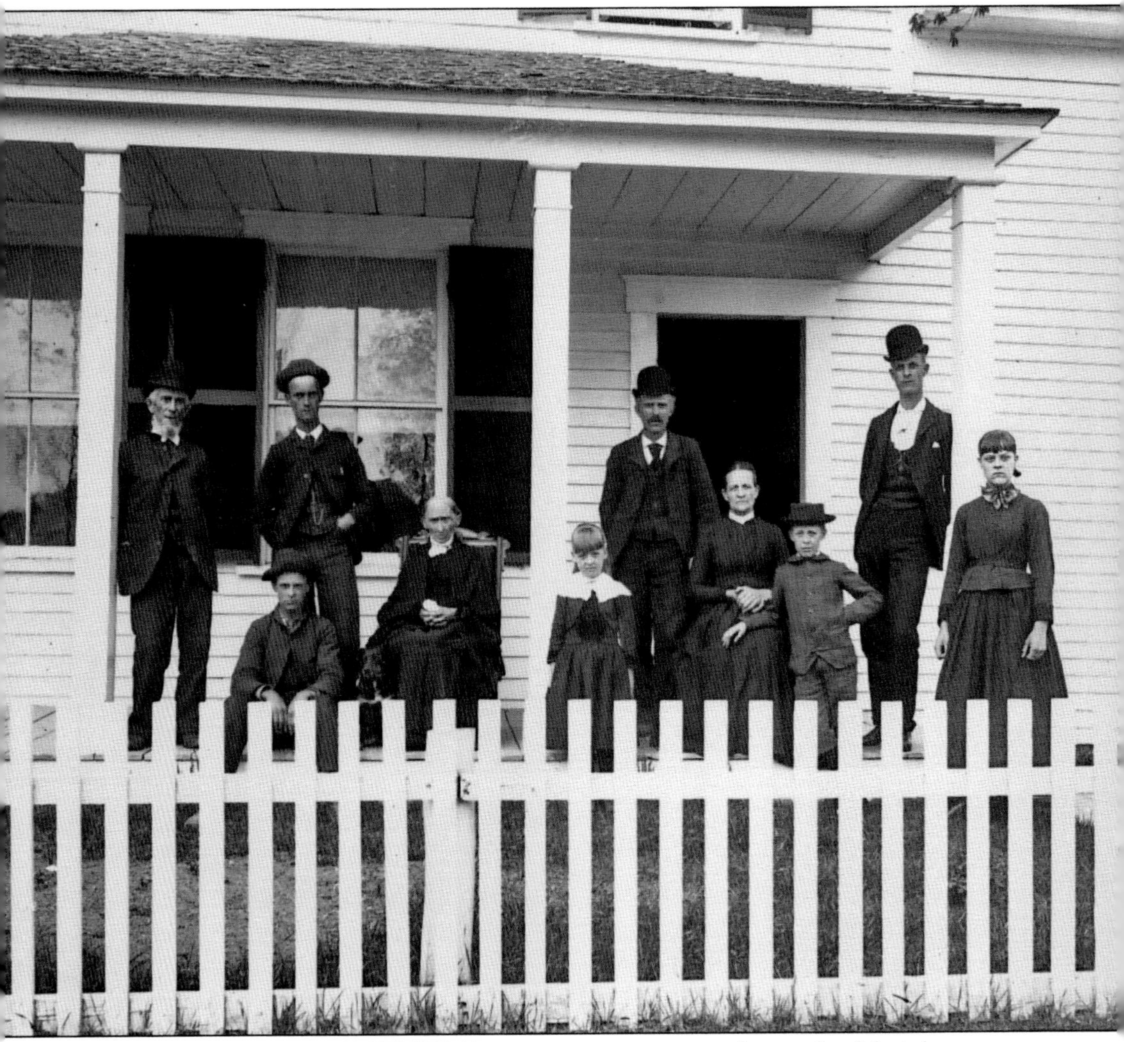

A FAMILY PICTURE. Four generations pose on the porch of their home.

THE WILLIAM PALMER HOME, SOUTH CONWAY. It's difficult to image a prouder looking couple than the one pictured above. South Conway or "Goshen" families were noted both for their ingenuity and their rugged independence.

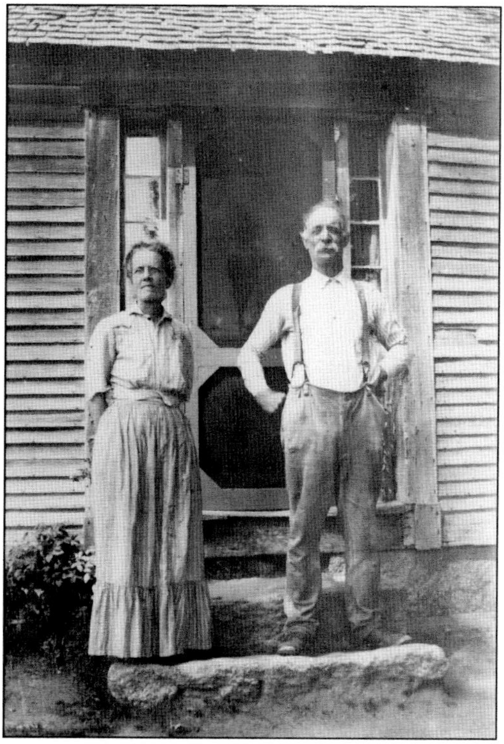

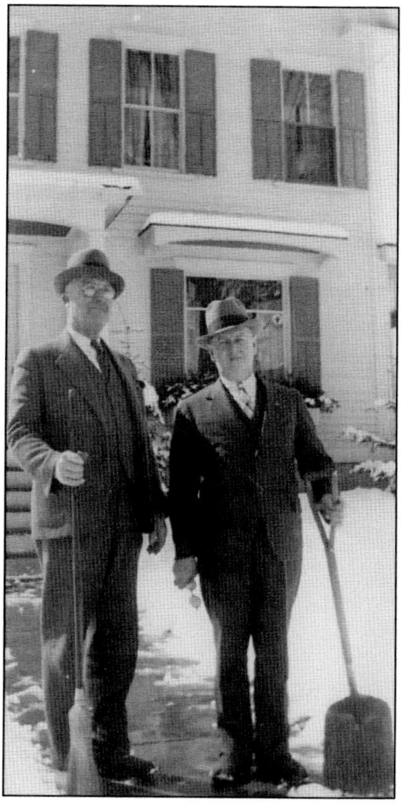

WALTER THURSTON AND GEORGE STONE. Two Conway Village businessmen are shown clearing the walk in front of Mr. Stone's Main Street home.

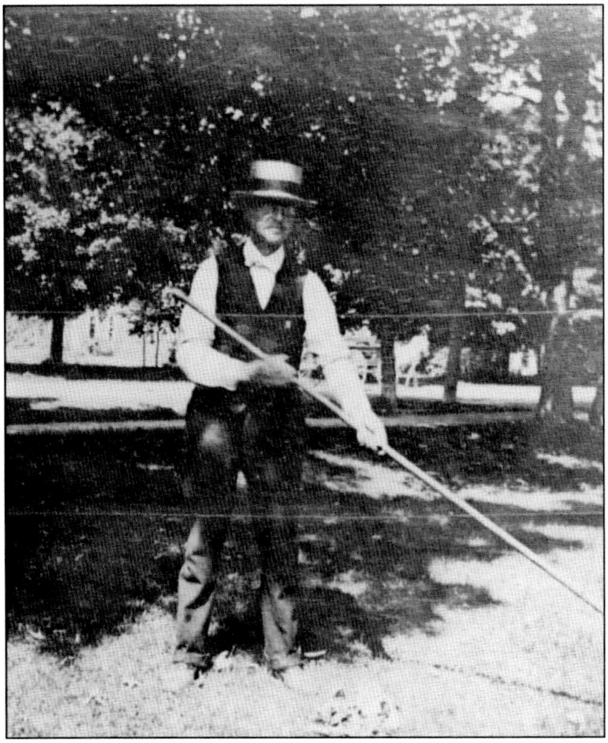

LEVI RICKER, c. 1930. Levi Jules Ricker was the proprietor of Kearsarge Hall, North Conway.

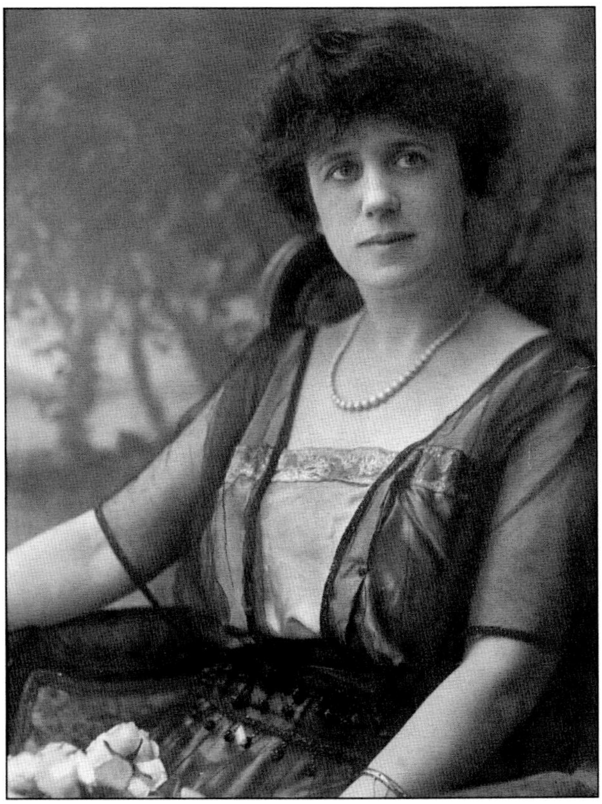

PEARL LORD (1888–1953). The daughter of Eben and Mary (Daniels) Lord, Flora Pearl became a private duty nurse, working out of Boston, New Haven, and New York.

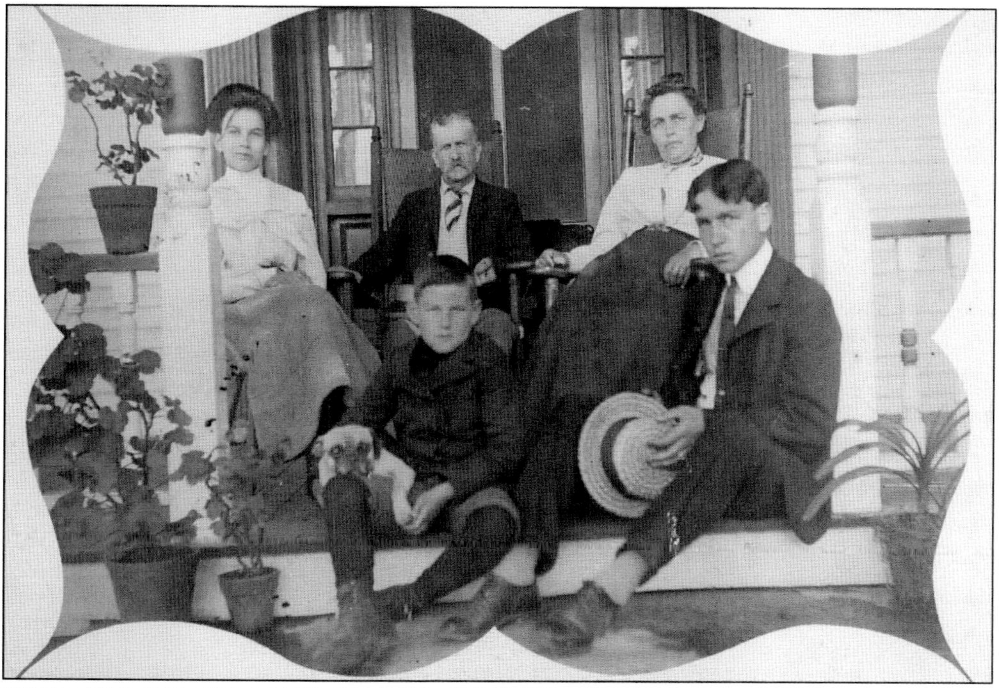

THE LORD FAMILY, MAIN STREET, CONWAY VILLAGE. From left to right are Flora Pearl, Eben, and Mary (Daniels) Lord. Leon and Robert Raymond (Bowser) Lord are seated on the step. The Lords owned the Eastman-Lord House from 1900 until 1962.

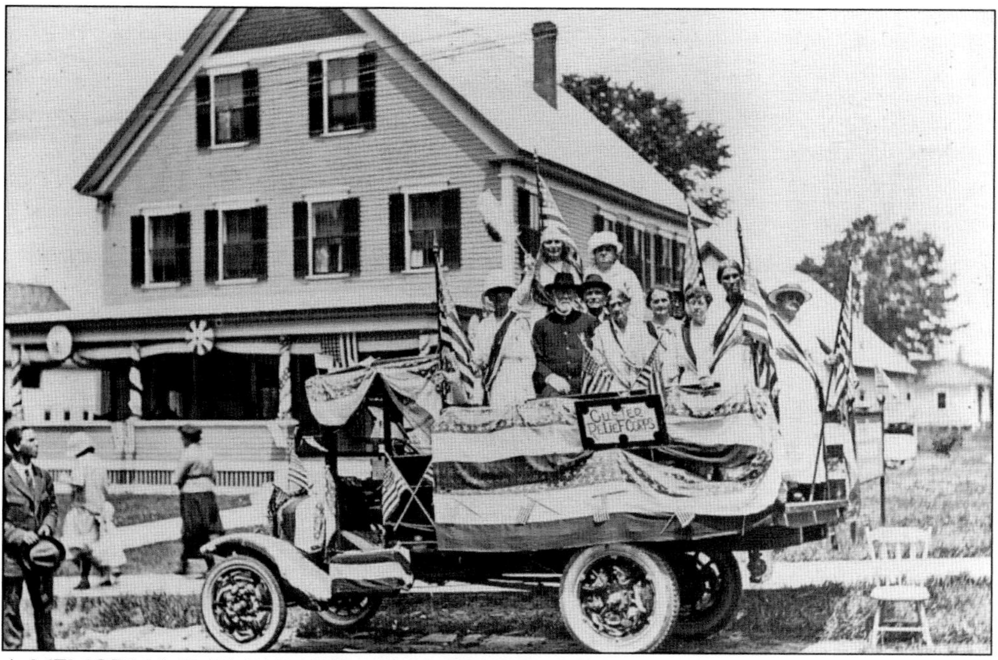

A MEMORIAL DAY PARADE, MAIN STREET, CONWAY VILLAGE. The Custer Relief Corps, auxiliary of the Custer Post GAR, boards its float before the Prescott house (previously the Conway House stables, later called the Conway Cafe Annex). Note the two Civil War veterans seated in the center.

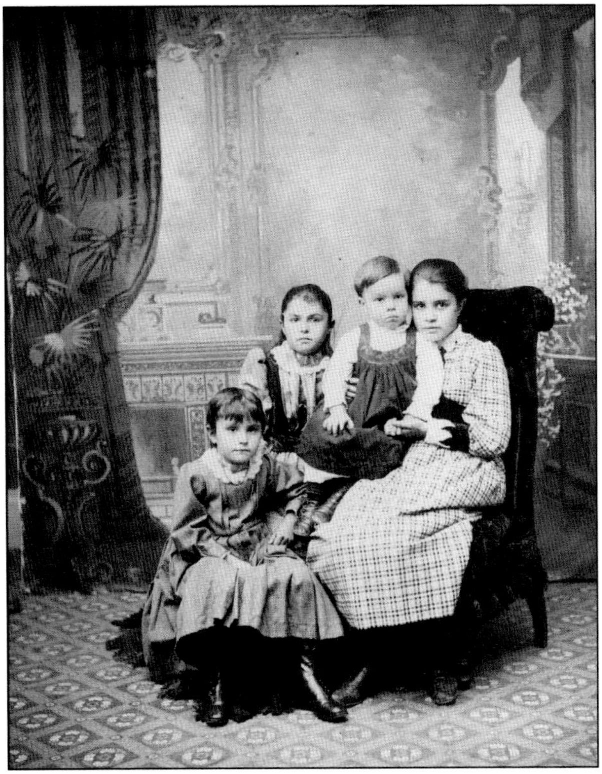

THE RICKER CHILDREN. Edna, Anna C. (Nan), Mary, and Russell Ricker pose before an elaborate background curtain in a photography studio.

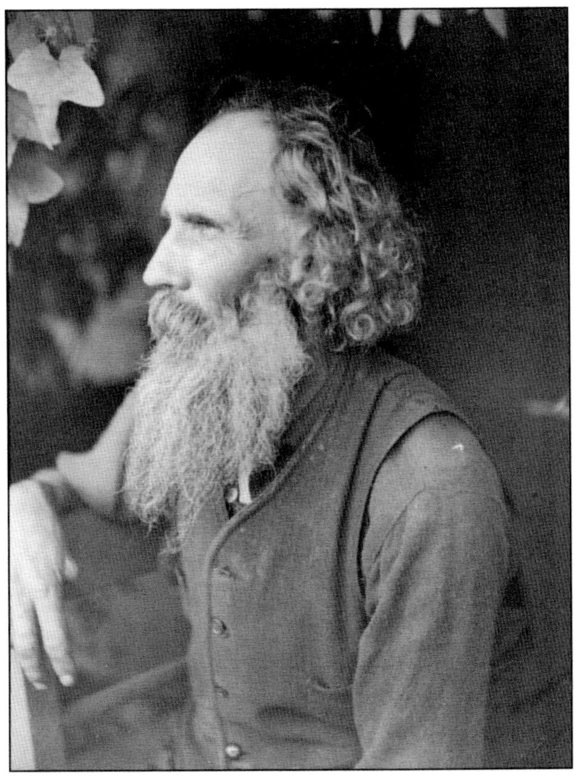

AMOS THOMPSON (1839–1936). A brilliant and eccentric inventor, Amos Thompson was credited with inventing both the electric light and the victrola before Edison. One of his inventions was a steam-powered automobile built during the 1860s. Mr. Thompson never seemed interested in patenting any of his inventions and so gained little profit from his genius.

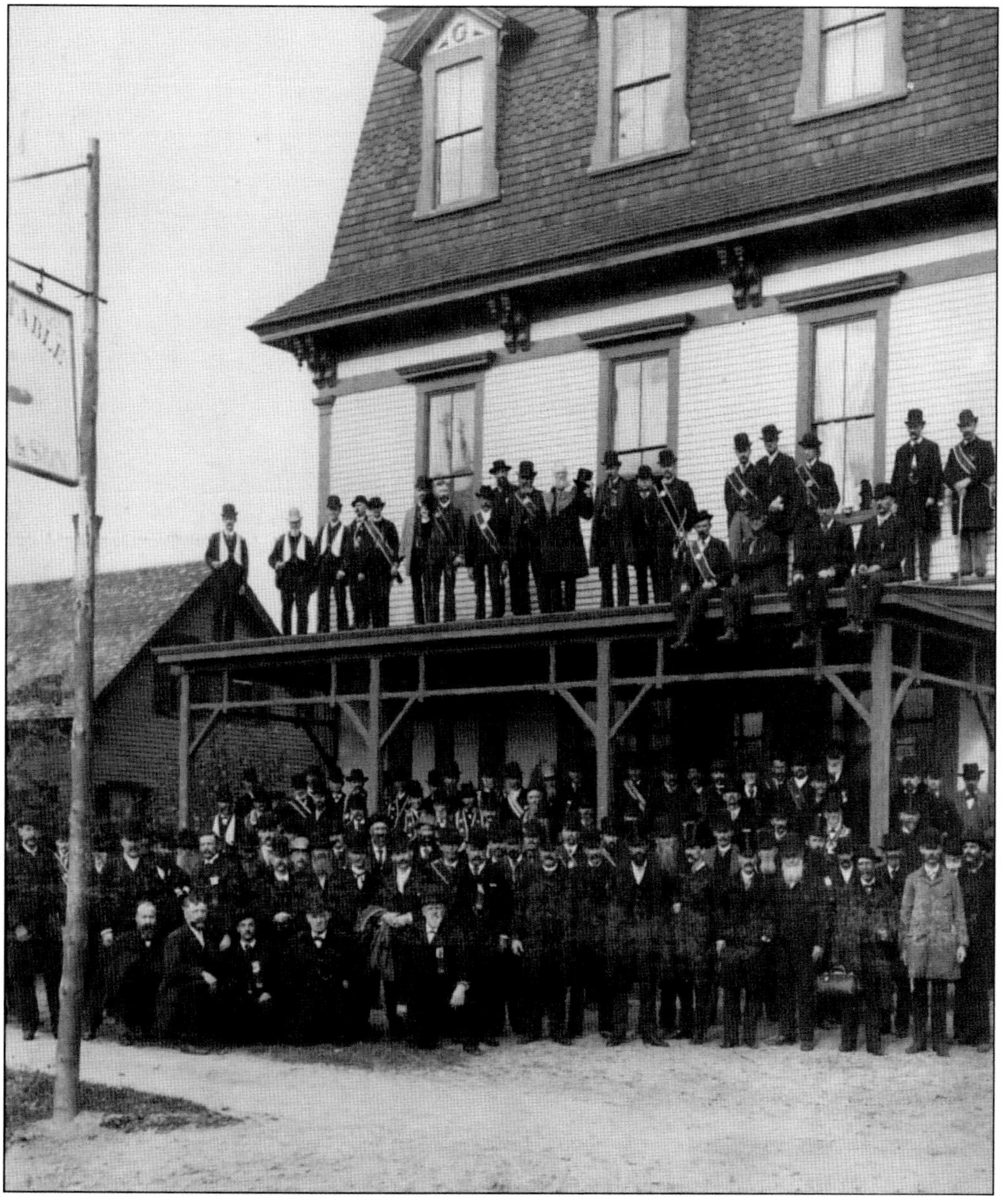

THE 46TH ANNUAL SESSION OF THE GRAND LODGE. In October 1889, the International Order of Odd Fellows met in North Conway. They were photographed in front of the original Masonic Temple (1873–1929).

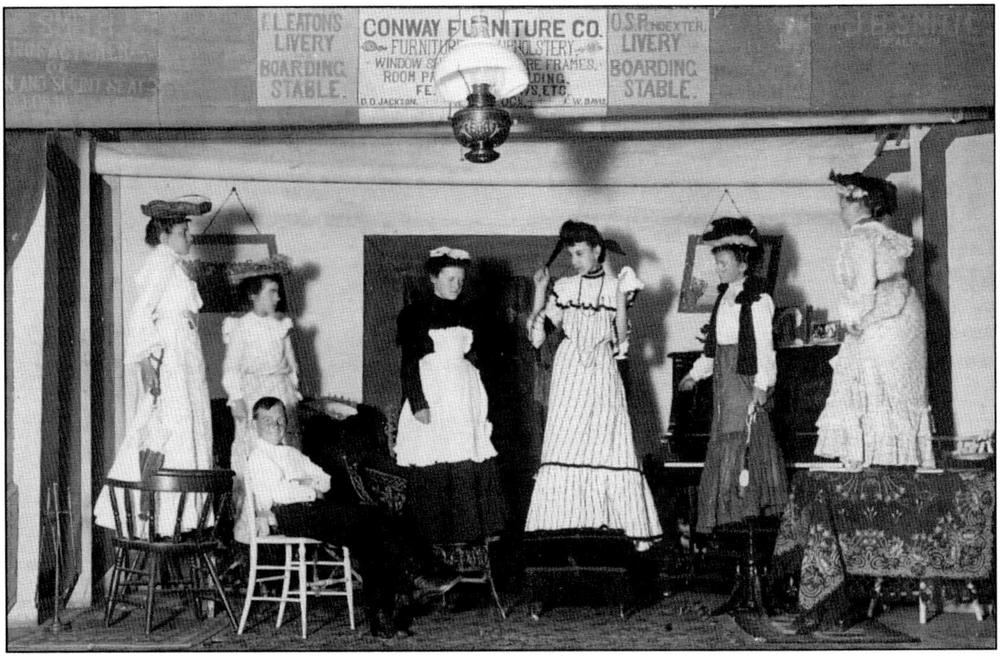

A CONGREGATIONAL CHURCH PLAY. Ready for the footlights are, from left to right, Nina Hiscock, Gladys Roberts, Rachel Jackson, Pearl Lord, Ruby Jackson, Martha Fifield, and Ernest Fifield.

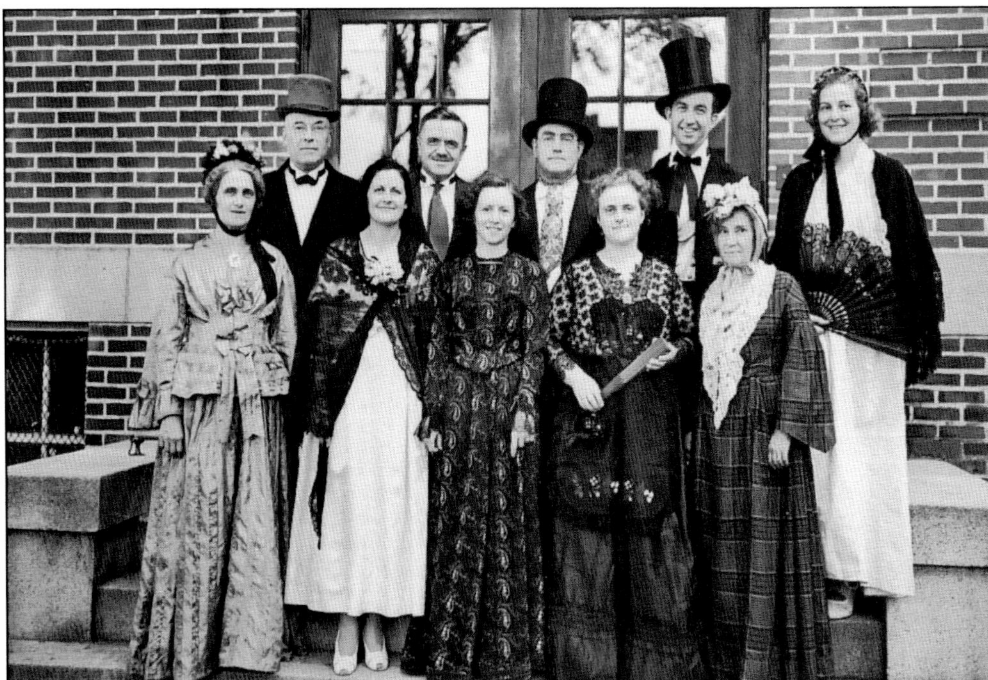

THE HISTORICAL SOCIETY, JULY 1938. Pictured in period garb are Mrs. Mudgett, Etta Kennett, Doris Newton, Rebecca Shedd, Florence Crockett, Arthur Furber, Frank Kennett, Bill Parker, Maurice Lovejoy, and Paula Lovejoy.

JOHN SEERY. Mr. Seery was a long-time station agent at the B&M Station in North Conway Village. Note the baggage wagons which could be rolled along a boardwalk between the station and the Kearsarge Hotel.

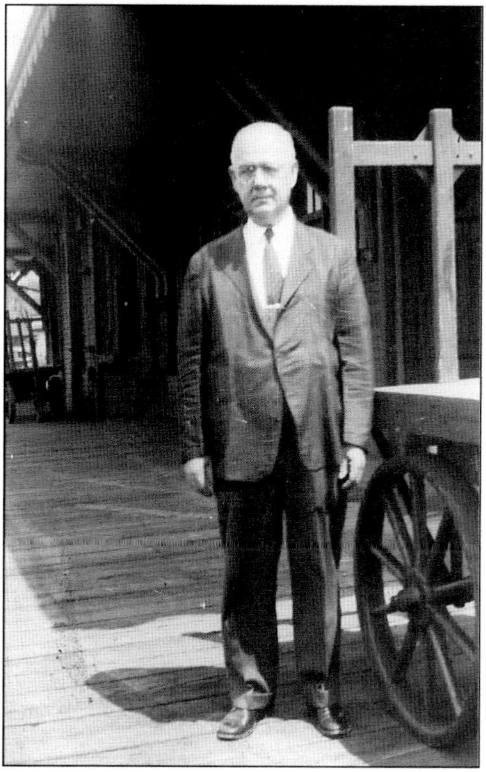

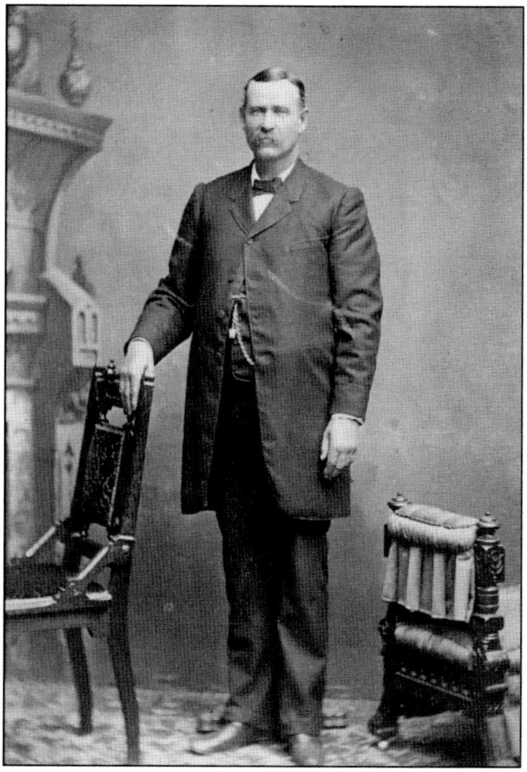

GEORGE W. WAGG. Maine Central Roadmaster George Wagg, noticing the exquisite quality of the granite in local bridges, brought it to the attention of Payson Tucker and J.H. Emery. Mr. Wagg was made president of the Maine and New Hampshire Granite Company and was greatly responsible for the building of Redstone Village. George Wagg Jr. followed his father as president of the company.

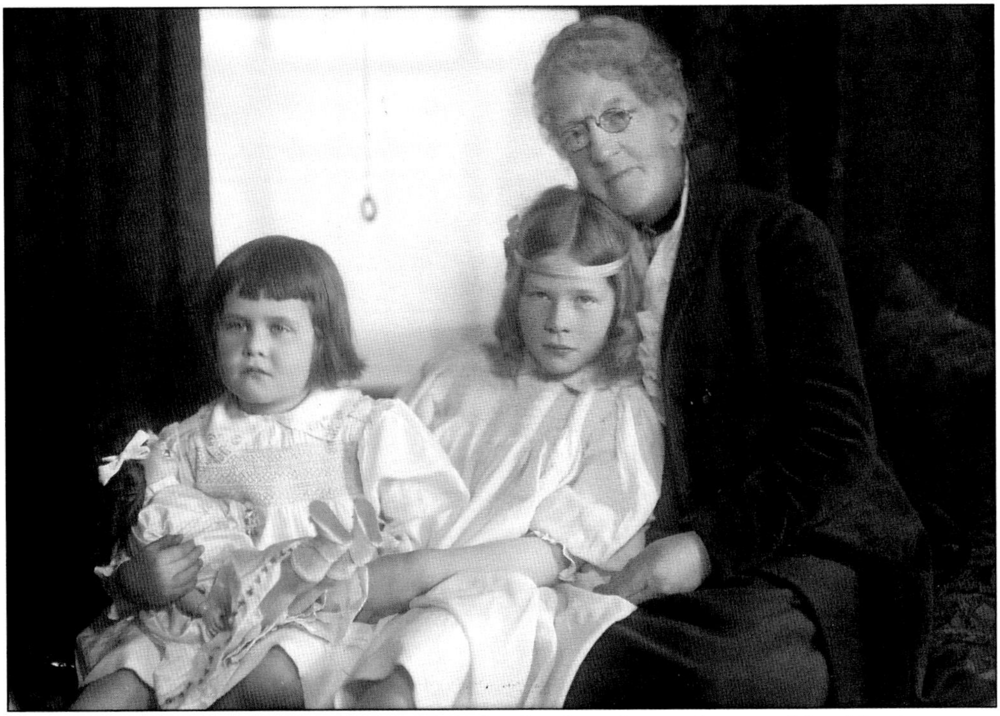

HELEN BIGELOW MERRIMAN. Heir to the Bigelow Carpet fortune, Mrs. Merriman was a North Conway social leader and philanthropist. She was instrumental in the building of Memorial Hospital and the new North Meetinghouse (First Church of Christ Congregational). Mrs. Merriman is shown here with her granddaughters.

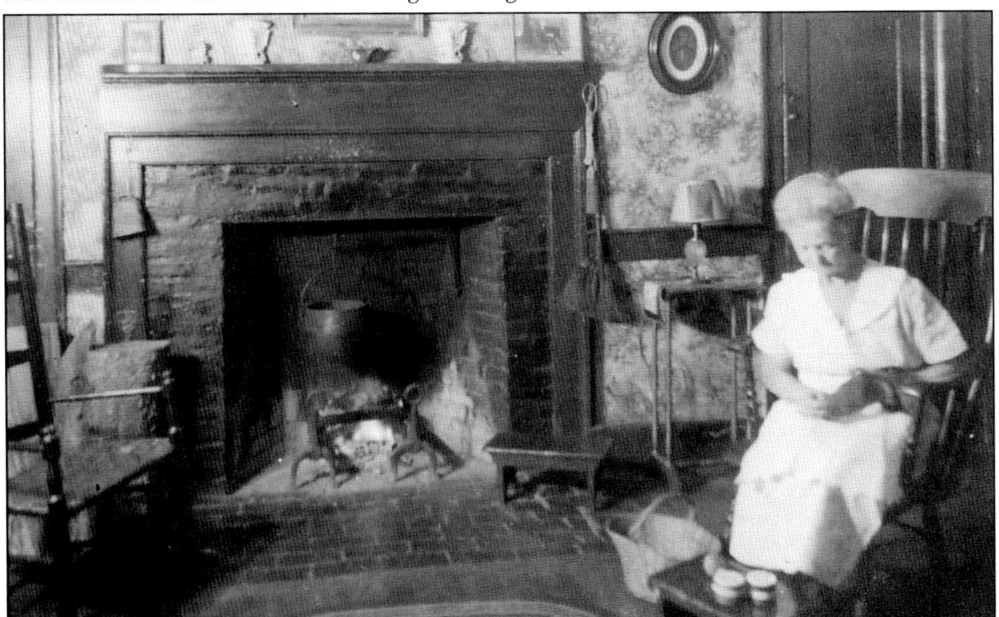

THE PARLOR, KEARSARGE HALL, NORTH CONWAY. After the Kearsarge Hotel burned in 1917, Mrs. Ricker, daughter of Samuel Thompson, moved across the street and carried on business on a smaller scale in Kearsarge Hall.

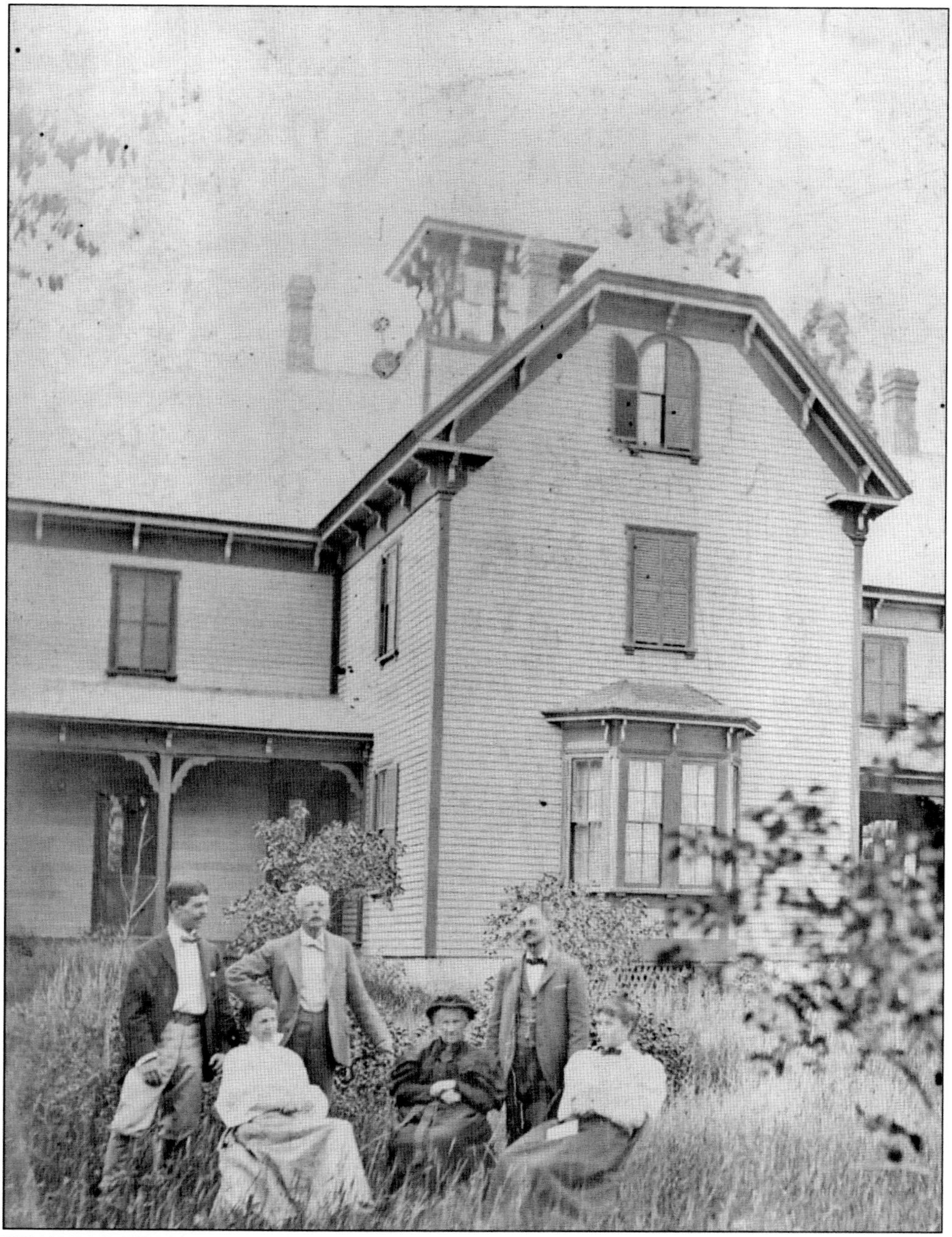

KEARSARGE HALL. A matriarch sits surrounded by Victorian gentlefolk on the south side of Kearsarge Hall. Kearsarge Hall, not to be confused with the Kearsarge House, stood on the site of the North Conway Bank's main office.

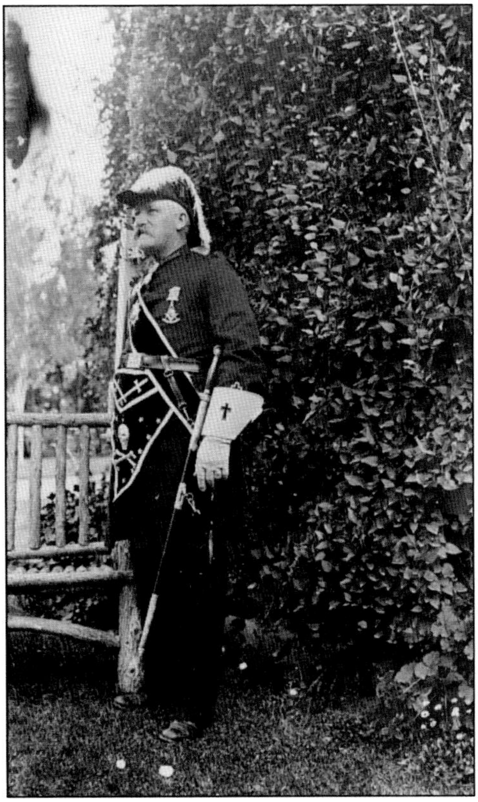

JAMES GIBSON. Despite this overwhelming view of him in full Masonic regalia, James Lewis Gibson was outshone by his very prominent son, Harvey Dow Gibson, and his somewhat eccentric father, James M. Gibson.

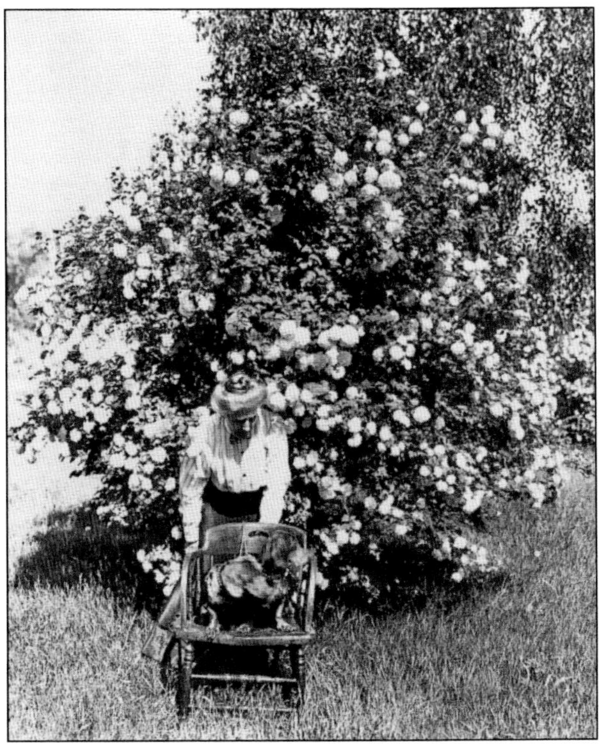

A WOMAN AND HER DOG. Long exposure times made it difficult to photograph fidgety animals without distortion. Here a Victorian matron tries to restrain her dog.

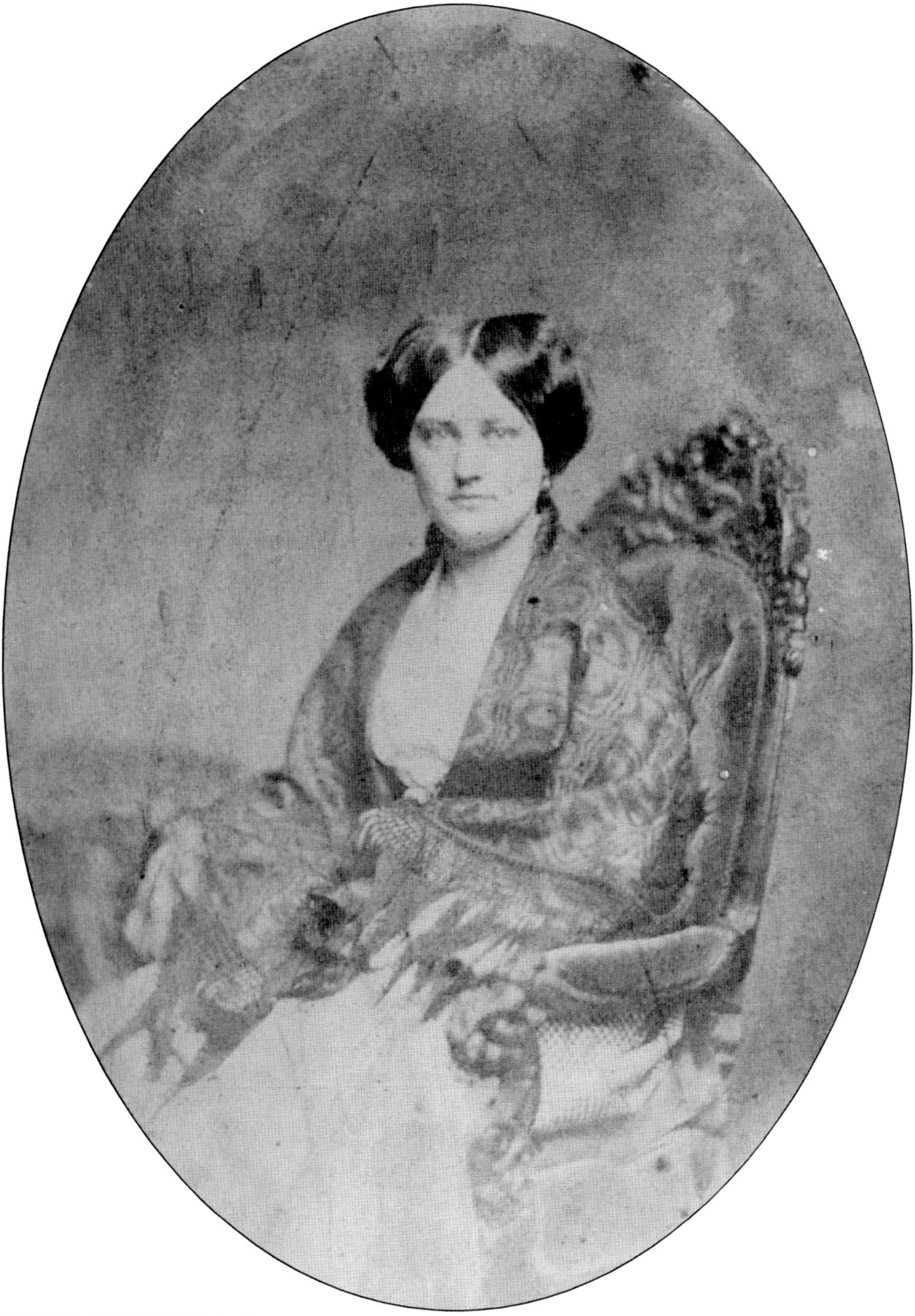

SUSAN LOVEJOY EASTMAN, NORTH CONWAY. In 1855, Susan Randall (Lovejoy) married William Wallace Eastman, fourth son of Conway businessman William Kimball Eastman. Susan and William moved first to California and then to Minneapolis, where he met with great success in the milling business.

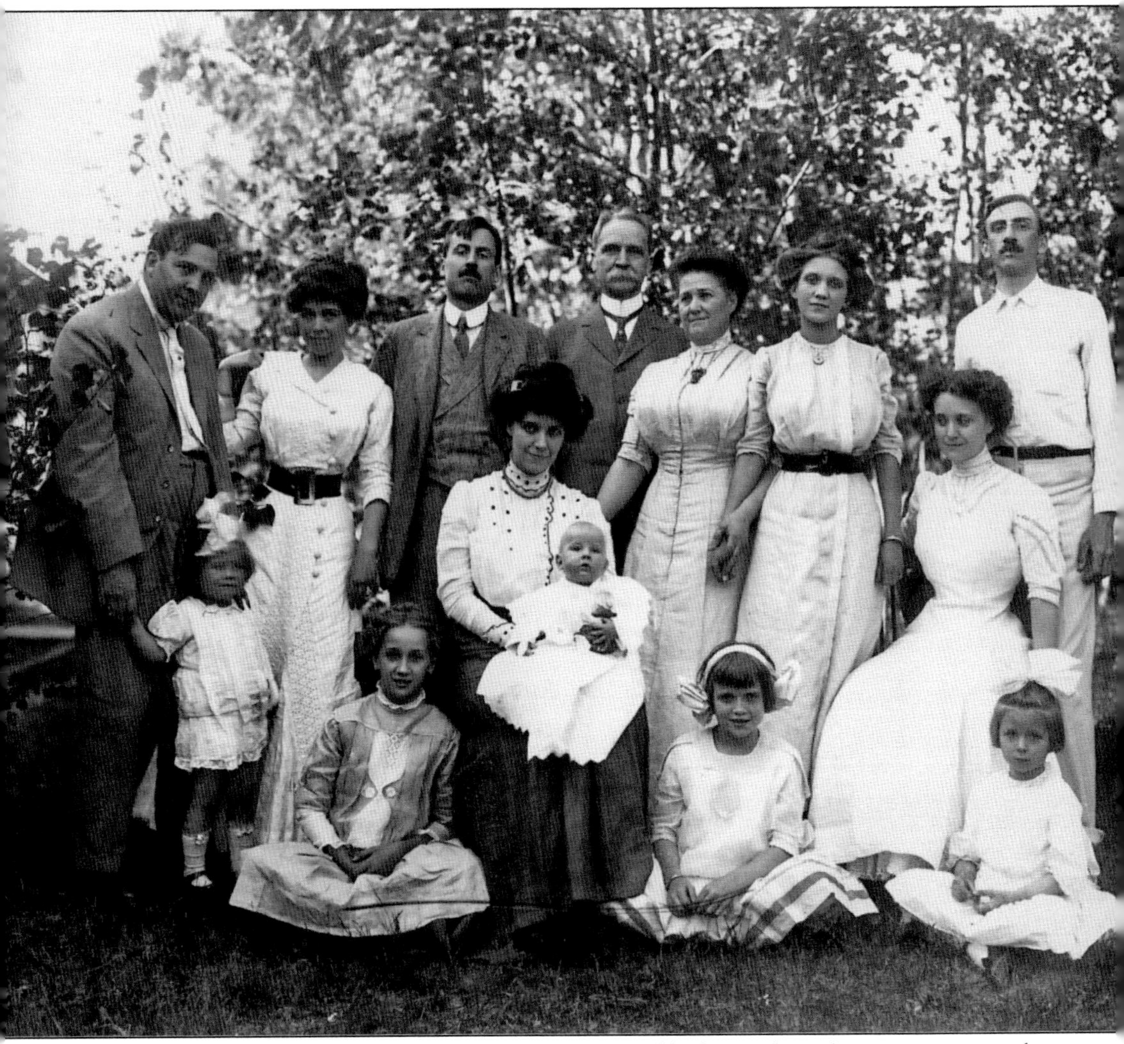

A FAMILY OUTING. This unidentified group posed before a glass plate camera on a pleasant summer day.

Ten

AND ALL THE REST

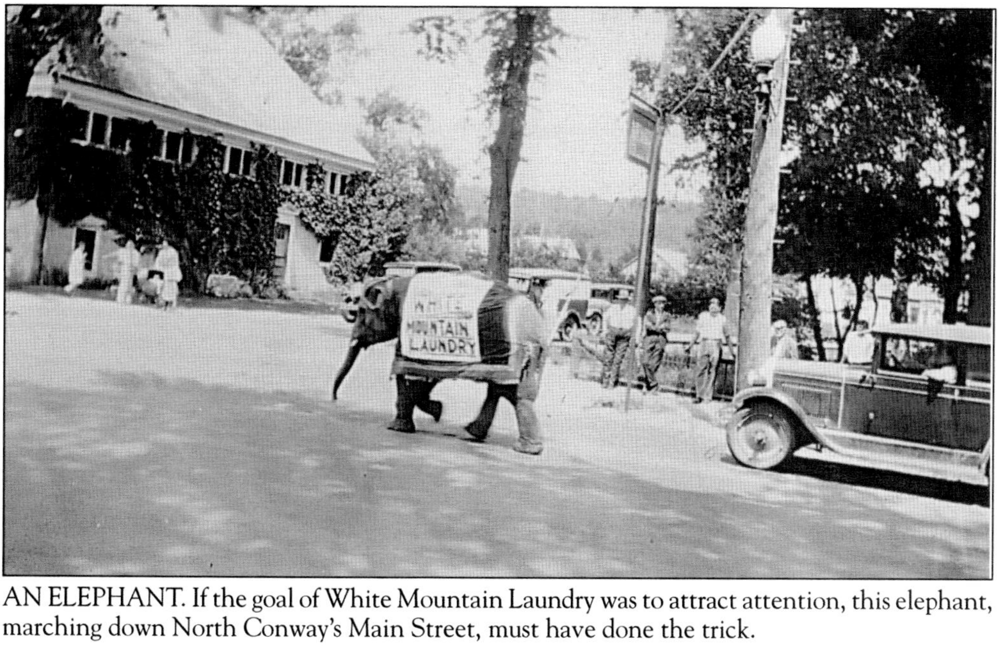

AN ELEPHANT. If the goal of White Mountain Laundry was to attract attention, this elephant, marching down North Conway's Main Street, must have done the trick.

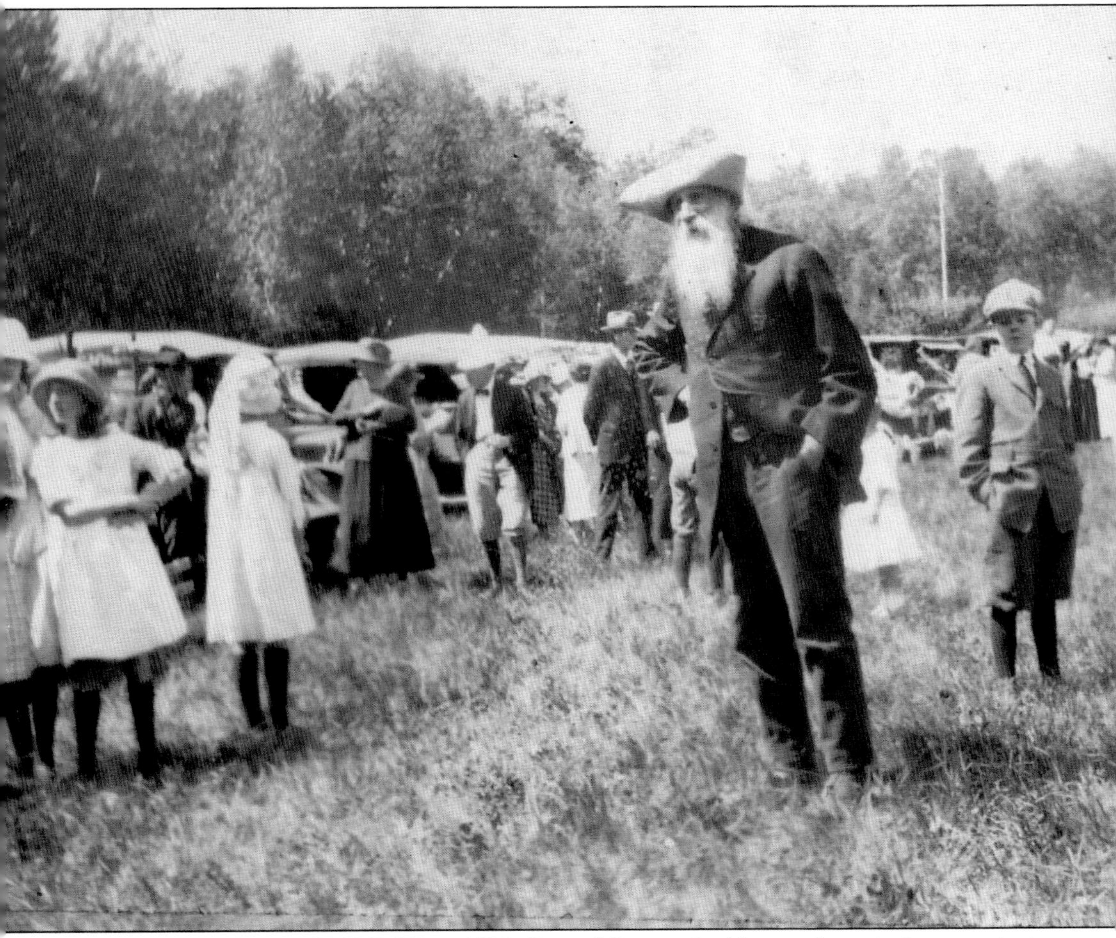

CONWAY OLD HOME DAY, *c.* 1922. One of Conway's older residents is shown enjoying an outing at the White Mountain Mineral Springs in Redstone.

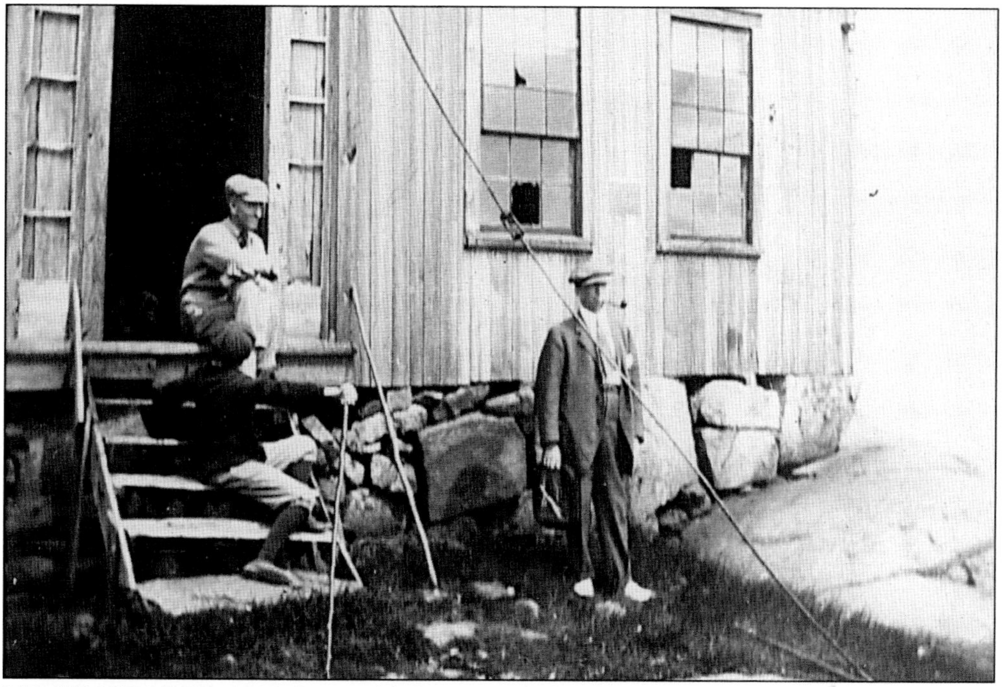

MT. KEARSARGE, 1912. Intrepid hikers pose before the second Kearsarge Summit House which replaced a larger structure, blown apart by high winds in 1883. Andrew Dinsmore built the structure, pictured above, from the relics of the original.

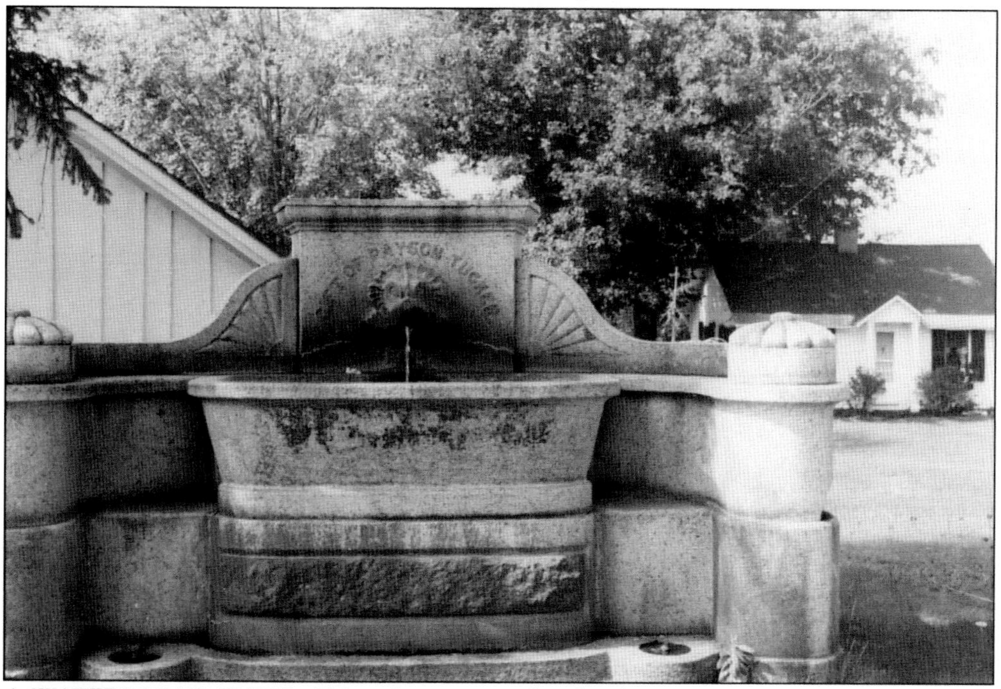

A WATERING TROUGH. Although now considered only quaint reminders of bygone days, watering troughs were once an important part of daily life. The one shown above is across the street from Payson Tucker's estate, Birchmont (now the Red Jacket).

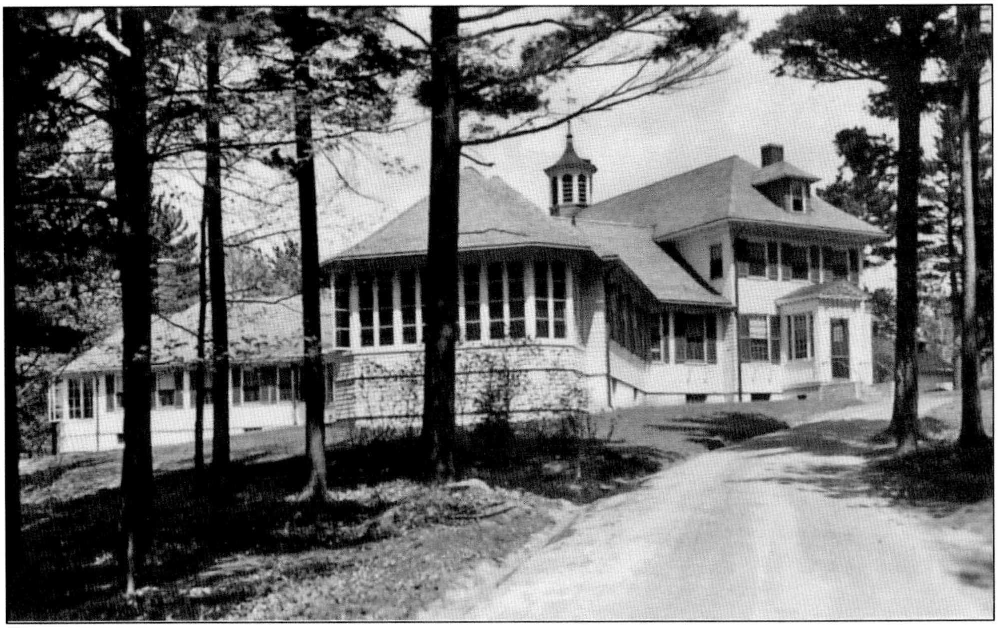

MEMORIAL HOSPITAL. When the hospital opened its doors in 1911, it advertised itself "open to all classes of patients, both medical and surgical except those suffering from contagious or chronic disease."

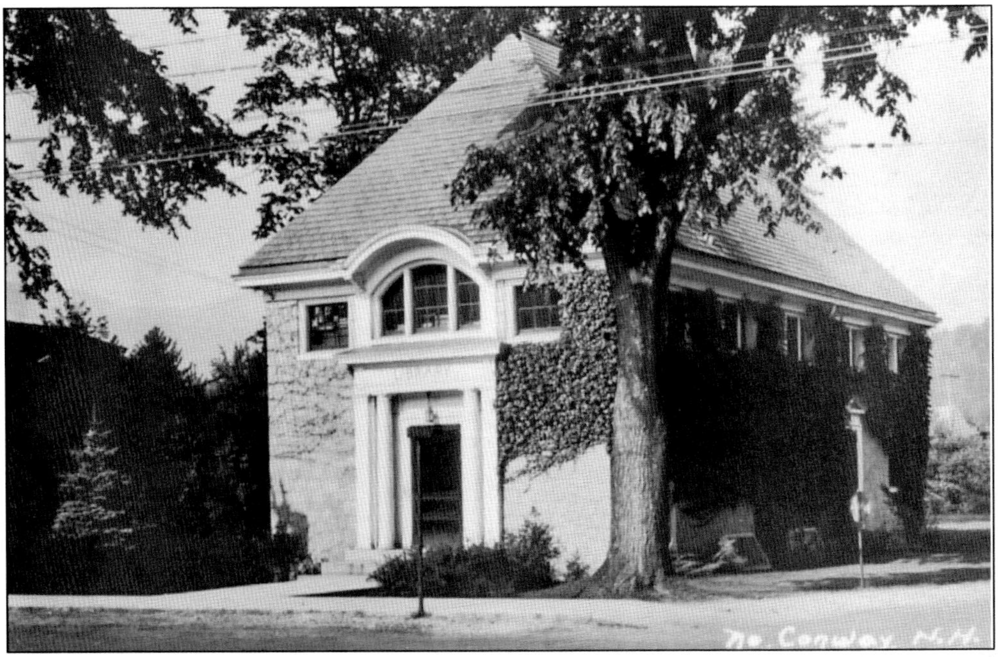

THE NORTH CONWAY PUBLIC LIBRARY. Granite donated by J.A. Whitaker was used in the construction of this library in 1911, built by James Schouler in memory of his wife. The land, on the comers of Mechanic and Main Streets, had been purchased in 1905 at a cost of $1,500. The architect was the world-renowned C.C. Zantzinger. Additions were added in 1917 and 1988.

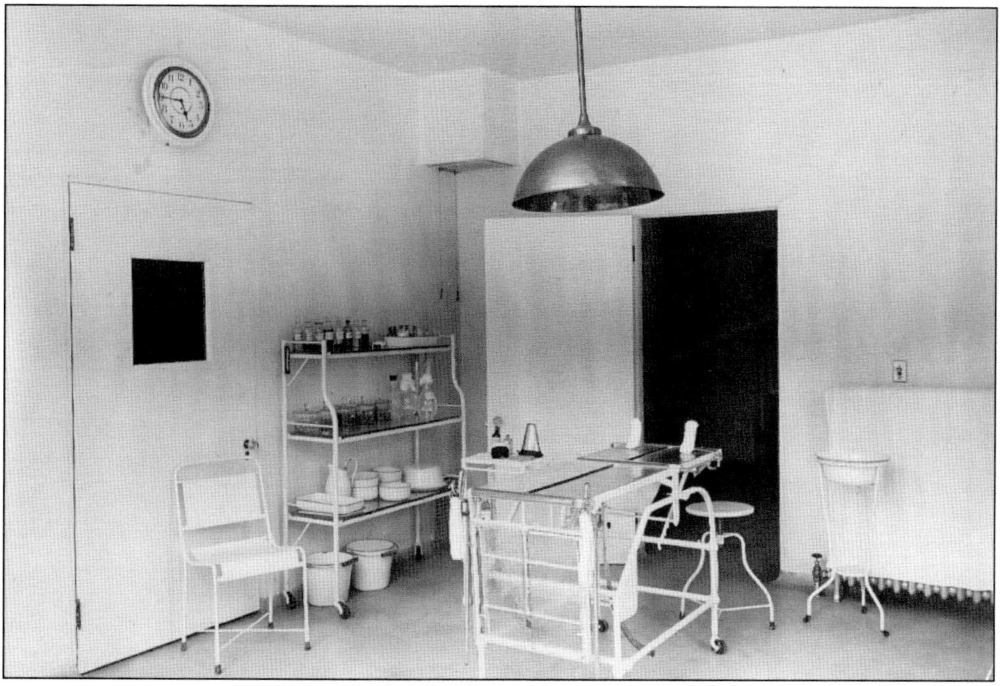

MEMORIAL HOSPITAL. Enameled dishes and glass-stoppered bottles were standard in this early operating or examination room. The radiator has been covered to facilitate cleaning.

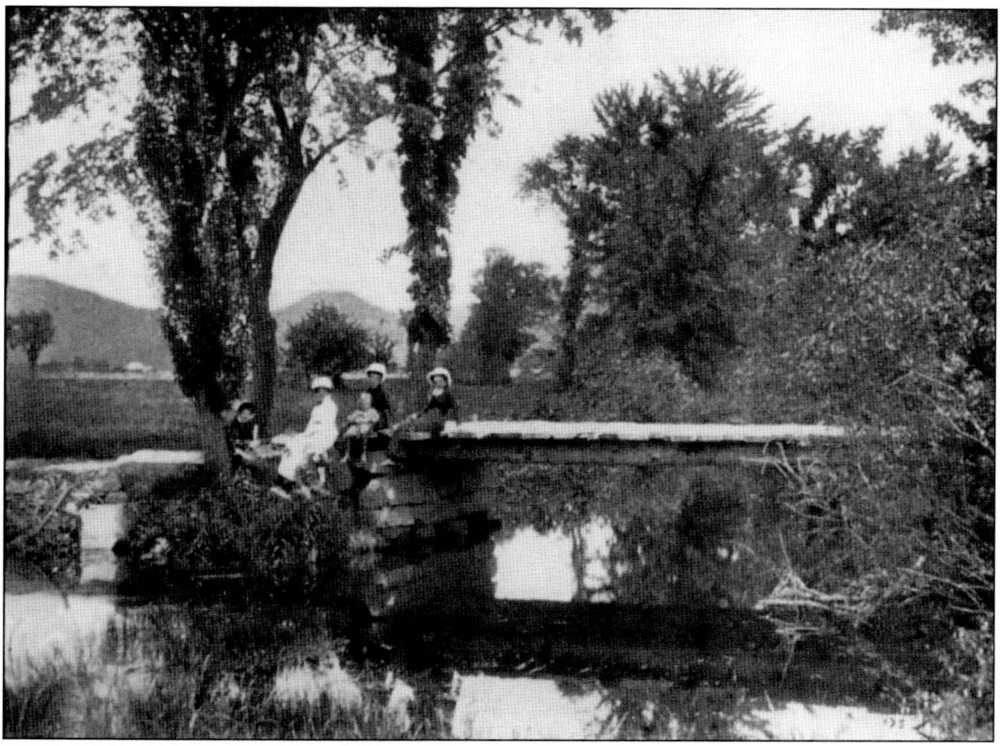

THE INTERVALE BROOK BRIDGE, c. 1890. Summer boarders delighted in being photographed amid pastoral Conway scenes.

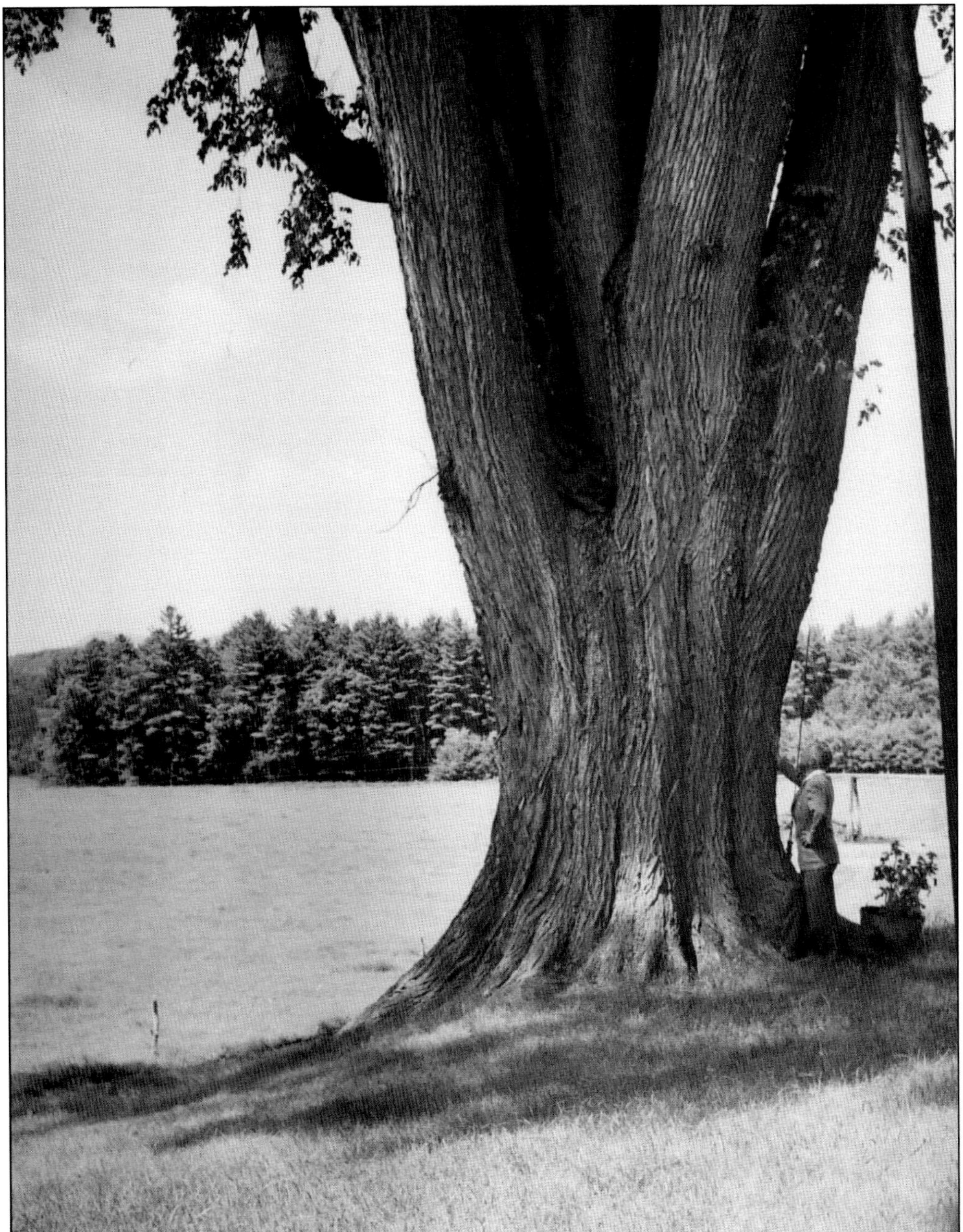

NEW HAMPSHIRE'S LARGEST ELM. The gargantuan elm that stood on the West Side until 1966 dwarfs an admirer.

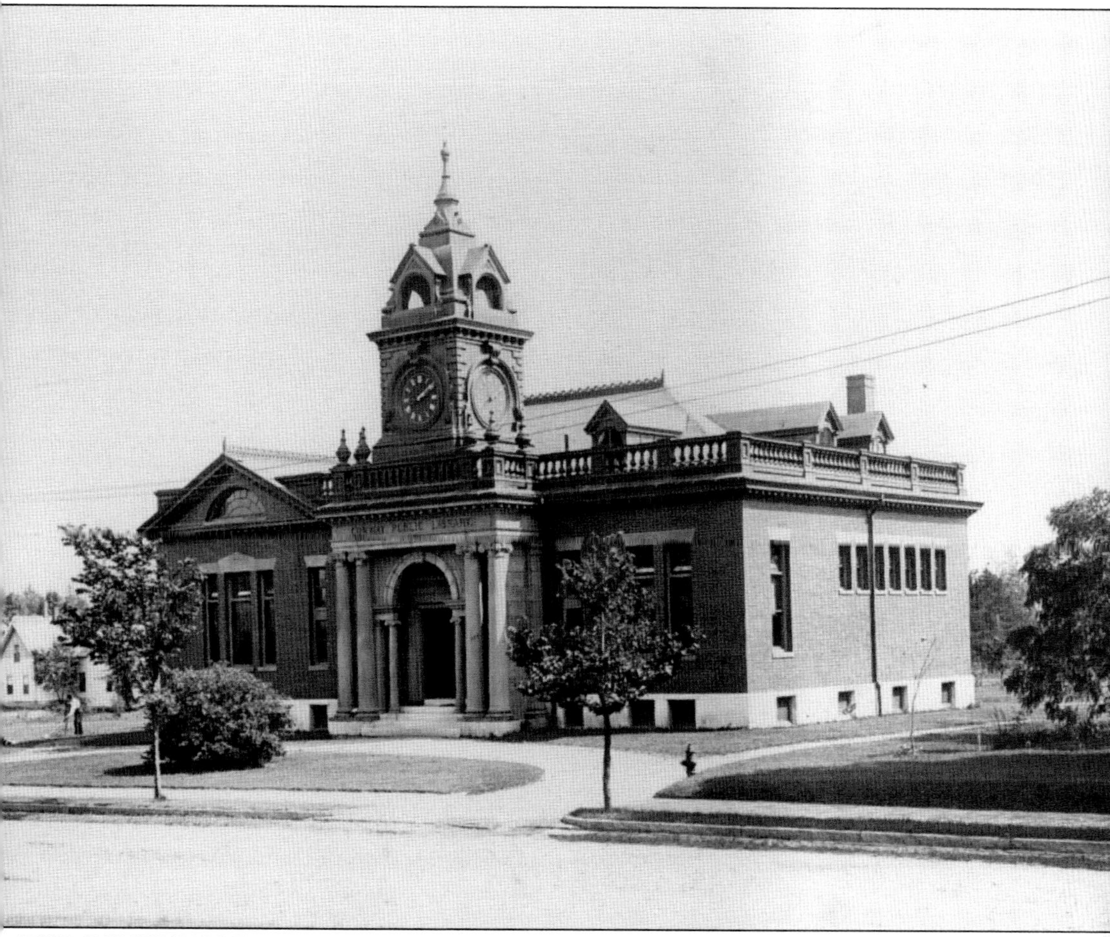

THE CONWAY PUBLIC LIBRARY, CONWAY VILLAGE. In 1900, the widow and daughter of Dr. Thomas Jenks approached the Town of Conway with their intention of fulfilling Dr. Jenks' dream. He had lived in Conway Village as a small boy and had long intended to present the town with a library. The building was dedicated in 1901. Few of the villagers remembered the doctor's brief residence in the Village but his memories were apparently fond.

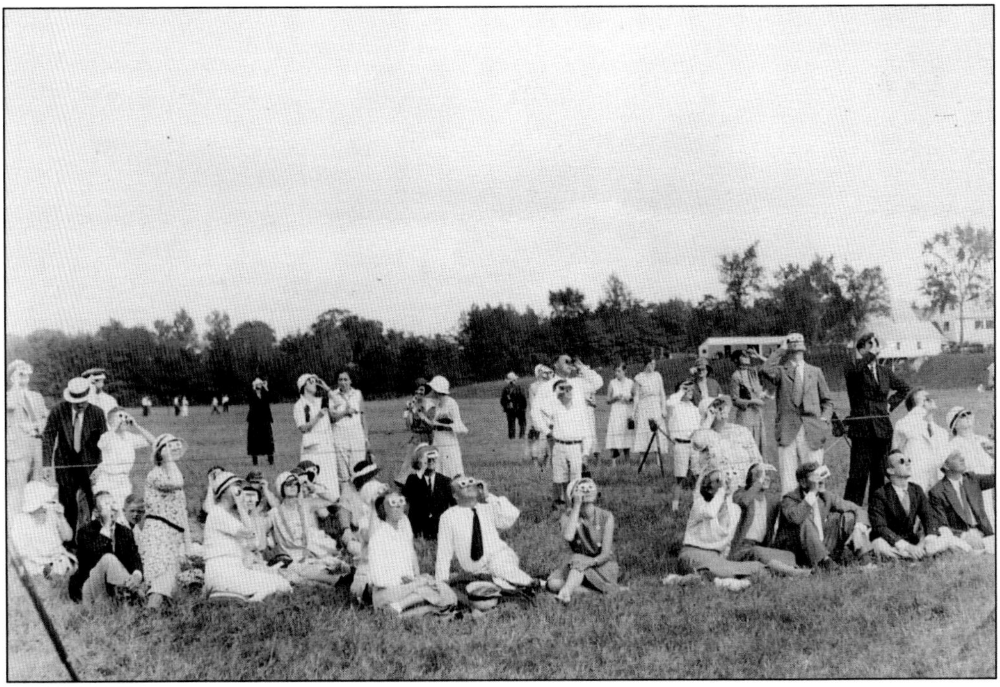

THE ECLIPSE. Astronomers predicted that the best spot to view the 1932 eclipse was in the Conway-Fryeburg area. Preparations were made for a huge throng of eclipse viewers. Restaurants hired extra workers and a viewing ground was set up behind the high school. The throngs appeared as predicted with no reports of panic or pandemonium.

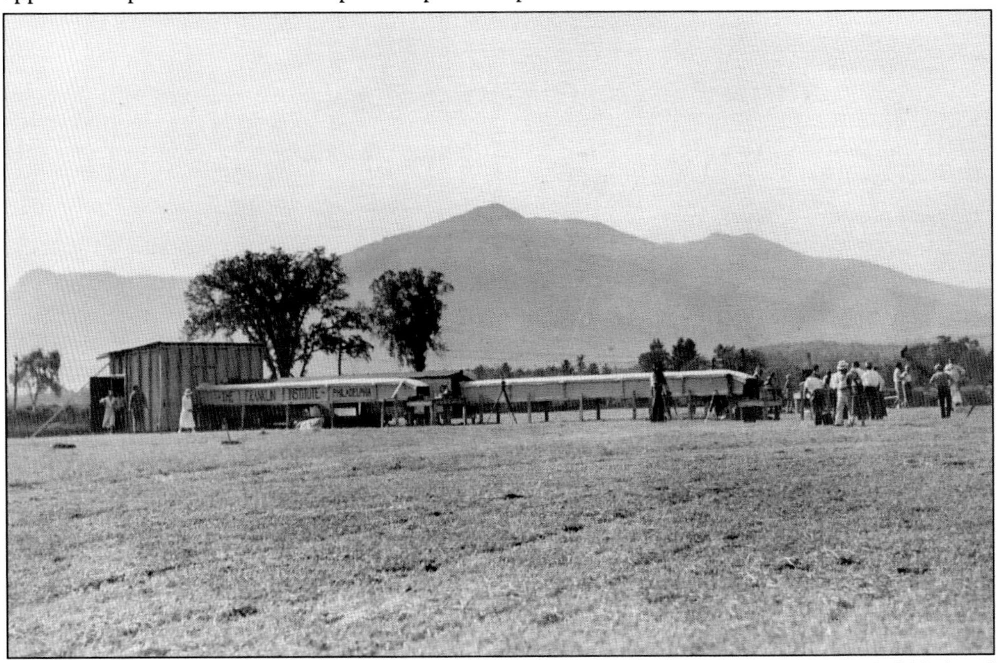

THE ECLIPSE, 1932. Philadelphia's Franklin Institute set up an observatory in the field behind Kennett High School to observe the much touted eclipse centered in Conway. Note the movie reel camera in the center of the photograph.

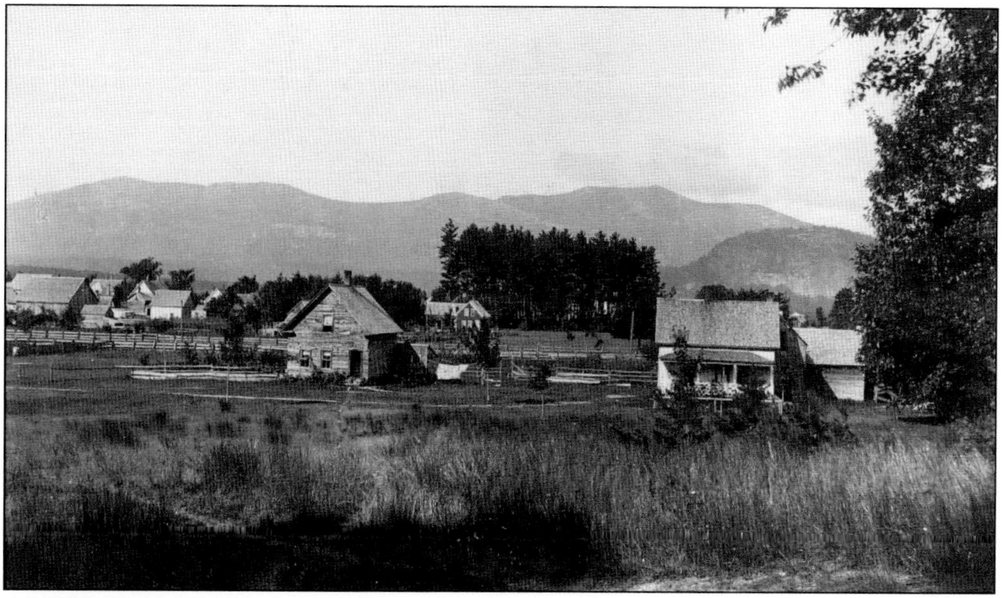

A VIEW FROM NORTH CONWAY. White Horse Ledge and Moat Mountain can be seen in the background.

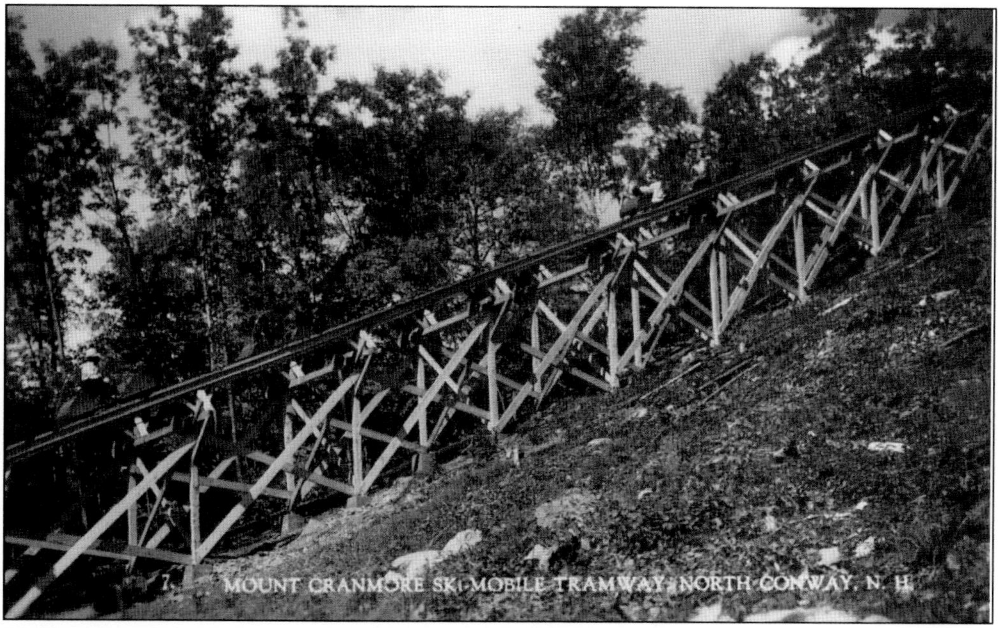

THE MT. CRANMORE SKI-MOBILE TRAMWAY, NORTH CONWAY. Invented by George Morton for Harvey Dow Gibson, the Ski-Mobile was long a North Conway landmark. Opened in 1938, it was the oldest continually running ski lift in North America until its discontinuation and dismantling in 1989.

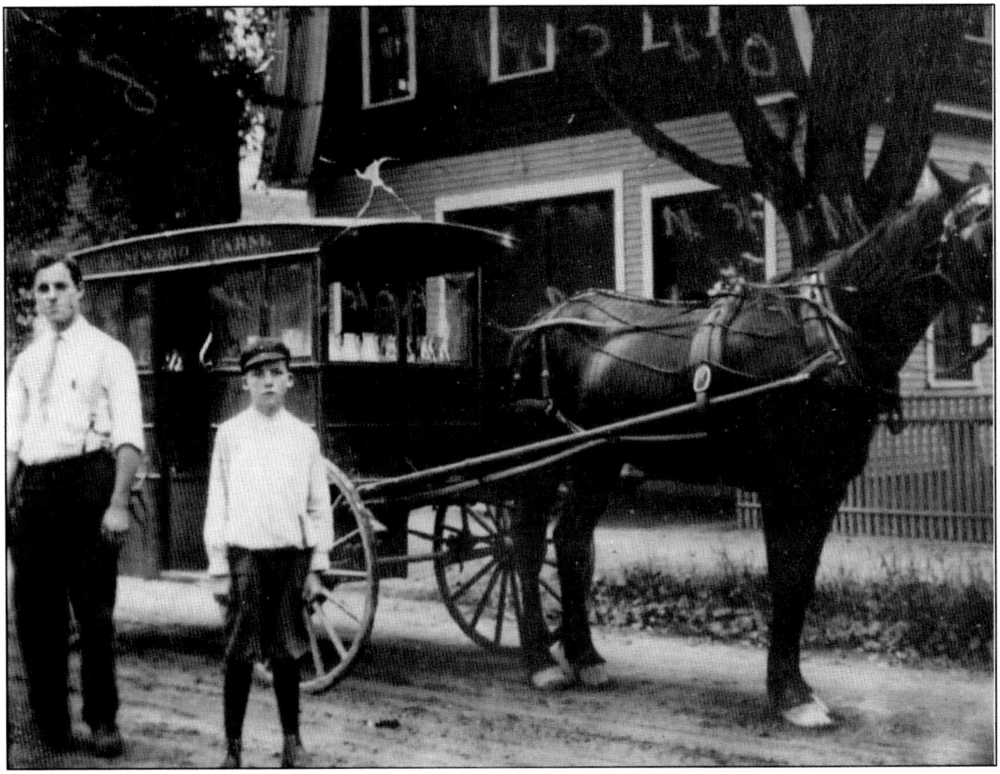

ARTHUR JACKSON. Arthur Jackson poses with the Elmwood Farm milk wagon in front of the Kennett garage on West Main Street in Conway Village.

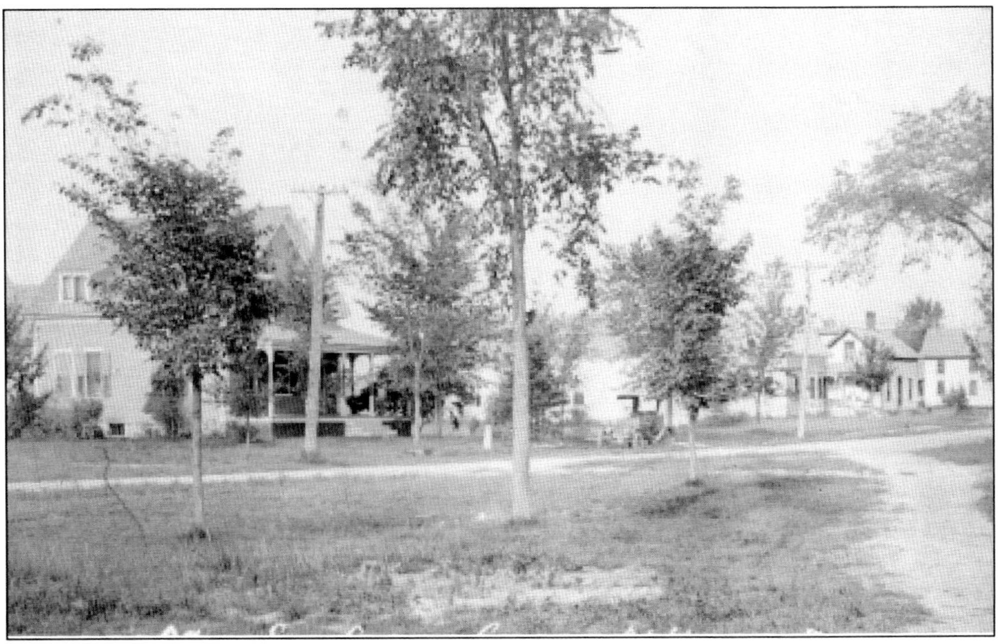

MAIN STREET, CENTER CONWAY, *c.* 1915. When this photograph was taken, elms still graced the unpaved streets of the Conways.